Lou Who?

J Johnson

Lou Who?

Two countries, two names, many men...
A memoir of self-discovery

Louise Johnson

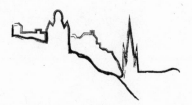

Louise Johnson
Lou Who?

First edition

ISBN 978-1-7772503-0-0

Book design: Stephanie MacDougall
Editor: Kelsey Straight
Author Portrait Photography: Grady Mitchell
Publishing support: TSPA The Self Publishing Agency Inc.

Dedicated to the one who birthed me, the one who raised me, the one whose love and support and energy knows no bounds, Mama Johnson. Thank you for teaching me that every challenging situation is simply a learning curve.

To all those life lessons, thank you, I wouldn't change a thing.

Forewarned is Forearmed

If you know me professionally, or maybe in a brotherly/sisterly way, some of the stories and details in this memoir may be "eye opening" for you to read. I'm comfortable sharing the stories, regardless of whether you're comfortable knowing them! If you can't look me in the eye afterwards, well, as my friend James would say, that sounds like a "you" problem.

With Love, Lou.

Contents

Part 3

Part 4

[1] This is *not* a typo.

Lou Who?

Part 1

One

How the West Won

"You can't outrun your problems. Moving to Canada won't make you a different person suddenly." I love when my friends don't pull any punches. My first thought in response to that comment was: *But wouldn't it be bloody lovely if that were the case!* My second, more sobering, thought was: *Oh god,..is that what I'm doing?*

Sitting in the bar of a cliff-top hotel on the southwest coast of England, with my colleague and friend Danae, it was the type of difficult conversation that I knew would come up as I told more people about my plans to move to Canada. It wasn't yet confirmed by way of a booked flight, but the decision was pretty much made. So, while telling work still a ways off, Danae was more than a colleague. She was the friend who I lined up for hours on end with when Krispy Kreme first opened in Edinburgh, the one who paid good money to devour gourmet burgers when a historic Edinburgh library turned into a popup restaurant, and the first person to make me prioritise my mental health. This is not a British trait (but she is American, so it figures).

I'd never truly considered that my sanity should be a higher priority than getting my ass to work and paying a mortgage. My mum[2] was an exceptionally hard worker and showed up for herself every day during her divorce: she showed up for work; she showed up for her kids; and she showed up for everyone who relied on her. I guess that's where I got it from—not only the hardworking bit, but the unfortunate turn of falling in love, getting married and then getting divorced. Sometimes, the people we love come to see, treat, and value love differently than us; and sometimes this changes us forever.

[2] I call any North American mother "Mom"; but I call any other mother "Mum." It's a distinction I make to respect both tendencies.

Rarely, however, do our past relationships hurtle us across the Atlantic Ocean to Canada.

Walking into work the morning after my marriage ended, I remember how Danae swiftly took me to the coffee shop across the street. She'd seen the panic cross my face as I walked into the office, and I *had* been questioning how I was going to function at work, now that my life was falling apart. She recognised the shortness of breath, the fear in my eyes and my complete inability to make a coherent decision regarding whether work was something I could manage that day. Over coffee, she assured me that taking some "me time" was not a sign of weakness: prioritising my emotional wellbeing was not only the kindest but also the most healing thing on my plate. Work could wait.

But in that grand English country hotel near Cornwall, having returned to work from my time off, Danae was now asking the hard questions re: my plans for the future. And I'd have expected nothing less from her. As lovely as it would have been to think a flight to another country could solve all my problems, I wasn't that naive. Regardless of where in the world I ended up, I knew there would still be work to do. There were wounds that I thought would never heal, mental trauma that I might never make peace with in full. Honestly, it would take much more than a ten-hour flight and an eight-hour time change to soothe my level of emotional devastation.

What was I hoping to achieve by choosing to move to a city I had never visited, where I knew no one, at a moment when nurturing a support network was not only sensible but necessary? Searching for the right words, I tried to explain myself to Danae, starting with the tangible, the part that I hoped she and others would get: *I didn't honestly know how to start my life again in Edinburgh.* Despite having all of my friends and family there, staying and rebuilding at home truly seemed more daunting than starting new somewhere else.

I was also finding myself in an entirely different time of my life; all my friends were married (or getting married) with kids (or having kids) and I was…well, I was back home living with my mum, looking for any excuse to get shit-faced drunk and relying on the *but-life-is-so-tough line* when I didn't want to face reality. Essentially I'd regressed to a teenager. While they were wonderful for support, my friends and I were looking for different things in life now, and you know what friends really don't like? When you suggest that you might need to make new friends....

My explanation for Danae then moved onto the less tangible and slightly more unhinged note of: *I actually hadn't really thought that much about it.* I mean, I had, obviously, but there wasn't really a decision to make. The only thing I could see helping me in that moment was getting out of the eternally familiar but now alien-feeling bubble of Edinburgh. It just *felt* right; and when the mind has suffered a break with the way things *once* were but are no longer, sometimes following a feeling in the body is the best resource we have.

Vancouver specifically came about after a school friend of mine, Sophie, told me how much she'd loved her four months living there—not to mention her complete assuredness that I'd love it too. I'd gone through a few other options: Australia or New Zealand (too far away), London (just didn't feel far enough), somewhere else in Europe (I didn't want to deal with a language barrier), or the Middle East (not ideal as a single white female, even if I had grown up in Egypt). I had moved to Cairo as a seven-year-old with my family, for my dad's work, and we ended up staying for seven years. It was very different to move somewhere by myself as a single, twenty-eight-year old female.

Having said that, my parents' conviction to uproot their family to move to a country as "colourful" as Egypt definitely galvanised me into feeling like I could do this. We'd moved to Egypt from an area of Edinburgh where people don't even leave that part of town, never mind move to the other side of the world; and we arrived in Egypt at a time of political instability (has there ever been political stability there?) when electricity and water were patchy to say the least. The summer before we made the move, my parents decided that we should take our first ever trip on a plane to somewhere else, somewhere a little more *family friendly*, before they landed us in the Middle East. And so we visited Toronto.

Hence why Canada *just made sense* to me as a destination. We ended up taking a couple of family holidays to Toronto during my childhood as well, to visit some extended family who moved to Ontario in the eighties, but I don't know how I would have felt moving to Toronto—a big, anonymous city—by myself. From what I'd read, Vancouver sounded like Edinburgh: a small, walkable city with the ocean and mountains (albeit in Edinburgh, they are more like hills). I'd registered for information about moving to Canada less than a month after my marriage ended. So quick was my want to get the hell out of dodge.

I take that back, Edinburgh will never be dodge to me, but in that moment it wasn't the place for me; and, like I said, Canada just seemed to make sense. Danae wasn't overly convinced by my arguments yet she accepted them. As we returned home to Edinburgh and the reality of feeling so alone in a place where I knew so many people returned to me, I knew for sure that I'd rather feel lonely in a place where I didn't know anyone, because at least that would make sense. Looking back now, it pains me to know that I made this decision out of so much sadness, rather than hope for what a future in Vancouver could bring. I just knew that I couldn't stay in Edinburgh.

I applied for a year-long working holiday visa once they became available that January, but they were kind of like Coachella or Glastonbury tickets: the first batch was gone in forty-five minutes, with the site crashing multiple times. Who knew so many people wanted to move to Canada? But I got a lucky golden ticket on the next round and managed to apply. This was the first time that I recognised how lucky I was that my marriage ended before I turned thirty. "Lucky" is maybe a funny way to put it, however. Did it feel lucky at the time? *Abso-fucking-lutely not*. But the type of visa I was applying for was only applicable if you were thirty years old or under, so if I'd been much older, it wouldn't have been an option for me. Honestly, not having that opportunity would have been devastating.

A month after my conversation with Danae in Cornwall, my visa came through and on April 25th 2013, I booked a one-way ticket to Vancouver. I would be leaving for Canada on September 25th 2013, as the Moon in Gemini was sextile with Uranus in Aries and Mars in Leo. I didn't know much about astrology, but according to Google, the formations above me that day sketched a helpful framework for this next chapter of my life, forces that brought ease to my relationship with independence, with willpower, with courage, confidence, openness, and ultimately going my own way.

Perhaps my instinct to move to Vancouver was only a gut feeling, but then it must have been one hell of a gut feeling, to have also written itself in the stars. At the time, instead of looking up, and like so many who came before me, I decided to look west, across the ocean to Canada.

Two

The End of the World as I Know It

The end of my marriage was not something I'd planned (I mean who does? Gold-diggers maybe?) But it was shocking to me. Six weeks —not months, not years—after our wedding in April of 2010, I found out that my husband had cheated on me, in numerous fashions. Before we even got married, he'd slept with at least one other person; and since we'd been married, he'd been texting a whole host of females, mutual contacts of us both and strangers from online. The texts would have raised eyebrows even if he hadn't been married.

The way I found out was...a mess. It wasn't long after we were back from our honeymoon, and I was still recovering from the gastroenteritis that had landed me in a Mexican hospital. (Who knew the marriage was going to end in as much shit as I witnessed during those few days of illness?!) I got home from work on a Friday night and he tried to pick a fight with me almost instantly. It was so odd and out of character, as if it were a joke. I tried to reason with him but he ended up storming out of the house, although not before he'd changed clothes and planned to meet friends, all in about five minutes flat. Honestly, how many guys make plans that quickly?

Despite the unpleasantness of the whole situation, I was glad that he left. I was confused by his outburst. Being alone gave me time to figure out whether or not I'd just completely lost my mind. This would turn out to be one of the first examples of gaslighting that I can recall. Gaslighting is a topical word these days, defined as: *to manipulate (someone) by psychological means into questioning their own sanity*. But it's not just one's sanity that gaslighting calls into question; it's also the core aspects of who we are.

I didn't hear from him all night, until finally he came stumbling in the door at four am. Now, I'd seen him drunk before (neither of us held back while drinking in each others' company, which wasn't the healthiest thing for our relationship), but this was some next-level intoxication. This was *incoherent, couldn't see, couldn't undress himself* drunk. I let him sleep on the sofa until the uneasy feeling in my gut made me give up on sleep altogether. I moved the dead weight of his body to the bed, allowing myself to take the living room, and undressed him.

That's when his phone fell out his jeans pocket.

I had never checked his phone before; the thought had literally never entered my head. I guess it didn't align with my consciousness until then. I looked at his phone staring up at me from the bedroom carpet. I looked at him lying on the bed, temporarily dead to the world, rocked by a feeling that I still cannot explain. Something felt different. Call it women's intuition or gut instinct, but I picked up that phone and took it into the lounge with me.

I couldn't have known that what I found would trigger the biggest life shift I'd ever experienced, even bigger than my parents' divorce eleven years earlier. The reality is: certain things cannot be unseen, certain truths cannot be untold, certain hurt cannot be reversed. What is it that they say? *Don't ask questions that you don't want the answers to?* Regardless of the outcome, I did want the answer. I've always hated being kept in the dark. Rather than being made the fool, given the choice between knowing something shitty or not knowing at all, I'll always go with the "know something shitty" option. Being blind to something doesn't make it untrue so why not know where things stand?

And so, I sat on the sofa with the early morning Edinburgh sun streaming into our first floor flat (yes, we do sometimes get sun in Scotland) and delved into his phone. It's hard to believe that something simple like creeping someone's messages can change your life forever, yet it happens all the time. Instantly I read texts to some girl from the previous night, suggesting that she travel through from Glasgow and he would book them a hotel room. It was a back and forth, sexually-charged text exchange, full of banter and flirting, which only let up once, when she wrote, *I thought you just got married? Lol.* He replied with, *Oh yeah, so I did.*

Like, talk about a punch in the gut. Or how about a stab in the heart? How do I talk about a pain that I never thought words on a screen could cause?

There is no way to describe the hurt of the person you love so callously referring to your newly minted marriage, the one you thought was built on love and trust. Over the course of the next few days, as I held his phone hostage, I discovered more texts. I even had someone confirm that they'd slept with him before we were married and were still regularly in touch.

He denied it all, claiming that none of it was true, at least until I presented him with enough black-and-white evidence that he had no choice but to come clean. None of it was information he gave up easily, however. He made me work for every single confirmation; I had to go digging through months of texts; I had to hold his phone like a time bomb and text people back as if I were him; I had to confront my husband with the names of women whom he might have inappropriately texted. All this energy expended, just in getting him to admit it.

And so, before the official wedding photos were posted online, before the gift-list delivery had arrived or the thank-you cards were sent, I was questioning whether I could stay married to my husband. It hit me like a train.

I moved to my mum's and gathered my best friends around me, the same girls who'd stood by me at the altar just seven weeks earlier. They were the first to hear what had happened; and upon hearing the news, people rallied around me. Work was understanding, and my husband was desperately sorry, inconsolable almost. Me? I was numb. I could not understand how this was my life. How had this happened? How could I have married someone that would do this kind of thing? I'd known my ex-husband since I was nine years old, so how did I end up married to a stranger?

Our families had met in Cairo, during a period when his parents were living there as well. He and his three siblings were all back home in boarding school as our parents became firm golf-and-gin friends in the Egyptian sun. Though the first time I actually met him was one summer back in Scotland when his family came to visit us at our holiday home in the middle of Perthshire. It was a lodge timeshare on the grounds of a beautiful country-house hotel. We fought from the first moment we met. We bickered and picked on each other, and none of that would change over the subsequent twenty years during which he became a fixture in my life.

He'd been the older "cooler" kid I'd always had a crush on. He was loud, funny, and cheeky, as I imagined my father was as a teenager. Always the life of the party, always ready with a joke, but his energy could be a little overbearing. (He was also the person who eventually made you feel like lying down in a darkened room alone to recover from the onslaught of jokes and banter.)

When we moved back to Scotland from Cairo, our parents' friendship was impacted by the physical distance, but the rest of us became closer. He became best friends with my brother; and my parents actually became his godparents once he chose to be Confirmed (one of the three sacraments of initiation into the Catholic Church, alongside Baptism and Holy Communion) in his senior years of school. His family provided immense support when my parents divorced; his one sister lived with my mum for a period of time during which she and I became incredibly close; and he lived with my mum for another duration of time. Our families were interwoven in such a way that marriage between the two of us seemed like a suitable solidification of familial bonds.

It had just felt right, like a fairy tale. We got married in the cathedral at the bottom of the driveway of the country-house hotel, the same place we'd met sixteen years earlier. We'd never really discussed the location choice, because we'd always just known; it felt as if things were exactly as they were meant to be. That said, my father, who'd been an integral part of our two families coming together, was not part of the day. (In retrospect, I wonder if I should have made a connection between the two of them. If it hadn't worked out with me and my father, why would it with my husband?) We can heal from anything, transform into whatever we need to become, but first we need to know and understand from what we are healing.

Interestingly, both his father and my mother had given him the *if-you-ever-do-anything-to-hurt-her* chat, but it had seemingly fallen on deaf ears. When I found myself back at my mum's place, excused from work for stress, she understood all the same. I spent a lot of time thinking/questioning/denying/talking things out with family, friends, and work colleagues. I just remember being in turmoil—and I hated living at my mum's. Yes, it was comfortable and she is always a welcoming hostess to family and friends alike, sometimes even complete strangers, but I missed my own home. I missed my bed. I missed having all my things. It was just an added layer of *shitty-ness* in an already shitty situation.

Lost in this world full of people asking me constantly how I was doing—not knowing whether I'd be able to move when I woke up every morning (because stress was physically taking over my body) not to mention having dreams so tormenting that proper rest became a long-lost memory—I made the decision to suck it up. No more moping around alone, absorbing advice from people who thought they had all the answers for me, while wondering if I'd ever have answers for myself again. When my great uncle married us in front of 131 cathedral guests, I'd taken my vows to heart. Testing the strength of those vows so soon into our marriage was never something I foresaw, but there we were, and now I had a decision to make.

At the time, I made the decision that I personally felt was the only option— go back and try to make it work. While I wasn't morally opposed to divorce or separation, I couldn't even begin to think about how my life would look if I didn't go back. What was I supposed to do? Start all over again? By myself? That wasn't the plan. That wasn't to be my life. I had just applied for my name change, for fuck's sake. I was moving on from Louise Johnson and becoming Louise Moodie. How do you even reverse a name change?! Sometimes change comes in such a way that it yanks an entire world out from under our feet, and our first instinct might be to go and find the original world; but our second instinct is often to create the world anew.

The biggest difficulty I faced was the naivety of my earlier perspectives. Before all this shit went down, I never truly understood the depths of commitment nor the nature of life's extremes. I always said that if someone were to cheat on me, the relationship would be over before the conversation began. Mostly, I said this thinking about my parents' marriage and how long my mother put up with my father's infidelity. Little did I know that it wasn't so black-or-white, so in-or-out, so stay-or-go. Context, feelings, emotions, logistics. All of these things made the decision far more difficult and complex, much more of a head fuck than I'd ever anticipated back when I thought a cheating partner would automatically mean the end of a relationship.

Esther Perel, a Belgian psychotherapist who specialises in relationships and sexuality, once made the comment that *the old shame used to be divorce; the new shame is staying when you can* leave. Her words smacked me in the face like a wet fish. I found myself between a rock and a hard place, because there is still an element of shame tied to divorce. But Esther's not wrong, there is also a shame in staying with someone once they've cheated on you. People presume that you are weak of character if you choose to stay, that you should want more for yourself. You're damned if you do and damned if you don't.

I never thought going back would be easy, but I never could have imagined how much it would tax me. To live everyday second guessing what my partner was telling me, trying to determine if he was lying, looking for telltale signs of actions repeating themselves. Meanwhile, I was dealing with the fallout from various friends who thought I'd made a mistake by going back, or who'd made their feelings clear vociferously enough when we were separated that they couldn't backtrack on whatever they'd said about the man I was shacking up with again.

We went to couples counselling, well, mostly I went. I think he joined for two sessions. I was familiar with counselling already, having gone after my parents' divorce and seeing a life coach before we got married. I'm not sure how much this particular instance of therapy helped, but I felt that it was the right thing to do. When it comes to therapy, even going and being unsure of whether it has actually helped afterwards is still somehow helpful, because either way, you learn enough to determine whether another mechanism might be more effective for your healing.

I also lost my job during that time (just another tidbit of fun for my first year of marriage). It took around six months for me to stop checking his phone. I did it almost daily for the first few months, and then slowly I weaned myself off. I have since considered that maybe I shouldn't have gone back if I couldn't stop checking his phone, but it seemed like the minimum viable action to being present in the marriage while feeling a tiny bit of peace.

One of my best friends is wonderfully German, and as the rain turned to snow and sleet pouring down on my wedding day, Katrin had provided me with a translation of a German saying: *Rain on your wedding day is all the tears of your marriage clearing out now.* Obviously, when it came to my marriage, that was utter bullshit.

Peace was hard to come by those days. My brain, my thoughts, and my dreams ran wild. I was in a constant state of turmoil, feeling like I wasn't trying hard enough to make things work, not appreciating enough that he'd seemingly changed, not fully feeling like myself. I wasn't sure I'd ever feel like her again. In fact, at this stage, I wondered who she even was. *Little Lou Who* had lost her groove.

We got through his thirtieth birthday in Vegas with family, his parents' wedding anniversary in Portugal, and our first anniversary, which fell in the midst of other events, thus we didn't get to properly celebrate. To me, that

came as a relief. I didn't know if the first year of our marriage was worth celebrating. Sure, we'd made it, but at what cost?

Perhaps I wasn't feeling like myself because the person I'd been up until
then was off doing something else now, living out her married life in a different
dimension of time, one where her husband never cheated on her and they had
given birth to a baby dragon that breathed hearts of fire—for all I know. But
jokes aside, there is something to be said about having the intention to remain
the same version of yourself for good, only to be cast off the tracks by some
circumstance that nobody saw coming. By returning to live with my husband,
I'd returned to a version of reality that I didn't believe was just, and this neces-
sitated subjugating the aspect of myself that longed for more.

My husband and I moved through spring and past that one particular date
in May that was forever ingrained in my head (it didn't help that the fateful
night where I'd read his phone was also my cousin's birthday) because the
only thing for me to deal with around that time was a medical procedure for
an abnormal smear result. Hospital visits had never been something I'd experienced in the past. Pretty much ever since I'd left the hospital as a baby, I'd
had no reason to return. Yet since I'd been married, I had been to the hospital
twice. Can we say *omen*? My mum had gone with me to have the colposcopy
done, as I needed someone to drive me home. It turned out to be just as well,
as anesthesia doesn't seem to agree with me. While I was grateful for the
numbing *prior* to someone digging around down there, I quickly felt as if I
were about to pass out. It's hard to relax if you can't feel where those instruments are going exactly. Lord, it's fun to be a lady!

The day afterwards, as I took a sick day to recover, I lay in bed still snoozing
while my husband took a shower (at the same time that I would normally
shower); and his phone pinged with a message. At last I'd grown able to ignore
his phone, so I ignored the message as well and avoided jumping to stom-
ach-churning conclusions. But then I heard the second ping on his iPhone,
reminding him of the new message; and I thought it might have something
to do with work, perhaps an issue that needed his immediate attention, even
at this early hour of the morning (a frequent occurrence in his line of work).

There is something ironic in the acknowledgement that I only looked at
his phone to make sure his day wasn't going to be fucked up; and instead it
fully fucked up, not just my day, but my life. *Again.* Damn that motherfucking

phone. I saw a text from a name that could have been male or female, along-side the name of his company, making me think it was a work text—so I opened the message and instead was faced with a picture of a woman's thong-clad ass. There it was, just staring back at me at seven am in the morning: some women's half naked arse, on my husband's phone.

I put the phone down, rolled back over and pulled the covers over my head. I couldn't bear to deal with it, especially not with the pulverizing cramps in my belly. I almost, for a split second, thought about ignoring it. I was in so much physical pain that the thought of dealing with an issue that I already knew had no good outcome was far more than I felt up to at that precise moment in time. Instead, I waited until he was almost dressed, and then I half sat up in bed and said: "You got a text message while you were in the shower. I checked it because I thought it might be about work; but it wasn't, it was a girl's arse. I can't do this."

With panic flashing across his face, he picked up his phone and instantly tried to excuse it as a joke from one of the guys. But I knew all the guys he worked with and hadn't heard this person's name before. Then he tried to tell me it was a contact he'd met through work; and obviously they'd sent it to the wrong number. He asserted that I was ridiculous for thinking that a girl would just send a photo like that to him on a Thursday morning.

Again, gaslighting in full effect. With no one around to validate your posi-tion and the person you love more than anyone in the world towering over you and saying you're wrong, that you're crazy and making a silly mistake, it's hard not to doubt yourself. It's funny how your mind can beat you up, even as the memory of a lacy thong burns a hole in your brain. But I really didn't have the energy to fight him on this. "Just go to work," I told him, but I could see he didn't trust that things were okay, nor whether I could accept what he'd told me. Me, I just wanted him out of the house. I wanted to not deal with it. He finally left for work and promised to come back at lunchtime. As I heard the car drive away, I called my mum and had her come over from work and pick me up (*with* my suitcases).

For the second time in fourteen months of marriage, I was back living at my mum's. This time, I told even fewer people. I couldn't bear the ques-tions, the judgment, the pity. I couldn't stand having to dissect my marriage all over again. So I kept going to work. I avoided most social situations and instead hibernated at my mum's, while she wondered how her daughter would navigate this particular trapdoor in her life. The way I caught my husband had been less cut and dry this time: all I had to go on was one picture and not all the mounting evidence. I hadn't witnessed any other inappropriate behaviours and his constant denial re: the truth was really making me question myself. Nonetheless, it was the same situation unraveling all over again.

After I moved out, he continued telling me that I was wrong. He didn't give me my space and begged me to come back. While not motivated by my vows this time, at least not so much, I still struggled to comprehend the alternative of not going back, but mostly due to logistical reasons. We had negative equity on our house, credit-card debt, and friends' weddings we were already booked to attend later in the summer. So, because of stupid financial, travel, and RSVP reasons, I returned to my cheating husband for a second time.

I cannot adequately explain my decision, because it barely felt like a decision, more like an obligation. Suffice to say, I have never felt so stuck and out of options as I did then, like I couldn't see a suitable way out. I'm not suggesting that there was domestic abuse in my marriage, but I understood in that moment how victims end up in situations which, to the outside, are clearly situations they should leave. Take it from me and avoid any "hands-on" research: it's the most isolating and terrifying place to find ourselves, and it doesn't take a violent partner to make us feel that way.

In returning to my husband *again*, while other people were certainly judging me big time, nobody judged me more harshly than I did myself. In deciding to give my marriage another shot, I lost respect for myself. I put my marriage first because that's what marriage is, but it turns out that I should have been putting myself first all along. My husband certainly wasn't denying himself the freedom to be free, so why should I?

Nonetheless, I moved back in with him sometime that August. At first it wasn't that bad. I felt numbed by my own defenses and had compartmentalised a lot of what had happened. I tried to focus on other things, but I was different and I knew it. I was incredibly tightly wound and simply couldn't relax nor enjoy simple pleasures. Life became more and more bland. Where I'd once found happiness, I now found tears. Escaping from a room full of friends laughing and chatting, I would tuck myself away in the bathroom and allow myself to silently weep. For what? I didn't even know anymore.

I persevered in silence for around six months, before noticing that the anxiety rising within me was becoming unavoidable. Frequently I experienced

the feeling of my breath being sucked from my body, usually when I was
wondering how I'd possibly spend the rest of my life like this. I had the startling realisation that this could be my new normal, for years to come, and the
fear that came with it did a number on my muscles and tissues. This kind
of thing was happening more and more often. I'd even started to have panic
attacks in the shower before work. I'd scream in tears but no noise came out.
I'd fold into the corner of my shower, feeling trapped in a life that I'd trusted
to be mine forever. I needed help; I needed to be rescued; I longed for an out,
but I couldn't make a sound.

By the beginning of summer, I realised that I needed to get real help.
Paranoia was making me crazy, and I truly mean that. So convinced that my
husband was doing things behind my back, I'd begun to try and catch him out.
I'd feign sickness at work to head home at lunchtime in case he returned to
the house. I would make the bed a certain way, so that I'd know if he'd been in
bed with someone else. Not to mention, I started sniffing the seat belt every
time we rode in his car together.

I know it sounds crazy, but the seat-belt thing is what gave away my dad's
final affair. I remember how he picked me up from school one day, which was
an unusual occurrence in and of itself, and I happened to smell the seat belt as
I was pulling it across my body. It was a perfume scent that I'd never smelled
before. In all fairness, it was lovely, but it wasn't among the perfumes my mum
wore. I remember thinking that a person would need to be in the car a lot for
the seat belt to smell so strongly of their fragrance. Long story short, seat belts
can be the downfall of a cheater.

Mostly, my husband's passenger seat belt smelled of me, though it didn't
stop me from having a quick sniff every time I got into the car. Yet with every
lunchtime stakeout, precision bed-making or seat-belt whiff, I was slowly
losing my mind. It was the start of what could have ended up in certifiable
insanity—I can entirely understand how people go there. Imagine the mind as
a ball of yarn: mental illness is when it starts to unravel, and insanity is when
somebody grabs a hold of the loose thread and runs in circles around the room.
In this case, regardless of my husband's cheating, that somebody was me.

After one particularly tough morning, unsure of whether I could even make
it to work, I texted my mum and asked her if we could meet for coffee. Our
offices were close, in the West End of Edinburgh, with a perfectly placed
Starbucks right in the middle. Sitting with our coffees at a little corner table,

I explained to Mum how bad things were: the panic attacks, the resignation to a joyless marriage, the anxiety. She was shocked, because everyone thought we were doing so much better. In some respects, I'm glad that we'd managed to create such a facade, because I didn't like the thought of people going through things with us. But it meant that if/when I told people about the reality, they were likely to be surprised.

I explained that I'd wanted to wring his neck in the supermarket, for no apparent reason. I told her that I had begun to flinch whenever he wanted to have sex, that he felt like a stranger. And I noted that, unlike in the beginning, I no longer felt safe in his arms. I so longed to feel secure, protected, safe. *Could I give those gifts to myself,* I wondered, *if I gave myself enough space to open them?*

My mum, having gone through a tumultuous marriage plus a divorce with my father, was well placed to offer good advice. She suggested that I set myself a time frame, be it two months, ten months, whatever I felt comfortable with; and in that time, to really be aware of what was causing me to feel the way I felt. Was it solely what happened in the past, or were there other external factors, ones that could just amount to a bad day for somebody else?

I'd been trying like a motherfucker to make it work, but she wanted me to be triple sure that I'd done everything I could before calling the game. She knew how important this would turn out to be, in the long run—to know for sure. But she was emphatic as well, saying that if I'd done all I could and things weren't better, I had to walk away for my own sanity. It was hard for her to say those words to me, and I knew it. She believes in the sanctity of marriage, despite her divorce, and she would have done anything for us to simply work and stay together. She loved both of us, even after all he'd done; but her concern, ultimately, was for me.

In my head, I gave myself six months, taking us to November; but in reality I wasn't sure how things would look then, nor how I would end it. Like, how do you just blow up your marriage? That was really more *his* forte. For the first time since we'd been married, I hoped that we could at least make it through the summer. Our first year, the shit had blown up in May, and the second year in June. But summer really wasn't to be our season.

On the last day of July, we returned home from a weekend away with friends. While he unpacked, I settled into the sofa with our laptop. Opening the web browser, I saw an unfamiliar login screen for an MSN account, with an email address pre-populated in the login field. It was a nickname of his from university, one that I'd incidentally always fucking hated. Wondering why he had an email address that I didn't know about, I called him through from the bedroom to ask about it. My spidey-senses were now on full alert.

Had he come through and just admitted it was his email address, who knows how things might have ended up. However, the story he tried to spin me was... incredulous. Initially, he said that he knew nothing about the email address. Then, after five or ten minutes of back and forth, he admitted that he'd previously had that email address but hadn't used it since university. When I pressed him regarding how it had ended up on a login screen on our laptop, he proceeded to tell me what I can only describe as a tall, tall tale.

Essentially, he suggested that someone had logged into our Wi-Fi, hacked into our laptop through the Wi-Fi, and then finally hacked into an MSN email address that he used to have at university. Did he hear himself? Did he genuinely think I was going to believe a single word of his story? At this stage, I was working in the tech industry, but I'm hopeful that I would have been wise to his big pile of stinking bullshit anyways. Nonetheless, this was his story and he stuck to it. In fact, as far as I know, he still sticks to it today. The delusion was fascinating to me.

I suppose the alternative—taking responsibility—would have required him to admit that he'd done something wrong and to apologise for his choices, or else be seen as a total asshole who actually didn't see anything wrong with cheating on his wife yet *again*. Maybe the latter option applied for my husband, thus the delusion was his preferred reality; because in my version of reality, he simply wasn't worth my energy, space, or time. I gave him every opportunity to tell the truth and backtrack on what he'd said without further repercussions. But no, he was adamant. *Deny, deny, deny.* He stormed out of the flat after an hour of relentless back and forth, hurt by the accusations I'd leveled at him, apparently. *As if he didn't have any priors...*

While he was out, I made myself busy hacking into his email account, the one he insisted not to know anything about—at least until he miraculously did, but apparently he didn't remember the password. I went through all of the security questions, tracked down the backup email account, reset the password, and added new security questions. Not long after he returned to the apartment, I was in. I didn't say anything to him about my extreme password-reset skills; instead, I gave him one last opportunity to come clean. I remember looking over the back of the sofa and saying: "I don't think you understand how crucial what's happening right now is to our marriage." But yet again, he flat out denied the possibility that he might have something to tell me and took himself to bed.

I don't think he was lying awake with any concern for the situation. So, while he was presumably drifting off to sleep, I delved into an online world that felt dark and secret and disgusting. The email was registered under a type of MSN account that I'd never before seen, almost a Facebook-type, "friends" network. I didn't even know MSN still existed at this point—but turns out it did and my husband was a seasoned user. All of the people on his friends' list were female, mostly with profile pics of them in their underwear. There were also a few names of women whom I knew (friends of his sisters and a woman from his work).

I'd hit the motherlode as far as evidence goes; there was literally so much information. I was taking screenshots and trying to get timestamp clarifications to put together a timeline. If it said February, was I to presume it was February of that year? Could all of these conversations be from his university days? Writing this now, I'm aware that it didn't fucking matter! It was shady as shit either way. Clearly he'd lied about something and I didn't need anymore proof. Still, I wanted to be sure and fact-check everything one-hundred percent before I effectively blew apart my marriage—this time for the absolute *last* time.

I went from looking at his MSN account to Googling how to conduct a deep dive of the laptop's history. Sure, I knew the browsing history could be easily wiped, but this wouldn't completely clear it either. So, I spent hours reading articles and doing all sorts of things in the depths of my laptop. Truly, I was on a mission. When I finally discovered some browsing history that confirmed my previous inclinations (he had, in fact, been coming home at lunchtime), I also discovered that it wasn't necessarily to have sex with people (though who knows). He'd been coming home and logging into this MSN account. He'd also been partaking in dating sites. *Wow.*

With a chill, I realised that this didn't even hurt me. My overriding feeling was actually one of relief. Relief that I finally had a reason to walk out, validation that my subsequent choices were the right ones, and gratitude that I could end this on my own terms. That night, I barely slept. As soon as I heard his car leave the next morning, I called my mum at work. I gave her a brief overview of the previous night's cyberspace investigation and asked if she'd find out from a colleague in the IT department whether there might be another, more feasible explanation for my discoveries. The guy must have been like: *WTF, why are you pulling me into your family drama?* But I didn't even care. I sent my mum the details of what I needed to know, word for word, in a text ending with: *Can there be any other explanation?* which she relayed to him. Her reply about half an hour later came back no.

Trying to make a relationship work after cheating is like getting shot with the bullet still lodged in your flesh. The doctor says you can probably survive with the bullet inside your body, so you try to heal, hoping time will take care of the wound. But the long term effects of having the bullet lodged deep inside you end up causing complications, thus you choose to remove it. You know the act of removing it will cause far more short-term pain than if the bullet were left to rot, but doing so will leave a vacuum that floods with blood, pain, and tears in the meantime—and this could well kill you.

Nonetheless, I decided to remove the bullet that day, to be one with the flood—come what may. I didn't have time left to build an ark or find God or take one of everything I wanted to replicate once I'd gone away. I simply let the waters rise around me, finding myself, in time, awash on the shores of British Columbia.

Three

The Big Move

Months after moving out of my marital home for the last time, I learned how one *physically* experiences emotional pain. My body manifested stress in multiple ways, all of which I tried to remedy with conventional medicine, chiropractors (even Reiki), and a lot of alcohol. I stopped short of antidepressants, after a shitty experience with them following my parents' divorce, and discovered that sleep could leave you feeling more exhausted than rested, if it were filled with tormented dreams and dark thoughts.

I experienced a feeling of not belonging, like Holden Caulfield or Esther Greenwood, as if I didn't fully exist. I could no longer tell what was true and what was attempting to mislead me, so instead I chose to presume the worst in people at all times. Regardless of the context and content, everything anybody told me was a lie. A friend asks me to go to the movies with them? *They probably don't want to go.* My mum says that she's working late? *She's probably going to meet someone.* A work colleague gives me kudos for a job well done? *They probably want me fired.* You tell me that Antarctica is white? *Yeah, okay, it must be black.* These were dark times, juxtaposed with an uncanny sense of relief that I was no longer tormented as I'd been in my marriage. But clearly, I was still suffering the effects.

It had been a long, pointless, and weirdly heartbreaking struggle to get my husband to accept that I wasn't coming back. When 365 days had passed since I'd moved out, I sent the papers to initiate the divorce process, as Scottish law permits, making the final check mark on my list of to-do's. The only thing left was moving to Canada. Naturally, my husband didn't take it well. He told me that I'd made a mistake and encouraged me to give it another go.

To me, it was unfathomable for him to think there was any chance of recon-
ciliation. Didn't he understand the extent to which he'd hurt and traumatised
me? It was narcissism at its finest, and choosing to move was the best thing I
could do.

When I told people about my move to Canada, I heard so many people
say: *Oh, you're so brave.* The silent implication I took from this (given my
severe distrust of everything that anyone said back then) was more like: *Wow,
you're nuts.* But I never let it deter me. I ignored the fact that I was giving up
my great job, with an awesome company that I was proud of and colleagues
I loved working with every day. People also often said: *Your mum is going to
miss you so much,* and I had to block out their words, for this was the most
painstaking aspect of my decision.

I'd been lucky to move back in with my mum, multiple times. For some
people, moving back in with their parents is absolute no-no. But when I
couldn't eat, my mum would entice me with dinners of cheese boards, crisps,
and dip—my all-time favourite snacks. Over the course of the summer, we
watched the Olympics and Wimbledon together, perfecting our skills when
it came to whipping up a fresh pitcher of Pimms as the players changed ends
or between one heat and the next—a wonderful skill. Like, really, does your
mum have a bar in her house? Does she organise gin-tasting sessions for you
and your friends?

She and I lived together like friends more than we did mother / daughter.
She was a saving grace for me in a desperate time of need, but rooming with
my mum wasn't a long term solution. As I swiftly headed towards thirty, I
knew that I didn't want to reach that milestone while living with my mum, for
fear that I may never leave.

Once I'd booked my flight, and with one eye on September 25th, I set about
doing all the things I'd never made time to do in Edinburgh. I enjoyed far too
many "leaving" celebrations with various groups of friends, sometimes twice.
I prepared for my life in Vancouver long before I landed on Canadian soil,
securing myself both a job and an apartment. What can I say? I'm a planner.
For me, pitching up somewhere new with no confirmed income, starting my
life in a hostel or on somebody's couch, was simply not an option.

After a particularly emotional last day of work (where I received maybe the
greatest leaving gift of all time: a photo-shopped picture of me, dressed as a
Mountie and riding a bear...yeah, you read that right), and some incredibly

expert-packing requiring of endless vacuum packs, it was time to drive to Glasgow and board my flight to Vancouver. OOF though, that drive. I hated it on the best of days and this was definitely not the best of days. Victoria, one of my best friends, accompanied my mum and me. The thought of the additional (and inevitable) persons's tears at the airport concerned me, but she'd be an exceptional distraction for us on the way through and a much needed comfort for my mum on the drive home to Edinburgh.

Walking out of my mum's house for the last time, there were a lot of deep breaths and deferring eye contact with Mum and Victoria, plus a few last glances at the kitchen countertop, which I'd sat at so many times debating the trials of life, not to mention the bedroom that had witnessed all my sleepless nights, the home that I still couldn't believe I wouldn't see again until…well, I didn't know when exactly. I'd booked a one-way ticket because I didn't want to give myself an "out." If I had a return ticket and things got even a little tough in Vancouver, I might just change the date and fly home before I knew it. But I wanted to make a go of it, and I think it was psychologically beneficial for everyone that we didn't get pointlessly attached to a return date.

I had also booked flights to Katrin's German-Argentinian wedding in Spain that April, from Vancouver to Valencia, so if nothing else, I had to make it five months. It seemed totally doable and although I wouldn't be going back to Edinburgh on the trip, I would be seeing my mum, as she was coming with me to the wedding. There was comfort in knowing that at least we had that planned. I would come to find this would be key, always knowing when we'd see each other again, even if it felt like ages away.

An hour's drive later, with some forced laughs and a lot of *don't start crying yet(s)*, we said goodbye. My mum was inconsolable and I felt for Victoria—it was going to be a long drive home. Meanwhile, I made my way up the escalator, not knowing what the fuck I was getting myself into but feeling as if this was the first positive thing I'd done in an incredibly long time. Ultimately, I knew that if all else failed and Vancouver turned out to be a stinking hole, home wasn't going anywhere.

I'd felt so lost for so long, but at least this feeling of the unknown made sense. It was to be expected, and there was comfort in that. Whatever experience arose from this decision, it would be the result of a choice I had made, not an outcome of some situation that got out of my hands. I'd done this; I'd chosen this; and I was going to make this work.

Unbeknownst to me, at the same time that I was flying to Canada, there was a judge back in Edinburgh signing my divorce papers. I'd done all the necessary paperwork and court visits and I'd just been waiting for the divorce certificate to come through, desperately hoping that I'd have it before leaving. Every day, I'd pray for the postman to bring me the one piece of mail that no girl should want so much, by the order of which I would return to being Louise Johnson.

When I left for the airport it was still MIA, so I took off into the sky as *Little Lou Who* and received my name change as the first piece of mail to my Vancouver address from my mum. Amongst a care package of other fun stuff, of course (such was her want for my divorce certificate to not be her first letter to me in Canada). Having my marriage officially end on the same day I left the country was poetically epic. It almost made it okay that it hadn't happened before I left, because the date of September 25, 2013 will forever be the day that my life changed forever.

Four

Welcome to Vancouver

When they say that Canadians are friendly, they aren't kidding. I arrived to the most Canadian welcome ever. My new boss came to pick me up at the airport and dropped me off at my new apartment in Yaletown, where my new landlord was waiting for me. To top it off, she'd stocked the fridge with essentials, in knowingness that I was arriving from Scotland that day. *Who are these people?!* I thought. Were they always this nice, or was the whole nine yards reserved for blonde-haired Scottish divorcees with healthy password-hacking skills?

I'd already researched the shit out of the area around my downtown apartment, so once my landlord gave me her final piece of neighbourhood insight (and told me for the third time to call my mum), I already knew where I was headed. Noodlebox was right across the street, and having already scoped out their menu before I even left Edinburgh, I knew that Pad Thai would be my first "Canadian" meal. Actual Canadian cuisine is much harder to put your finger on, however, since it's such a multicultural country and the traditional foods vary across the wide expanse of the continent.

In the Province of British Columbia (B.C.), the "traditional" cuisine is rooted in locally abundant resources like freshly-caught salmon, other fish, and dishes indigenous to the Aboriginal groups still in the area today. In Vancouver, you can find people and cuisines from literally all over the world, but a traditional Pacific-Northwest menu will probably include such specialities as bannock, boar, elk, shellfish, and fresh made berry jam—just to name a few things. Nonetheless, the traditional foods of Aboriginal groups in B.C. are rooted in the locally abundant resources of the area, certain of which are harder to fine these days, as our natural resources have been over consumed by the local "powers that be."

While other people may have gone out for a walk to discover their new neighbourhood, I should probably explain that, at this point in my life, I wasn't particularly confident in unknown situations. I liked familiarity, comfort zones, and control. "Exploring" felt uncomfortable and I'd had a long day, but I made it across the street and back again to watch some ice hockey on TV (my first experience of the Vancouver Canucks losing, though it would not be my last). But yeah, I moved to a new city and I didn't like the unknown... *This would be fun!*

As a result, it probably took me longer to discover the city than it does most newcomers, and as I found the areas I liked, I became a regular on those streets and in those shops (yes, I frequented The Cross in Yaletown on a weekly basis, just looking at all the prettiness), finding comfort bit by bit, like *The Little-Train-That-Could.* While I allowed myself a slow burn with regard to city exploration, I also made a deal with myself that if I got invited anywhere, I would say yes. My mum always taught me not to go with strangers, but I was hoping it would work out a little better in Canada, and not at all like taking sweets from a creepy guy in the park.

The great thing about having my apartment and job lined up was that at no time did I feel as if I were on vacation; it truly felt like starting a new life. I arrived on Wednesday, went to visit my new office and had lunch with my new colleagues on Thursday, and started work on Monday. *Pro tip: Don't underestimate jet lag when starting a new life with an eight-hour time difference.*

My apartment was a tiny but perfectly formed 500-square-foot condo in a high-rise building, right in the middle of the Downtown area, across the street from the Vancouver Public Library, and between the Gastown and Yaletown neighbourhoods. It was fully furnished, right down to the hangers and Tupperware, which was handy considering that I'd arrived with little more than clothing. And I loved it.

I'd had a life goal ever since I was a child that I wanted to live in a high-rise building, somewhere downtown in a North American city. I cannot be sure which movie inspired the idea, but being able to tick it off my list felt fabulous. Obviously, there are more important goals in life than living in a trendy high-rise building, but it was important to me because I'd never thought it could happen. When I saw the reality take shape before me, it was a sign that I'd cleared a new life path for myself. People tend to *ooh* and *ahh* at the thought of history, upon hearing that I grew up in Edinburgh and Cairo, but living in a city of glass, purpose-built for the 21st Century, was absolute bliss for me. For starters, there was so much parking, and I didn't even have a car!

It was also the first time that I'd lived alone. *Ever.* From home, to boarding school, to shared flats in university, to living with my ex, there was no time when I didn't live with someone, if not multiple people (or eighty-nine other girls in a boarding house). I was a little apprehensive about how I'd find things yet excited about the new experience. Thankfully, the apartment was small enough that I couldn't possibly freak myself out by coming back to an empty, dark apartment, and I don't think I ever missed coming home to someone. The choice to live alone meant that I really needed to make an effort to be social; otherwise, living by myself, paired with my dislike for the unknown, might have rendered me a hermit.

My job was doing sales and marketing at a yoga company that made and sold yoga products. Up until this point, I thought the only thing you needed for yoga was a mat and some flexibility. Apparently though, there are blocks and straps and bolsters involved. *What the fuck is a bolster?* For those who haven't been to Vancouver or don't know anything about the area, it's a typical west-coast city in the sense of having a healthy mentality towards lifestyle. Yoga, green juice, kale, hiking, crazy exercise fads—it's a whole thing. A whole thing that I had never experienced because for those who don't know Scotland well, healthy isn't really a widely practiced concept there.

My new colleagues were amazing, introducing me to a whole host of Vancouver habits, culture and terminology. And when work suggested that I take up yoga, given that, you know, we worked in the yoga industry, I figured it would be a good learning curve and a great chance to go "full Vancouver."

Okay, so, yoga is hard. It's not the relaxing lie down kind of activity that I thought it was. And yes, I spent most of my first class in the YYoga Downtown studio trying not to fart (the internet memes are not lying). But I'd found my type of yoga studio, at least: it was bougie as shit and felt more like a spa; while the studios that smelled like moth balls were less up my alley.

I also went to my first singing-bowl meditation at one of the yogi shops to which my company sold (definitely not bougie and definitely not a spa, but who says I didn't leave my comfort zone?). To be frank, this cynic fully drank the Kool-Aid; I was zen as shit when I left that place, despite having spent an hour and a half lying on a dusty shop floor, surrounded by musty smelling hand-woven clothing. Such is the spectrum of yoga-type experiences available here in Vancouver.

My job also registered me for a course, within the first few weeks of starting work. It was a Coaching and Leadership Training Intensive that all of their new employees took (talk about abandoning my comfort zone). Bearing in mind, I was "fresh off the boat" from Britain, the land of the stiff upper lip, where the want to brush things under the carpet—especially emotions and hard conversations—reigned superior. This was everything we are not about; and stupidly, I hadn't considered that in order to coach people, we'd have to act as willing subjects for each other to practice on as well. Not long into the weekend-intensive course, people were bearing their souls to each other in the downtown hotel conference room. Needless to say, it all got very uncomfortable very fast, at least for me. Meanwhile, these North Americans were more than happy to spill their guts.

Thankfully I met two wonderful humans who made the whole thing much easier. Kim had moved to Vancouver from the East Coast after her own divorce, and Jenni had come to town for the course from Alaska. *Alaska!* When would I have otherwise met someone from Alaska? Both were people I could get on board with, finding some element of comfort in their presence, in the midst of exercises like standing in a circle while people gave us compliments. *What in the merry hell was that about?* Oh Canada, you are like a riddle and a joker all at the same time, trying to explain the jokes you play on yourself.

Alas, the act of explaining a joke tends to destroy its humour! Years later, I'd learn from a friend who'd grown up in the city that their high school gym teacher had tried to teach them all a bit more attitude, after noticing the high incidence at which students would apologise to desks—like, after bumping into them—as if they were people. My friend told me that this gym teacher (who came out of the closet as queer a few years later, after a ninth grade student at the school came out as queer himself) had long curly blonde hair and once made a joke about how men couldn't have breasts because they'd just play with them all the time. The story was quintessentially Vancouver: the older generation was always lying in wait to help the younger generation forward the movements that they themselves had begun as individuals years ago, and everywhere everyone was apologizing to inanimate objects, as if there were a hidden spirit keeping them alive.

The irony of Canada's niceness, that home-bred collective resistance to causing trouble, is that there were histories and legacies of behaviors that most Canadians preferred to leave in the shadows. If and when the shadows came out, well, Canadians were really good at apologizing to whomever they concerned—perhaps *too good* at apologizing. The workshop that my company had us take together was about digging deep and looking at all that was really happening inside us, with the knowledge that this was fueling our professional and personal behaviours. As I spent more time in the city, getting to know its history in the process, I wondered if perhaps these workshops would benefit from being held with respect to the identity of place and community as well, versus simply person and corporation.

In the weeks following the course, after Jenni had returned to the snow of Anchorage, Kim and I met for a drink. Looking out over Canada Place with cocktails, she became my first proper Canadian friend outside of work. So far, the "new experiences" thing was working out for me. Before leaving Edinburgh, I'd also done the dreaded thing of joining a Facebook group for people moving to Vancouver on working holiday visas. In theory, it's a great idea, getting a bunch of people together who are going through a mutual experience. In reality, mostly it's just people asking the same questions over and over again, usually ones they could have simply googled, all while scare-mongering about how difficult it is to get visas, how hard it is to find jobs, and how expensive Vancouver is once you get there. So, for the most part, I ignored it.

However, a few weeks after I arrived, a Scottish girl whom I'd met through the group invited me over to her apartment in the West End—a neighbour-hood in the Downtown area known for its painted rainbow-flag crosswalks and proximity to both beach and forest—along with another couple of girls who'd recently moved from the UK. As lovely as it was to get out and meet people, it's hard when you meet entirely based on everybody having one thing in common and then just hoping there'll be more stuff to connect on in person. It was safe to say that had we not all been there on the same visa, our paths wouldn't have crossed (or if they had, there wouldn't have been any lasting friendships built).

All the same, one English girl, Michelle, despite being fairly quiet, seemed more like "my sort of people." So I was glad that I made it out, despite moments of discomfort while navigating the crowds in The Pint, a bar in

Gastown where we ended our night. Thankfully, it was near enough to my apartment that I could slink off home easily, but that discomfort around the unknown was never far away.

A few weeks later, I met up with my not-so-kindred Scottish spirit for the Christmas festival in Yaletown. We'd made it about halfway along Mainland Street, passing most of the attractions and stalls, when I saw someone that I didn't know but still recognised. Weird. Turns out she was another Brit, an English girl from the Facebook group. After brief introductions to her and her Scottish boyfriend, we made the very quick but not at all surprising decision (as a group of Brits) to ditch the festivities and head to the nearest pub. *Ah-h-h-h my kind of people!* It would be the first of many afternoons spent drinking craft beer at Yaletown Brewery.

Laura and Sam were absolutely the type of friends I could get along with; and it was lovely to find out that Sam was from a town not far from where I'd gone to school. Michelle, the other English girl I'd met on the previous night, joined us as well. Thus five Brits sat in a pub on a Saturday afternoon and had numerous beers. Now it felt like home! The drinking culture was one of the most definitive differences I could pinpoint in Vancouver, right from the start. After work drinks were not a thing here. I'd heard numerous people decline evening invitations because they had [*insert any type of workout here*] early the next morning.

On my Christmas night-out with work friends, we went for dinner and drinks straight after leaving the office, and everyone cleared out and went home by seven pm. A day later, my mum told me that her Christmas night-out had ended when their group from work got thrown out of the pub at one am for drug use (note, my mum was an innocent bystander). *Yup,* this is not the UK. But here were people who understood what we'd left behind at home, and Sam had already found his way to a rugby club filled with the Irish and French and Aussies. Through my friendship with them, a community of fellow drinkers was just an invite away.

By the time that Christmas arrived, just three short months after I touched down in Vancouver, I was comfortable with my choice to stay in the city over The Holidays, knowing that going home so soon might be unsettling. I'd received a number of invites to spend Christmas with new acquaintances and their families, but they were just that—acquaintances—and it didn't feel right to impose myself on their Christmases. Instead, I bought a fuck tonne of cheese from Whole Foods (*hi, Canada, why is your cheese so expensive?*) and every type of alcohol I could conceivably want to drink, before settling in for a day of watching the Disney parade, Christmas movies, and the inexplicably comforting fireplace channel. (What is it about the crackle and spit of a fresh log on the fire that's so enjoyable, even on a screen?)

Skyping home, while my family enjoyed their Christmas dinner together, was lovely albeit tinged with sadness and some serious FOMO. Was it better or worse than the previous Christmas, when the separation was still super fresh and I'd persuaded (forced might be a better word) my mum to spend Christmas with me in Vegas? Hard to tell. At face value, one might presume that Christmas would be the toughest part of The Holidays, but for a Scottish person, the New Year (Hogmanay, as we call it) is almost as big of a deal. December was about coming to terms with the reality that this would be the first Hogmanay I'd celebrate outside of Scotland. Despite the many Christmases I'd spent abroad, I was always home by the 31st. *Always.* Edinburgh was home to the largest New Year's Eve street party in the world; from as young as I could remember, our family traditions during the New Year were far more robust than those of Christmas.

As adults, New Year is so often a let down—long lines to enter venues, expensive bar tabs, and no means of transportation when it's time to go home. But to this day, my childhood memories of New Year's are ones that I cherish. Familial relations are hard during The Holidays (this is not brand new information, I know), and recollecting the happier times after too many scandals and skeletons have broken is basically Mission Impossible. Yet I love recollecting those New Years memories, steeped in Scottish traditions, like when my uncle would stand outside my Nana and Grandpa's house with one minute to go before midnight, in order to "first foot" us after the bells.

Scottish tradition dictates that the first person of the year to visit your house (the first foot) should bring something to eat (normally shortbread), something to keep warm (a log for the fire, or a lump of coal, in my earliest memories) and something to drink (obviously whisky). So, my uncle's return to the hearth, just one minute after midnight, granted us food and good luck for the year. My family managed to make a whopping amount of lovely New Year's memories like this one. Once at my Great Gran's (who'd lost her legs due to medical complications), my other uncle walked out of the bathroom into the dark hallway after a few too many drinks, finding nothing but a pair of legs staring back at him. *Yeah,* he almost had a heart attack.

Nonetheless, booking myself a prized stay at the Fairmont Hotel in Vancouver, just a couple of blocks from my apartment, was the perfect anti-dote to missing my first Scottish Hogmanay. My friend Kim came to stay and we enjoyed cocktails at the bar, followed by steak dinner and a ball dropping in New York City (at nine pm re: the East Coast/West Coast time difference... then they just replay it again at midnight Pacific Time...okay, then). It wasn't quite home but it was a lovely and a brand new experience all the same.

I'd had an interesting first few months discovering how to be by myself. I remember deciding how to introduce myself to other people. Early on I decided I'd intro myself as Lou instead of Louise. I'd always liked it as a nick-name but my ex used to hate it, said it sounded like I was a toilet, so I think it only galvanised me more to use it going forward. Does divorce always have to be the answer to the question: *Why did you move here?* There was freedom in how much I chose to tell new people, knowing that they had no other context. For the most part, I never shied away from the story, feeling in some way that it might make some aspects of me more understandable to people—back when I still felt like that was my responsibility.

During my first season in Vancouver, I also popped my post-divorce sex cherry, as it were. Men were wholly off my radar for eighteen months, not through choice but simply because my brain had forgotten about their very existence (at least in the form of romantic or sexual interests). I hadn't missed the intimacy, such was the subconscious nature of my decision to put an ocean and a continent between me and my old life. My brain was occupied with far bigger, pressing things.

So, getting back in the saddle, if you will, was not an insignificant occur-rence. It was a pretty big deal. One I was happy to experience blackout drunk. Romantic, *right?* Sensible, *eh?* The opportunity, or should I say the Irishman, presented itself during the rugby team's Twelve Pubs of Christmas Day of Drinking (which is exactly what it sounds like). My "confidence" rose with my level of intoxication, and a cheeky snog in one of the latter twelve bars somehow swept us back to my place in the rain, fully decked out in Santa hat gear and ugly Christmas sweaters.

Despite my level of drunkenness, mine was a hugely conflict-fueled experience. He was funny, attractive, and a great snuggler, but I felt self-conscious and unsure, barely convinced that I even remembered how to have sex (given my eighteen-month hiatus since the last time with my husband). This was just some random guy and there were a lot of *what-the-fuck-am-I-doing* thoughts running through my head. One night stands aren't exactly familiar territory when you're recently divorced from the person who witnessed your inaugural coming-of-age.

My consternation was marginally eased when, in a moment of pure mid-sex comedy that fully speaks to my level of inebriation, I fell off the bed. Given the compact nature of my bedroom, I landed ass first in the window blinds. Thankfully, we both laughed it off. There would forever be a peach-shaped dent in those blinds, but who doesn't love a good sex memento? Ultimately, while not sound advice nor medically supported in any way, I'd say that being drunk for sex following my divorce might have been the only way to slip back under the sheets. I cannot imagine carrying out the act in full awareness; my brain was in overdrive already, but at least I blocked most of it out! *Gotta' love a healthy approach to sex, right?*

Everything would've been fine if I'd just come to a full stop the next morning, if we'd simply waved goodbye as he hobbled out the door in two different shoes (the result of one of yesterday's pub-crawl challenges), wearing his intentionally ugly Christmas sweater complete with battery-operated festive lights. But the sex, the snuggling through the night, the hugely open and honest chats we'd had as the morning light flooded into my bedroom, the kind of chats that you only have on the cusp of drunkenness and hangover, all left me feeling as if there must be more. *Surely, right?* Could you really do all those things and just wave goodbye the next morning?

Instead, I attempted to make something of it. I wanted to extend our post-coitus communication, presuming there'd be a follow-up meeting, that he might have been so dazzled by me that he couldn't help but see me again. Oh wait, *right,* I'd been a drunken, rain-soaked, hot mess that fell off the bed mid-sex and poured my heart out the following morning—about my divorce and how he was the first guy I'd slept with since my ex-husband. *Hot.*

Sam Smith sings: *Guess it's true, I'm not good at a one-night stand,* and it seemed like the same could be said for me. How was I to know? I'd been with my ex since I was nineteen years old and there hadn't been a whole lot of experiences before then (in fact, a total of one). Nor would it be the first time that I would attach far more significance to an experience than the man with whom I'd shared the night. But if nothing else, it was nice to get the monkey off my back, as far as *post-ex-husband sex* went. Though I wouldn't be rushing to seek it out again, which was in no way a reflection of the guy, but rather the emotional complications waiting on the other side of the orgasms.

Five

The Resettlement of 2014

I made it through Christmas and Hogmanay (or The Holidays, as termed in North America with all the most politically correct of intentions,) and I was ready for my first full year of life in Vancouver. Almost two years had passed since I left my husband and initiated the divorce process, and three months had passed since I left Scotland. My trip to Spain for Katrin's wedding was coming up soon in April, and my mum's first visit was planned for June. The city was feeling strangely like home and I'd only been here for three months.

My want to stay within my comfort zone (the one that still somehow let me move to an entirely new country) was mostly kept in check. I was still embracing new experiences, like accepting Kim's offer to hike Lynn Canyon together, a park in the North Vancouver mountain area with trails of varying length and difficulty. Having, up until this point, only ever owned running shoes, I figured that they may not be ideal for the potentially muddy and slippery route. So, going into The North Face store on Granville Street, I purchased my first ever pair of trail shoes. I was pretty sure when I bought them that they were at least half a size too small, but they were on sale and how much did I really think I was going to use them anyways?

Like, what does one wear to hike? Again, I had running gear but I was pretty sure it wasn't really the same vibe. I needed comfy layers, ideally water-proof. Along with the trail shoes, I bought a North Face rain jacket, in bright pink. It wouldn't have been my first choice but, again, it was on sale and I hated rain jackets. That rubbery lining that just makes you sweat and lets condensation gather inside... I didn't get it.

Ugh, the outdoors. It wasn't my favourite place, but it was beautiful in Vancouver and I guessed that having the mountains on our doorstep meant that I should take advantage of the local parks. Though my preference was really a casual stroll, or run, around Stanley Park (Vancouver's city park, three times bigger than New York's Central Park and a convenient fifteen-minute walk from the middle of Downtown, with toilets, concession stands, and even a restaurant or two). Yeah, Stanley Park was about as close to nature as I really wanted to get. But there was no denying the beauty of Lynn Canyon and the peace that being in nature, surrounded by trees and the freshest of air, affords us. Maybe I could get used to it?

At the end of January, as Laura and Sam were celebrating their Christmas engagement, going to the bar for drinks in the middle of downtown, I felt marginally more confident than I had in a long time. It was also nice to go out with a handful of people that I knew. It's funny how quickly you can pick up a group of friends. From the outside, the celebratory drinks likely looked like a meet-up of expats, such was the number of Brits, Aussies, Kiwis, South Africans and Irish folks in attendance.

In the midst of far too many shots, I had my first encounter with the girls that would come to be known as AnnaB and Quyeneth. They were English and had arrived a few months earlier than me, and both of them seemed to have their Vancouver lives together. These girls, along with Laura, would turn out to be a fundamental part of my new life, providing me with more laughs, thought-provoking discussions and events/trips/dinners/plans than I ever could have imagined. But just as I was finding my feet, I would look down to find them swiftly swept off the ground.

My job, which was initially supposed to be a six-month contract, taking me to April, would now be ending in January. And my apartment, for which I'd signed a year's lease, was now being sold and I would have to move. Both were unexpected pieces of news, neither great, though I actually breathed a small sigh of relief when my landlord said that was her only reason for calling. The night before I got the call, I'd gone out for a "casual Sunday happy hour" with Laura in Yaletown. Meeting up at three pm at The Flying Pig, one of our favourite neighbourhood bars, we quickly realised that while we were there for some quiet drinks, the Whitecaps players who'd just walked in were there for anything but.

The Whitecaps are Vancouver's soccer (*cough* *football*) team, playing in the major league with the likes of LA Galaxy. There are plenty of ex-European players in the league, by which I mean Europeans who no longer play for European clubs. They often come to finish their careers in North America, knowing that it is less demanding on their ageing bodies yet still financially rewarding. I'm a huge sports fan and always have been, so I tried to watch as many of the local sports teams as possible upon moving to the city. I checked out the Vancouver Canucks hockey team (who allegedly were having a slump, but their run to the finals one year incited riots in the city), the BC Lions Canadian football team (like American football but with a few rule differences of which I'm still not entirely sure), the Vancouver Canadians Baseball team (a seed team for the Toronto Blue Jays that apparently provides perfect summer's evening entertainment), and then the Vancouver Whitecaps.

For the most part, if any of the players on those teams smacked me in the face, I wouldn't have the slightest idea of who they were, but on this occasion I recognised an ex-player of the English Premier League. (There are very few black men in Vancouver, so they're often obvious regardless of whether they're famous athletes.) Doing a top-down scan of the two guys with him, I recognised one of them as the rookie who'd made his debut in yesterday's game, and I figured the other must be a hinger-on, as my Nana would say. (As in, someone who hopes to get scraps from hanging out with people whose coat-tails they might be riding). I mean, he also could have been one of their managers (did MLS players have managers?) or coaching staff (did they drink with players?) or any number of other things, but that was the story I'd made up in my head and I was sticking to it.

The three well-dressed men clearly weren't experiencing any Sunday scaries before going back to their normal nine-to-five jobs, given the multiple shots they'd done at the bar, but in all fairness, we were also drinking on a Sunday. Who were we to judge? Likely due to our proximity at the bar, they offered to have us partake in the shots and thus somehow, a quiet Sunday-afternoon drink turned into something of a bar hop with these guys. The rookie was incredibly young, a Black American with beautiful piercing blue eyes. He'd just arrived in Vancouver and his English colleague was trying to welcome him to the city.

We moved through a couple of nearby bars and picked up two seemingly random girls by the fourth bar, when we found out that the hinger-on actually owned a bar in the neighbourhood. Okay, so my assumption had been a little off about him; naturally, we very much appreciated all the free drinks that he supplied us with at his bar. But Laura and I were both getting to the point where it was, like, nine pm on a Sunday night. A couple of happy-hour drinks had turned into what felt like a Saturday night, and we kinda felt like we should go home. One last bar, and we would.

However, as we were all walking along the street, with my apartment a mere two blocks away (god I loved living in Yaletown with its many bars in extreme proximity to my apartment), English boy and I were in conversation (again) about how different Vancouver was from the UK, and in a partially drunken, partially distracted fashion, he entirely missed the black-painted bike rack in front of him and went *arse over tit* (that expression is less of a Nana saying and more of a Scottish thing). I've never seen someone's legs so blatantly ejected from the ground. If you can imagine him bending at the knee and then envision that happening in the opposite direction with his body falling forwards, well, that's what it was like. Straight over the bike rack, face first. When I replay the scene in my head, it's still so clear: with him about half a foot away from me, mid-sentence, bailing out in such an epic fashion. I have used that memory to make myself smile on more than one occasion.

But at the time, it felt a little more serious. He had a huge gash on his head, and his black skin was peeling back to reveal the pinkest of flesh, now smeared with blood and dirt from the sidewalk. Laura took it upon herself to stem the blood flow, possibly knowing about my aversion to blood. Despite his protestations, we were both pretty sure that he was dazed if not concussed and should likely go to hospital. Unfortunately, as we tried to have a rational conversation with him about his injuries, the two women we'd picked up, who were visiting from South America, fell into hysteria and tried to hail cabs to Vancouver General Hospital (which, by the way, is not how you order a cab in Vancouver—pick up the phone, download an app, or consider yourself walking).

Seemingly, neither one of the men wanted to draw attention to themselves, perhaps because they'd been out drinking before their Monday morning training, or perhaps neither one of them knew how the RCMP would react to two Black guys bleeding on the street in a public area. Racially-motivated police brutality against the Black community was perhaps less of an issue in Vancouver, but there were also so few Black residents. So the rookie promised to take his fallen soldier home, staying with him in case he was concussed.

Laura and I weren't convinced that this was the best idea, but we also weren't about to argue. We were all drunk; they were grown men; and sometimes you just want to go to bed. Plus, Laura was now covered in a guy's blood and clearly our Sunday needed to end.

A few days later, the news made it to the press that our new friend had "tripped" and would be out for a couple of weeks with a head injury. Well, at least he hadn't died from his head injury! At least the incident hadn't created issues for them with law enforcement. In recent years, Vancouver's Black population has been growing, and the Black Lives Matter protests in the USA (which are happening as I write this) regarding the murder of George Floyd, have brought certain issues to light in Canada as well. Police brutality against Black and Aboriginal people is a problem in Canada too. When my coworkers gave me that going away card back in 2013—with me dressed as a Mountie, riding a bear—I knew that bears were not to be ridden, but I didn't know that the RCMP had essentially been created in Canada with the express purpose of policing Aboriginal communities.

But clearly, I was now comfortable in my new neighbourhood, maybe too comfortable, if all-afternoon Sunday drinking sessions were becoming the norm. Vancouver was set up to make me and people like me (that is to say: middle class, White, English-speaking and from a place people loved and knew from the movies) feel comfortable, so adjusting wasn't the hardest thing in the world. I had moved here for a clean slate, but I still wanted it to resemble the state of my old slate as well—just before it got shat on by my ex-husband. Still, it felt like my change in job and apartment could threaten my newfound comfort a bit.

Thankfully, I ended up getting a job with a tech start-up, which I'd begin on the Monday, after finishing my job at the yoga company that Friday. My new position took me back to the industry I'd been working in before leaving Edinburgh. It was a full-time, permanent position, which they'd offered to me on the spot when I went into their Gastown office for an interview. All this to say that it worked out for the better, because being in a permanent role allowed me to think about applying for residency.

The apartment piece was a little trickier. I loved where I was in Yaletown and knew I'd been lucky to get something so fully furnished, but Kim was a great partner in the hunt for a new place. After looking at more than a few unsatisfactory options (either they were dark as shit or expensive as hell, or, in one awful case, both), we talked through whether I should consider non-furnished places. This scared me more than just having to move apartments.

I would have to buy everything new. Like, absolutely everything. And how much was that going to cost me?! I'd been living on a pretty tight budget since arriving in Vancouver. Also, while I'd been able to secure a second year for my working visa, again in the Coachella-esque online release of that year's allocation, it still only guaranteed the next year and a half. And I didn't know what came after that. I'd be able to apply for Permanent Residency if I made that choice, but there was no guarantee that I'd get it. Buying all that furniture felt excessive if I'd potentially need to up and leave the country.

But you know what really made up my mind about going to IKEA to spend hundreds of dollars? Going to look at a brand new building, just three blocks from my current apartment, which would be part hotel and part residences, where I'd have a partial water view from my generously-sized balcony, plus a twenty-four-hour gym and a swimming pool in the building.

I saw it, I loved it, I signed for it. While my first apartment would always hold a special place in my heart, this one felt a lot more like me. For starters, I bloody love hotels and now I'd be living in one! Plus, with all the money I'd be shelling out at Ikea, it would at least be furnished with things that felt a bit more like me. I found this out to mean that everything would be white or gray except my couch, which would be bright pink. Because if I couldn't buy a bright pink couch at this point of my life, when could I?

I had been incredibly lucky with the way my life had turned out since moving to Vancouver. As one of the world's most "livable" cities, it can be an incredibly difficult place to live, and I had managed to get the foundations of a wonderful life in place—partly through my type-A organization skills and all the privileges afforded to me growing up. I'd ensured that I had an apartment and job secured before I arrived, but I'd also compromised on long-term financial saving. It has been said, and it's true, that living in Vancouver is an expensive hobby—a hobby because oftentimes people can't make it last a lifetime due to the cost.

I like to live comfortably, but as I grew up, I also faced times of financial hardship. I'm not ashamed to say that creature comforts and certain luxuries are important features in my life. In Eygpt, for one thing, I lived a very charmed life. But in order for me to have those creature comforts as an adult, I chose to give up on a lot of my other spending. I don't shop or travel half as much as I'd like, and when I go out, I know exactly how much I can spend. I live paycheck to paycheck and long-term financial planning isn't something I've been able to prioritise.

Whether most people, and by most people I mean my mum and brother, would agree with these choices is something I don't dwell on too much. Maybe, at some point, I'll turn into the "responsible adult" that the world says I'm supposed to become. I figured it wasn't impossible that some of the responsibilities I felt beholden to were functions of times or perspectives long gone by, and it wasn't necessarily so bad that I was doing things differently now. I had different priorities and with different priorities came different opportunities. For the time being, however, I had a move and my thirtieth birthday to focus on, and I could hardly wait for either one.

Six

Dirty Thirty

Before I turned thirty, there was the small matter of my trip to Valencia for Katrin's German/Argentinian/Spanish-wedding extravaganza. She was one of my closest friends from boarding school, and yes, it was still a mystery to me how a German brother and sister ended up at a boarding school in the middle of the Scottish countryside, while their parents lived in numerous far flung places all over the world.

She knew the date of her wedding prior to me leaving for Vancouver, and there was never a doubt in my mind that I would make it a priority to get there one way or another. Before I left Scotland, I made a list in my head of events that I would move hell or high water to attend, no matter the distance nor cost, and Katrin's wedding was undoubtedly one of those occasions. Plus, it would be the first time I'd seen my mum since that tearful goodbye in Glasgow Airport. I couldn't wait to spend a couple of days with familiar faces; but it really would be only a couple of days.

When I'd booked my flights, while still sitting on my mum's couch in Edinburgh, I wasn't sure what the situation would be with my job or holiday allocation; so I'd booked the shortest trip I could, which meant leaving Vancouver on Wednesday night and arriving in London on Thursday. There, I'd meet my mum and we'd fly to Valencia later that night, just before the welcome lunch on Friday and the wedding on Saturday. I'd have one recovery day on Sunday, and then it'd be all the way back to Vancouver for me, all in one go on Monday. Just looking at my itinerary gave me a headache, but it would be worth it. And there's something glamorous sounding about "flying to Spain for the weekend." The reality, however, is quite different.

I'd loved flying as a child, all those trips between Cairo and London and then up to Edinburgh; they were fun and the British Airways staff members were always so lovely to us kids. *Oh wait, maybe that was it, we were in Business Class....* Now, at this later stage of my life, when I would've actually appreciated the perks of the front of the plane, I couldn't afford it. Regardless, there has always been something exciting about flying—and don't get me started on how much I love airports. Maybe it's travel in general: flying, airports, hotels. I was always a huge fan. Arguably though, my experiences with all these things growing up in Egypt were on the luxury end of the scale, which never hurts to foster interest.

So, with no business class, not even an airport lounge in sight, I prepared for my overnight flight from Vancouver to London. I needed to sleep during the flight to make the following day a little less painful; so, promptly after dinner, I tucked up my table, put my eye mask down, and tried to get comfy against the window.

All was well until I woke up in the darkened cabin, with the two strangers next to me in seats B and C silently snoring. And me? Well, not feeling so great. I couldn't have been awake for more than a minute, but I knew something wasn't quite right. I couldn't decide if I was going to be sick or shit my pants. Regardless, I was prompted to do something I'd never done before. *Shock horror,* I pressed the button for cabin-crew assistance, hoping that one of them was still awake back there in the galley, although only a glimmer of light shone into the main cabin.

Honestly, I'd started to sweat profusely. As I tried to remove my eye mask and get the synthetic blanket off my knees—in attempt to pull my sweater up and over my head—the tall tanned server I'd seen helping people into their seats earlier appeared, leaning over the sleeping beauties beside me and asking how he could assist. I think I managed to say, "I really don't feel very well"; and my words were answered with darkness.

It could have been twenty seconds or twenty minutes later before I opened my eyes and tried to figure out where the fuck I was. There were metal poles and limbs and, oh right, I was on a plane, and I was staring across the cabin floor at the bases of seats and sleeping passengers' legs. I was also somehow lying in the middle of the aisle, head pointed towards the cockpit, legs in the direction of the rear galley, oxygen mask firmly over my nose and mouth, and a soaking wet crotch...*Why was I wet? Had I pissed myself?* Before I could work out what had happened (oh Jesus, here it came) the thing that always happens when I faint happened. The last time I fainted, I'd been a child, and I always hoped that I'd outgrown this habit for good—but no, here came the tears. I was never sure why they occurred. I wasn't hurt; I knew from experience that this, for me, was normal. I'd always regain consciousness and cry. Most of the time I could tell that I was going to faint even before it happened but it had been so long since the last time.

The first time, though? I thought my body had been overtaken by aliens— either that or I was having a stroke. Nine-year-old me says aliens; adult me says stroke. It was our second visit to Toronto and we had just arrived back at my family's house from the airport. As we stood there chatting with some neighbours, I felt this black mist creep over my entire body, starting with my toes. My limbs were paralysed before I realised what was happening. I couldn't even speak. I was looking at my dad beside me, trying to yell out to him for help, but I guess it just didn't come. I hit the deck fast and face-planted on the sidewalk, only regaining consciousness when my dad carried me up the stairs to the mezzanine lounge overlooking the pool in my great aunt and uncle's air-conditioned Mississauga home.

It had been terrifying at the time, and for a good forty-eight hours after-wards I felt groggy. But now, seventeen years after the last time it happened, I was lying in the middle of a darkened plane aisle, crying and wondering if my bladder had involuntarily released itself, not to mention why I'd returned to this awful habit right now. My fellow seatmates, who were previously sleeping like babies beside me, now appeared to be standing at the front of the cabin, peering through the darkness and wondering what the hell had just happened to the girl in Seat A. Lord only knows how we all came to be out of our seats; I can only imagine what I would have looked like in the light.

Thankfully, I didn't need to be flying Business Class, nor traveling as a cute seven-year-old, for the British Airways staff to be as wonderful as I remem-bered from all my childhood flights. They moved me to a flatbed seat in First Class, which sounds idyllic but I was feeling like absolute death. Fainting had always left me with what I can only describe as a neurological hangover that took hours to wear off. Hours would pass before my legs could hold my weight and my stomach could keep down food well enough to move an inch in any one direction. I was also still trying to work out if I'd pissed my pants and now I was potentially sitting on a first class seat in pee-covered clothing. I was all class.

After surreptitiously trying to dry my leggings over the back of the seat in front of me (who says I don't belong in first class?!) and not being able to fully enjoy the flatbed because I was pretty sure I was going to vomit if I reclined too far, I got my stuff together as we prepared to land in London. This was not how I thought I'd be feeling on my first touchdown on UK soil in over six months.

Gingerly making my way through passport control, customs, then back through security to get into departures for my flight to Valencia, all the while not entirely convinced I wouldn't faint again, I finally found my mum waiting for me. What I'd imagined as a lovely reunion instead amounted to me bursting into tears and my mum wondering why I looked like absolute death. I was just relieved to be with someone who could help me, should my body give out on me again. Travelling alone has its drawbacks.

It was a shaky start to the weekend, and I felt less than ideal for the duration of my trip. In addition to discovering that despite my thinking I hadn't hurt myself in my mid-air escapade, I'd actually managed to bruise myself from my shoulder down to my arse cheek, presumably from hitting a plane seat while hitting the floor? If only they had CCTV on planes.... After an exceptionally fun couple of days with my closest friends—watching my best friend get surrounded by love, and eating an incredible amount of paella and cava—I was getting ready to take three flights back to Vancouver in one day. But I was realising that the lingering nausea I'd had that weekend was getting worse.

It seemed like a strange after effect from fainting that I'd never before experienced. But I soon realised that it was actually nerves. I was nervous about getting on a plane. The trauma of the flight to London had left more than just a physical mark and I was now concerned about having to go all the way back to Canada. Would I faint again? Would I have to repeat the experience? And while my mum would be travelling with me for the two shorter flights, I'd still have that one mammoth transatlantic flight to contend with all by myself.

Maybe moving to Vancouver, practically the furthest point west I could have chosen in Canada, was a stupid fucking idea. It was an inopportune time to develop a fear of flying. It not only seemed irrational at twenty-nine years old when I'd just moved to another continent, but knowing that I had another flight coming up in six weeks didn't bring me much comfort. Fortunately, in the end, everything worked out okay on my flights back home to Vancouver.

It wasn't that I was having a crisis about turning thirty, in fact I was quite looking forward to it. My twenties had been almost precisely punctuated by my relationship with my ex-husband; and it felt like moving into my thirties would give me a clean slate, shutting the door on the last decade of my life and all the trauma that went with it. So I wanted to make sure that I celebrated it well—Vegas seemed like a good option, but I was of the opinion that Vegas was **always** a good idea.

After Kim introduced me to the great outdoors of Vancouver, I was excited to introduce her to how to do Vegas right. We stayed at the Aria, where we made a birthday dinner reservation; and otherwise we would just enjoy the pool, the sunshine, and all the people-watching. My new colleague and friend, Jess, put me in touch with a club promoter she recommended and we lined up a couple of club options for our trip. I'm not a club goer, but there's something about Vegas....It's one of the things I love about it. You can go and be whoever you want. Everyone and no one is looking. You can be playing slots between a woman in a wedding dress and a guy in a Hooters tank top. You can go and do Vegas on a shoestring budget or splurge to your heart's content. Thus I find myself doing things in Vegas that I would ordinarily never do, before returning home and needing to recover for the next four weeks.

My thirtieth birthday was to be no different. I decided to start celebrations the night before my actual birthday, so that I could ring in my thirties in a suitably fun way. Plus, with the eight-hour time difference to the UK, my birthday actually started early for most of my family members anyways, so it just made sense! Over in Vegas, we started with a beautiful dinner, seated as a table of two between a bachelor party of eighteen men from Long Island and a group of eight guys who were there to watch their friend play poker. It was a super fun start to the night. There were a lot of comments flying and the entertainment was only punctuated by the servers checking that we weren't being unduly harassed. We also got sent shots of some of the nicest tequila I've ever tasted. (Like the kind you can actually enjoy without instantly wanting to burn your mouth off afterwards.)

On the conclusion of dinner and following a quick trip back to the room (because Vegas dresses and dinner bloating don't go well together), we went to Hyde, a club on the edge of the Fountains of Bellagio. Our club promoter contact had got us in for free with a few drinks tickets. We were soon asked to join a group of Swiss bankers at their table. They had a prime lake view and we barely hesitated. Did it feel like we were being pimped out? Yah, a little bit. Did we mind, considering the bottle service and the views we were enjoying, or far more importantly, the guarantee of seats all night? Not in the slightest.

Thankfully, the European financiers were all gentlemen, most of them married, and just in Vegas to celebrate a birthday. At midnight, I recall a lot of extra shots being brought to the table. After that, well, it's murky. Kim would likely be able to fill in the details, since she'd been the responsible one while I got fully white-girl drunk. What started as such a civilised and classy celebration descended into an alcohol-fuelled mess, resulting in me leaving all of my belongings at the club while we returned to our hotel further down the Strip. And I mean *everything:* my bag complete with my wallet, room key, make up, and phone.

Waking up the day after I was supposed to have elegantly entered my thirties and instead having to crawl up the Strip with the Nevada sunlight burning my eyes, needing to take the very kind Bellagio concierge's offer of a bottle of water while security went to retrieve my belongings from the vault (which took almost forty minutes, given the level of security involved) was certainly not what I'd planned. I'd have put it off until later in the day, if it wasn't for the fact that my phone was in the bag and I was sure my mum was likely moving into the "missing presumed dead" stage of her panic re: not hearing from me.

Of course, my phone was beautifully smashed when I got it back, which prompted me to recall the moment when I'd dropped it screen first on the marble club floor. I didn't want to tell the staff at the Bellagio that they really shouldn't have bothered putting my bag in the vault. Despite it being a beautiful emerald green BCBG Max Azria clutch, the value of the contents was a whopping 150 dollars maximum. The rest of the day was spent in full recovery mode and while it definitely wasn't the start to my thirties that I'd hoped for all these years, perhaps it would be the last drunken mess of my life—you know, because I'd miraculously grown up overnight? One could only hope.

Either way, it was a memorable birthday, and after buying myself a Tiffany infinity bracelet and ring—with money that I'd accumulated from my slot wins over the last three days—I was grateful to finally be living on my own terms. I had a ways to go before I felt truly happy and settled, and I

knew that. My twenties had been a struggle, but I was hopeful that my thirties would hook me up with happiness in a way that I'd never planned on but
was one-hundred percent ready for now.

Part 2

Seven

Calm Waters

This new decade of life came with a welcome sense of calm, and the rest of 2014 was filled with affirming experiences. My mum was in the city for her first trip to Vancouver and it couldn't have gone better. After chowing down at Noodlebox for her inaugural meal (because tradition), we walked along the seawall in English Bay—and even on that overcast June day, I'll never forget her saying: "I get it. I get why you love it so much."

Her words were everything. Having my mum understand why living in Vancouver made me so happy, how it had given me a new life beyond Edinburgh, all while knowing that she likely wouldn't have her daughter back in Scotland anytime soon in consequence, made me feel so much more at ease with my choice. Sure, the ability to have self-confidence regardless of whether my mum understood my decisions was important, but with her understanding came greater closeness all the same. Greater closeness, in this way, was uniquely valuable, given the geographical distance already placed between her and me.

In over six years of life in Vancouver, I've now come to learn that the guilt about leaving will never entirely dissipate. Every flight back to YVR, every family occasion I miss, every time I wave my mum off in tears at Vancouver airport, I know this is a choice that I made. I did this, and I can't imagine how hard it is for my mum to have me so far away. I'd known that she'd need to personally witness why Vancouver was a better place for me than anywhere else, to see things through my eyes. Receiving that note of understanding on her very first trip allowed me to breathe a sigh of relief.

Arguably, it's hard not to love Vancouver. When I took Mum to Whistler, which is practically on our doorstep, we got to experience our first bear sightings together (a total of eight bears over the weekend)! She was bitten by the Canada bug, even more so than she'd been on our family holidays to Toronto decades earlier. British Columbia, as a province, is so much different from Ontario. Living in Vancouver versus Toronto is kind of like living on a different planet, the main difference being the land itself. Toronto is urban and inland, while Vancouver is an island-like city surrounded by water and towering mountains, which lend their energy to the city's personality and inner life.

My mum saw my new apartment, got to know the neighbourhood and all the places I kept telling her about on Skype. She met my now growing circle of friends and all these things put her mind at ease. Not to mention, I loved sharing all those things with her. At the time, we were looking forward to the arrival of a new generation in our family: my sister-in-law was expecting a baby in October. So, before my mum left, I booked my flights home for Christmas; it would be my first trip back since moving to Canada, and I'd have the treat of meeting my new niece or nephew.

When said niece arrived a few months later, I was more in love than I'd ever thought possible (especially for a baby I'd only ever glimpsed over Skype and in photos). It was another difficult thing to miss out on in person, but I was glad that she'd been born after I'd moved—or else there was a very real chance that I wouldn't have managed to pick up and go with her already in existence! I want to be the aunt who embodies strong, female values and reinforces her purpose and strengths, someone she can look up to with a grin, perhaps as an example of a road less travelled that can still provide happiness, love, and fulfillment. I'll simply have to do all of that from afar.

Before my Christmas trip home, however, there was the small matter of a half-marathon plus a bachelorette in Vegas to attend to (yes, I was going to Vegas again), and I had Laura to thank for both. After Laura and Sam had gotten engaged at Christmas, they'd made the decision to get married in London in twelve-months time. In turn, Laura decided that she needed a fitness goal to work towards in the lead up to her wedding, thus we signed up to run a half-marathon in late October. Sam also joined us, along with Kim, who brought her friend and her new boyfriend, bringing our running group to six "athletes", of which I was definitely the most reluctant participant. I'd never imagined myself running a half-marathon. Like, it was never on my bucket list.

I'd taken up running before my wedding, with the Couch to 5K app to thank for getting my ass out the door. Previously, the furthest I'd ever run was for a bus. I'd never tried to run more than five kilometers and even that had felt like a marathon at the time. Upon moving to Vancouver (and only once I'd plucked up enough courage to haul my ass to the seawall for a run all by myself), I continued with my short-distance running. I figured a half-marathon would truly be an effort, but it turns out that you can train yourself to do unimaginable things. And my body was clearly more capable than I thought. Growing up, I'd never thought my body was built for much at all.

Since the plane "fainting" episode in April, my propensity for dropping to the ground like a swatted fly had only increased—mostly when I was showering after working out, but then I started to feel it during yoga. One time, I woke up face down on the floor of my gym, and another time I thought I was going to faint while watching the 2014 Football World Cup Final with friends over brunch. Without even waiting for the final whistle, my friends decided on my behalf that I should probably go to a doctor. Thus I found myself undergoing neuro and cardio tests while training for a half-marathon. It wasn't a whole lot of fun and I cursed all the training and the approach of race day.

The race wasn't fun either, especially upon witnessing two runners suffer heart attacks at different points during the course, as we wound our way through Stanley Park. But I did it. We all did it, and holy shit what a sense of achievement! In fact, so much so that in the hours afterwards, somewhere between brunch at White Spot (we weren't looking for class, we were looking for carbs) and me losing complete use of my legs (such was the effect of that first 21.1 kilometres on my body), I decided that I was going to run one half-marathon for every year of my thirties. But I made the mistake of making my goal known. It seemed like a good idea at the time, but I think that's what they call endorphins.

With the half-marathon out of the way, Laura's bachelorette was up next. AnnaB, Quyeneth, and I had told her that we'd planned a civilised wine-tasting trip to San Francisco and Napa, but perhaps we pulled it off too well because that trip sounded quite lovely. In reality, we were going to Vegas; Laura's sister and some of her best friends from home were flying in to surprise her for the party.

This trip would cement my friendship with Laura, Quyeneth, and AnnaB— gals who'd come to be known as the "Winning @ Life Ladies." From the rainy drive over the border, to the motel in Bellingham before our flight the next morning, and the room that we shared together while the neighboring room played a family game of Twister, to endless in-jokes, onion ring towers, and going the long way round, it was truly one of the best trips I've ever taken. Laura, AnnaB, and Quyeneth are some of the smartest and funniest women I've ever met, and now I was lucky to call them some of my best friends.

Quyeneth couldn't make it to England for Laura's wedding a few months later, but AnnaB and I were more than a little excited about being the Vancouver contingent at their UK wedding. They got married over the Winter Holidays. It was a fun-filled, pork-pie fuelled, drunken joy of a celebration— a classic city wedding in beautiful London, during December, which ultimately sent me home with one of the bridesmaids' brothers. More drunken sex ensued. The month prior, I'd enjoyed yet another sexscapade with yet another rugby player, but it seemed like men were only on my mind when I was drunk. Did this mean I wasn't really interested in them, or was I repressing those feelings when sober to avoid dealing with them?

Still, the thought of dating seemed daunting. Only on my third experience of casual sex (post-marriage) was I finally able to shake the feeling that I was somehow cheating on my ex-husband. The irony is not lost on me that he'd been the cheater and yet, here I was, post-divorce, worrying about our vows. It's like being married to someone becomes such an inherent part of your identity that certain feelings about the connection become involuntary. In my rational mind, I knew it was over, but there was still this part of me, somewhere deep down inside, that felt connected to him. What if that lasts forever? What if I can never shake the feeling that we're part of each other?

Rather than trying to scrub him from memory, maybe I need to make my peace with it. Attachment was tricky, but all the benefits of a relationship still appealed to me. Who doesn't want someone to come home to now and then? Why wouldn't I want someone to share new experiences with in Vancouver? And wouldn't it be lovely, not always flying alone?

It's an interesting question, how to enjoy intimacy without getting mired in attachment. Vancouver holds a few potential answers, what with its ever-growing culture of free-spirited, ethical polyamory, but for now that isn't my side of the fence. My ex-husband might have jumped at the opportunity, given his history, but there was a framework to polyamory that went far beyond casual sex. I had lived out the two standard shames when it came to relation-ships—staying with a cheating husband and also getting divorced—but the third shame, these days, is having multiple relationships at once (and not, like, for religious reasons!). Vancouver was good at this; and I was slowly being brought up to speed.

I was thirty, dirty (I mean *flirty*) and thriving, but I missed not having *a person*, including someone to sit beside while flying thousands of miles high up in the air. Flights were again making me faint, and on my return to Edinburgh from Classic's (our new nickname for Laura) and Sam's London wedding, I'd almost made it through an hour-long flight when I awoke from a nap and started to feel "it" in my toes. Like a gray mist descending in reverse, the feeling had me convinced that I was about to spew my load or shit my pants. Fortunately, I'd end up doing neither and lose consciousness instead. The jury's still out on whether that was an improvement. This time, I was offered a wheelchair to get off the plane; but I politely declined, favouring my pride over what my body would've appreciated.

I only had a few days left in the UK before it was time to board another flight back to Vancouver. Thus, more anxiety ensued and a real fear of flying was certainly making itself known. Boarding a plane only increased my anxiety, which made me even more agitated, which in turn made me feel like I was going to pass out. What a vicious cycle, and one that made leaving home even more traumatic. In some ways, it took the shine off of what had been an incredible first trip home.

My aunt and uncle, who affectionately go by Auntie C and Big G, picked me up at the airport, because my mum was still in the dark about my early arrival. Complete strangers commented on the lovely sight of us all bursting into tears as I came through arrivals. Such was our excitement about seeing each other after fifteen months. They'd both been a huge part of my life before I moved to Canada. They'd been incredibly close to my ex-husband, and my uncle had even walked me down the aisle. Not seeing them for so long had been difficult; truly, there is nothing like seeing family.

Meeting my niece was definitely the highlight. She was the squiggliest bundle of joy with very definitive hair (think: a middle-aged woman called *Karen,* asking to see the manager). But looking past her locks, I had nothing but boundless love for my niece. From the moment I met ZIJ (her initials), she became my favourite person on the planet. But if we're being honest, she was an absolute pain in the ass as a baby—and I say that with all the love in the world. Nonetheless, that trip I observed my brother and sister-in-law doing an incredible job of coping with her forty-minute sleep cycle, something I didn't comprehend until I witnessed it for myself. In those moments, I was grateful to simply be her auntie, with the privilege of handing her back to her mum and dad.

Despite the persistent alarm clock of a crying baby, spending Christmas as a family made my heart fill with warm colours—pinks, purples, reds, greens, and blues. Spending time with relatives and old friends meant everything to me. I'd always worried how that first trip would turn out, how traumatic it might feel to leave again; and I got all the questions I'd expected from my loved ones. *When are you moving home? Aren't you sick of it out there yet?* But I had a feeling that while the relationships I'd left behind were still the same, something had shifted in my relationship to the city itself.

No longer did Edinburgh feel entirely like home. Perhaps by definition, it would always be "home," but I wasn't sure it was **my** home anymore. I felt like a visitor in my old life, similar to when my family came back to visit from Egypt and rotated between staying with my mum's parents versus my dad's parents. This time, I was back staying at my mum's, but not having all my things there made me feel like a visitor. So much was still the same, but a lot was different and the disconnect was plain to see.

There was a sadness that came with this realisation. I love Edinburgh as much as anyone can love their home city, and I am fiercely proud to be Scottish, but it just wasn't the place for me anymore—at least not for now. I, of course, kept this to myself. When it comes to friends and family, nobody wants to hear that you no longer feel at home where they are.

To top it off, I had anxiety about being back in the same city as my ex. I couldn't be sure if he was still in town, since we'd had no contact since our divorce. But even if he was back in Glasgow, Edinburgh and Glasgow are only one hour apart (I'll save you the Google mapping), so there was still a very real chance I could bump into him. There was certainly a much higher chance than there'd otherwise be with an ocean and a whole continent between us.

During that trip, I realised how paralysing it would've been to remain in Edinburgh. The freedom I'd given myself by knowing that I would never bump into my ex, nor anyone from his circle, was one of the best gifts I'd received in a long time.

I can't imagine the feeling of moving on from my marriage with the possibility of seeing that person around town or otherwise being faced with constant reminders. I know people do it all the time (hell, some people have no choice, if there are kids and pets involved). But I don't know whether I could have dealt with that—it just seemed like additional punishment, kicking someone when they're down or adding stress to an already heinous situation. So, to all those people moving on while still coming face to face with the past, I salute you.

The trip was a mixed bag. I felt huge amounts of love, mixed with the epiphany that things would likely never be the same again. But that year, I'd learned to train my body to do impossible things, like running half-marathons *for fun* on the weekend, so surely I could whip my mind and perspectives into new form as well. It would take a lot of self-work, patience, and reaching inside while looking outwards, but Vancouver provided a blessed environment in which to continue doing this.

Eight

Blessed But Depressed

After all the settling-in I'd done in 2014, I was hoping that 2015 would follow suit. Presumably as a result of the questions I'd answered at home (re: whether I was dating, what my "man situation" was, or why I hadn't found a Mountie yet), I'd started to feel as if maybe I *should* be dating and questioned why I wasn't.

Honestly, I didn't know why dating was giving me such trouble, even thinking about it was hard. Obviously, people figured that I'd be fully back in the swing of things at this point, but I wasn't (or if I was, I had my drunken nights out to thank for it). Part of the problem was that things would come to a halt as soon as I'd make a connection with someone, and I couldn't help but feel as if it had something to do with me—perhaps how I conducted or portrayed myself around potential partners, or perhaps just how likable I was in general.

Maybe I was doing it wrong? Is there a wrong way to date and be yourself? Perhaps I was just too eager. As soon as I met someone even remotely nice who had any form of interest in me, I became fixated on the possibility of it becoming more. I tried to ensure that my fixation didn't come across to the other party (as might have happened with that Irish, *Twelve-Pubs-on-Christ-Birthday* guy), but maybe bluffing isn't my game.

The hardest part was wanting to dive headfirst into the comfortable, easy relationship side of things. Of course, the exciting spark of a new relationship is great, but in reality my comfort level aligned more with knowing where I stood and doing routine things like cooking dinner together and hanging out after work. I caught myself jumping ahead and thinking about meeting their family and getting married. Perhaps because this was my most recent (and almost only) point of reference? I had become an all or nothing kind of gal: either men didn't exist, or I'd get stuck fantasizing about a long-term partnership with an almost stranger.... *Someone find Lou some chill.*

Did I want a relationship because I hated dating, or did I struggle with dating because I wanted to get straight to the relationship? Honestly, I didn't know. My friends had great success on Tinder and loved going on multiple dates a week. What was stopping me from having that? Myself? There's the saying: *you get back what you put out*, so was the problem what I was putting out there, that I wasn't open to dating? I was definitely open to meeting someone, but dating seemed like a cumbersome way to do it.

Meanwhile, I was really enjoying all the time and space to myself (hell, if someone had told me how fun living alone was earlier, I'd have done it years ago)! But I'd be lying if I said that I wouldn't have liked someone to hang out with, like, more than just as a friend. I was envious of those friends whose relationships provided them with the companionship I was missing. I never wanted to be jealous of my friends, but sometimes it was hard to see them coupled up.

Nonetheless, Spring was beautiful in Vancouver and that helped to marginally ease my dating confusion. I was struggling to decide on a favourite season, but this is a wonderful problem to have, especially coming from Scotland where there are essentially only two seasons: *gray* and *holy shit, it's sunny, let's all get sunburnt*, the second of which only appears for maybe twenty-one non-consecutive days each year.

Springtime also brought me a new friend, Keith (or Max, if he had his way at renaming himself in this book). He was Irish and had just moved to Vancouver to discover life as a young gay man, in a far more forgiving environment than he'd found back home. Albeit, our journeys were very different, but both of us were aware of the similarities from early on—they became the basis for an incredibly strong and supportive friendship. Lucky me, I now had two Irish guys as BFFS—positive, non-romantic relationships with men who provided a whole lot more value than I'd experienced in my relationships before.

Spring turned into Summer and I found myself heading back home for Victoria's wedding (another event that I wouldn't miss out on while living in Vancouver). Victoria is the same friend who'd driven with me and my mum to Glasgow Airport on September 25, 2013, a close friend from school who'd apparently lost her mind upon getting engaged. By this I mean that she'd asked her sister, who lived in Australia, and me, who lived in Vancouver, to be her bridesmaids. Talk about a logistical nightmare!

As I planned my trip home for the wedding, Lisa, another one of my best friends, was planning a vacation to Florida with her husband and daughter for around the same time. Well, her husband was planning it. When I was with my ex, and before Lisa and he had a baby, we all used to holiday together. He and I were always the planners. Meanwhile, Lisa and my ex would just show up and it worked best that way. This time around, he asked me whether I'd like to join them, as a surprise for Lisa and Hannah.

I'd already realised that the ability to surprise people was perhaps the best part about living abroad, so the trip was an opportunity I couldn't pass up, despite it meaning a lot more flights. The chance to make in-person memories with familiar faces had grown so small in my life, and being invited on their family holiday felt uniquely special. Despite Florida not being "on my way" anywhere, I adjusted my Skyscanner search and created a trip itinerary that made my eyes water. (The things you do for friends and guaranteed sunshine—Florida, I'm looking at you, cause Scotland sure as hell doesn't offer a constant stream of vitamin-D.)

A month or so before my trip, the anxiety I'd expected to experience upon boarding my plane had already started. I sat with it for a week or so, trying to understand why this trip was filling me up with so much excitement and equal dread. I spoke to my mum, talked through my plan for the trip (Disney World, then home, then wedding, then back to Van), and tried with her to reaffirm how much fun it'd be. But as I sat on the toilet at work one day, overcome by emotion (am I the only one who's had these moments?) I realised that my anxiety wasn't about the plane but the wedding day. Being a bridesmaid at one of my best friends' weddings had triggered some unexpected emotional anxiety.

I'd been to weddings since my divorce—this would be the fourth—but what caused me anxiety was the thought of standing in the front of a church. The last time I'd done that I was saying *I do*. Sure, understanding my problem was not a solution, but being able to pinpoint it was nonetheless a relief. I'd gotten better at listening to my feelings after moving to Vancouver. For the majority of my marriage, I'd related to my feelings like a little Tinker Bell versus a little Charlie Brown. Either I moved through them quickly, or else I let myself believe what other people said about my feelings being *wrong*, thus ignoring my emotional world for the "better" part of my marriage.

Being able to listen to my feelings and react accordingly gave me a clearer sense of myself, returning some of the self-assurance that had been otherwise worn down throughout my marriage. When somebody insists that your gut feeling is wrong and you sway between following it or not, you really start to second guess yourself. But like I said, knowing the source of my anxiety about being in the wedding party did not miraculously solve the problem. My symptoms might have been making me sick, but the trip was booked and I wouldn't bail on one of my best friend's weddings, especially not as a bridesmaid.

I had plenty of time during my flight to ruminate, analyze, and possibly overthink. *Who, me? Never.* But I came to realise that my main concern was what people thought about me. Did everyone know that the last time Victoria and I stood beside each other at the altar was when she'd been a bridesmaid to me? Would the same questions come to light as on my last trip home, like: *How's dating? Oh, you're not dating?* Society is so set on walking us through these monumental life moments, with each new milestone building on the next: meeting someone, getting engaged, being married, having kids, furthering professional careers, and perhaps buying a house somewhere; but couldn't we work towards alternative milestones as well?

Socially, most of us aren't programmed to offer acceptance when someone deviates from the established path. It's seen as an anomaly and comes with a unique tone of failure. We even talk about "failed" marriages, but how about the possibility that my marriage wasn't a failure? How about its absolute success in teaching me that I shouldn't stay married to someone who disrespects me? How about the emotional trauma that set me up for emotional maturity later in life? Sure, it's not the most conventional win, but every life experience is also a gift—albeit that some of them show up in dark and twisty ways.

Due to society's assumptions of the "right" way to do life, I worried about being massively judged in this social setting. After all, we'd be celebrating one of the most socially accepted milestones in the world. Perhaps it was all just me projecting, but whatever prejudices I had from my early social environments made things pretty tough. It's interesting how our fear of judgment is often based on our own prejudices. I was far less judgmental now than I'd been earlier in life, but still, there were clearly some lingering inbuilt narratives.

We only expect other people to judge things that we would judge; we only hate in others what we cannot love in ourselves. We hate our differences because we are different, and this frightens us because we're also the same in certain fundamental ways, and we long to reconcile this irreconcilable tenet someday. We long to love as one and express as another and life exists for that purpose, no matter what we believe about days of judgment or marriage or casual sex with fun-loving strangers.

Separation and diversity only exist because in truth we are capable of connection and oneness and these are things we learn on behalf of each other. Sometimes instead of reconciling the complexity in the reasons why we want to be connected but appear apart, we force distance between each other, because it's easier to feel connected to those who look or act the same. Some of us want to be connected so badly that we act as if the people who look different from us—who don't weave with our cloth of spirit—are less than us. But some of us are *wrong*, and they're exercising free will in staggering ways.

The sanctity of marriage is still something I believe in. I believe it has a place in the world for those who choose it, but I don't feel like it's a necessity for every relationship. Sadly, I do believe that most marriages are unlikely to last in harmony, at least until more people have dealt with their emotional baggage and nurtured more emotional maturity. On an imaginary scale of "marriage-optimist to marriage-pessimist," I'd like to think I'm a marriage realist.

Evidently, being so close to the altar again—albeit someone else's altar—had dredged up all these tricky thoughts. I knew there wouldn't be any close friends for me to lean on, other than the bride who might be a little busy, and that made everything harder. I looked at it as a job instead (which I strongly believe is what bridesmaids are meant for anyways—put them to work—especially if you're paying for all their stuff!). But if you're making them pay for their own dresses, the most you can hope for is that they turn up sober. These are just facts. Know what you're getting ladies!

Victoria was paying for everything and that coupled with my need for distraction meant that I went into full-on bridesmaid mode at any chance I had that weekend. A stepmother and birth mother needed to be kept apart in the church pews? Me and my ass were on it. The timing needed to be updated for dinner service? I was already talking to the catering manager. The remaining alcohol needed to be taken back into the castle from the marquee at the end of the night? My muscles and I needed a workout anyway. I realised that making myself busy and being productive was a typical thing that my mum would have done, so I guess the apple doesn't fall far from the tree. I guess that's how Adam ended up eating it.

It was a beautiful day, albeit blustery as hell, but that's what happens when you get married on top of a hill, and I was indescribably happy to witness Victoria saying her vows and celebrating with her afterwards. For me, it was a lesson in getting comfortable with the tough emotions lying just under the surface—and in fact overflowing at multiple times that weekend. Despite all the love surrounding two people pledging their lives to each other, it was hard not to remember when I'd said those words, with such hope about what they held for me. As I went to bed that night in the snuggest (and only) single room in the castle, with a gifted bottle of Edinburgh Gin half drunk on the antique bed stand and the draught whistling through the gap between the door and the stone-flagged floor, I wondered if that feeling would ever leave me alone at weddings again.

Nine

Depressed But (Still) Blessed

With every trip, home or otherwise, came the dreaded and inevitable anxiety I now associated with flying. It started with me becoming hyper-cognizant of how I was physically feeling: had I eaten, was I too hot, was I hungover, had I been standing up for too long? Though it seemed like that list was becoming longer and longer as to the things that could trigger my fainting, so it was hard to check them all off. In doing a body scan, I'd end up focusing on the tiniest pain, the slightest chest flutter. Then I'd start to worry. Then the worry would cause my heart to flutter and I'd get a headache. Thus when I redid the body scan, I had more reason to panic; and then, well, you see where I'm going with this.

I'd seen a doctor who wasn't a whole lot of help, but he did prescribe me some anti-anxiety meds to help with the flying. Yet the thought of taking them made me anxious (ironic, I know) and so they'd stayed in the bottle so far. However, by late Summer, the situation had become entirely debilitating and my life was severely impeded by what was now a chronic medical condition, not just tied to flying. I was doing no exercise, because everything was making me pass out or at least putting me on the verge of passing out, like, even the most serene of yoga classes.

By that point, it was happening numerous times a week. I'd also pretty much put myself under house arrest during the warmest months, such was my fear that going out in any climate above eighteen degrees would result in a poor experience, for me and those around me. I didn't want to be the person who gets airlifted off the mountain mid-hike due to a fainting episode, but eventually, I knew my friends would get tired of me turning down their suggestions for weekend activities.

The familiarity I had with my condition by then was scarily precise. I knew every aspect of the feeling that took over my body. I could foresee every development, as the episode progressed from a vague fuzziness to a full body fog. I'd lose all feeling in my hands and my feet as a blackness came over my eyes like a veil. I'd want absolutely nothing to do with anyone around me. I'd want to shed my clothes, get away from people and move as close to the ground as possible, in preparation for the moment when my heart rate would drop so low that I literally wouldn't be capable of staying upright.

To some degree I could control it, at least sometimes. If I got myself to the ground voluntarily and could control my breathing enough to regulate my heart rate back to "normal," I could postpone the faint. Though arguably, being able to stop myself from fully passing out was worse than just letting the blackness come and feeling my body hit the ground. It was like stopping a sneeze—it never felt natural to resist the veil. The act of stopping the episode in its tracks left me on the knife edge of passing out for hours afterwards.

At least my friends were becoming well versed in knowing that the moment I went quiet (which otherwise didn't happen often) was potentially the start of it. Then, if I uttered the words: *I really don't feel very well,* they knew it was a code red and went fully into "seat, water, air" mode. While those words don't sound very specific, it wasn't just *I don't feel great* or *I don't feel well;* it was exactly that sentence: *I really don't feel very well.* Those were often the last and only words to leave my mouth before I went in for a face-plant.

It took a more serious turn (*but was it not serious already?*) when I ended up in the emergency room at Vancouver General Hospital (VGH) one morning. I had woken up with no vision in my left eye and an incredibly severe headache. Actually, I couldn't even say it was a headache. It was a skull ache (a brain ache?). Regardless, it was horrific, and particularly traumatising because I'd never known what it was like not to see. *Yeah, good job taking things for granted.* I panicked, so much so that I called my boss, Don. I didn't know who else to call. Can you say, *that's fucking sad?* Actually, mostly it was because it was a weekday morning and there was no way I could work, so I felt like I should tell him that I was half blind and wouldn't be making it into the office.

Don is an embodiment of a Canadian Hockey Dad, and I loved working for him, not least because we shared an appreciation of good red wine. He was fairly concerned and suggested that I call an ambulance. That seemed extreme, but I did concede that maybe I couldn't drive myself to the Emergency Room. Instead I called a cab and soon I was at VGH, trying to explain my level of pain to the admittance desk. They wanted to start with an IV to get liquid Tylenol into my system and minimise my pain; so I mentioned my fainting habit, assuring them that inserting an IV into me would one-hundred percent result in a fainting episode.

I was squeamish to a fault. When I was a child, my weakness used to be blood—any sight of it and I was done. I'd start to feel my legs cease to serve their purpose as legs. But now it was about having anything put in me that was not instantly removed. That sounds like a sex story, but it's not. Injections? No problem. Taking any significant amount of blood (and by significant, I mean if they needed to fill even one vial, we were in trouble) was different. An IV that would remain in my arm for god knows how long? Absolutely not. I was having flashbacks to being in the hospital on my honeymoon and the air-conditioned room in Mexico causing the IV fluid to run like ice through my veins. I will never forget that feeling, just like you never forget your worst nightmare of all time.

Not that I didn't want the liquid Tylenol, such was my pain and concern for my sight. Thus I was willing to risk fainting for the hope of relief. The nurses said that would be great, because then they could monitor my reaction. *Oh, great, then we're all happy....* Sure enough, as soon as I felt the cold prick of the needle on my skin, something happened; and the next thing I knew there were four extra nurses in my room, my previously upright bed was fully reclined and I was feeling like an even bigger bag of crap than I had upon entering the ER. Of course, the tears came shortly afterwards.

While laying in bed, awaiting the initial test results and trying to ignore the needle in my arm, the nurse came through and said, "someone's here to see you." Needless to say, I was surprised to see my boss walking into my hospital room. *Seriously, these Canadians and their niceness! Whose boss turns up at the hospital?!* He wanted to check that I was okay, probably not least because when I'd called him that morning, I may have cried while on the phone; perhaps he also thought I was having an emotional breakdown. To be fair, it wouldn't have been far off.

I was exhausted from the months of fainting, terrified of what this searing head pain might be, and feeling incredibly alone. Lying in a bed at VGH was more isolation than I could bear. Of course I had friends, but it's not the same as calling "your person" or your mum. I had neither, at least nearby, but I was grateful for the compassionate support of my growing network of community in Vancouver.

Fortunately, the pain subsided as the liquid gold flowed through my veins, and my vision returned albeit still blurred in fashion (how do people with bad eyesight cope?!) and within the space of the afternoon, I ended up having all the tests the nurses could imagine, in hopes of getting to the bottom of the fainting. The vision and head pain seemed of lesser importance; they were mostly concerned that I'd been passing out so frequently. So, I ended up coming away from the hospital with both a neuro team *and* a cardio team looking into my symptoms.

As awful as it was to spend the day dealing with my pain in the hospital, at least my health insurance covered the expense. If I'd immigrated to a country that didn't provide free health care to all residents, waking up half blind would have been hugely problematic. I figured that my visit to VGH was worth it if something might be done about my fainting episodes. I also got a reminder that you don't always need "a person" or your mum, you just need good friends. Laura and Sam came to pick me up, taking me to their place to feed me before driving me home. They also got to meet the man who'd become my cardiologist, who Laura would later tell me wasn't as good looking as I was proclaiming. Clearly, my vision wasn't quite back to one-hundred percent yet. They were truly my closest friends in Vancouver, and I was eternally grateful for them.

It was an interesting time for our friend group. AnnaB had decided to return home to England, and Quyeneth was also planning to return back to London. It made total sense for both of them; but it was unsettling to say the least, as well as pretty devastating to lose two of my closest friends. AnnaB hadn't lived in the city, so she was frequently a guest at Hotel Lou (aptly named, considering that I lived in a hotel) especially on our nights out. I loved our Sunday mornings of tea and toast and our trips to Sephora. She was my girliest girlfriend, and we had the chattiest chats about makeup and clothes and relationships.

Quyeneth also had her time as a guest at Hotel Lou, mostly for our early morning wake-up calls to watch the Six Nations Rugby games. We would spend nights prepping breakfast for the six am games the next morning, and I have her to thank for the glory and presence of all my ten fingers (specifically after one particularly drunken night prepping a sausage casserole). I was still trying to expand my social circle and be sociable, but I was aware that it was becoming more of a struggle. Nights out with friends would often end with me in tears, mostly alone in bed at the end of the night. Whether it was the toll that fainting took, the feeling of being very alone, or the residual emotions from Victoria's wedding, I wasn't sure.

I was struggling to find joy in things and regressing from social situations. To be honest, I had little motivation to do things, which I'd initially put down to my concern of fainting, but I always knew that was only an excuse.

Instead of longing to go out and be social, I preferred to stay in the comfort and security of my apartment. Hermit Lou was making an aggressive return. At first, when my darker feelings were more fleeting, I just put them off to a bad day. But as their frequency increased and I became more acquainted with the experience of living under a black cloud, I made the connection to a previous time in my life when I had felt the same way. The days felt long, the nights felt longer, both were lonely, and there was no peace to be found at any time. There's a definite distinction between "a bad day" and "depression"; and I was erring on the side of the latter.

In time, it dawned on me that in planning my move to Vancouver, followed by travelling and setting up my new life, I hadn't actually addressed my divorce. I'd told Danae all those months ago that I knew moving to Canada didn't mean I'd leave my problems behind, but I'd done a pretty good job of putting them aside for a considerable amount of time. Maybe now was a good time to do something about them. The question was: *What would Lou do?*

Ten

Meet Julia

For a few weeks, I sat with the reality of my feelings and how to tackle them, before speaking to a friend who was also a registered therapist in Vancouver. I explained how I'd been feeling and asked whether she knew anyone I could go and see. I'd never asked a friend for a therapist recommendation, but we get recommendations for restaurants, travel destinations, and masseuses, so why should counselling be any different? Especially when my friend Jillian was already in that field of work; I trusted her judgment on the subject, implicitly. If I'd still been in the UK, this absolutely wouldn't have happened.

Back home, people barely talk about things like counselling, let alone ask for recommendations. Here it was like second nature. Jillian replied right off the bat: she agreed that it was a good idea for me to speak to someone and gave me the details of a therapist she knew, one her sister had been seeing and loved. It would be the single best recommendation I'd ever receive, as deciding to see Julia became a pivotal moment in my life. Going to her office on Granville Street in downtown Vancouver, I was pretty sure about what to expect. I'd been to a couple of therapists by this time in my life; so less than having nerves about asking someone for help, it was the thought of everything I needed to work through that incited dread.

Talking about my problems (or anything, really) has never been an issue for me. I'll tell anyone almost anything. Sometimes I wish that I had more of a filter, but it's how I am. *Sharing is caring*, right? So, going to "speak to someone" about things like my ex-husband cheating was not that difficult. (I know that for some people, the thought of being vulnerable or self-reflective is enough to make them run for the hills.) I'd seen counsellors back in the UK, both after my parents divorced and when the issues first surfaced in my marriage. I always thought of them as positive experiences, but I never had any real *Aha! Come to Jesus…* moments in those sessions. I never really came out feeling all that much different. Yes, I maybe learnt some new coping mechanisms or better ways to communicate, but in terms of feeling wholly better about the issue at hand? I wouldn't say there was an overwhelming feeling of change. I'd always let the time between sessions get longer and eventually stopped going altogether.

This time was different. My first few sessions with Julia were as to be expected when meeting a new therapist—me spilling my guts, a lot of ugly crying, mostly me just unloading all of my experiences (*we don't call it baggage*), and explaining the context of my struggles. There was a lot to unpack. I mean, I think three or four sessions passed before I ran out of life dramas to detail in providing her with pertinent context.

At the end of every session, Julia would ask, "What was something useful today?" And there would always be something. Either a question she'd asked that got me thinking about something differently, a comment she'd made, or a story she shared about her personal experiences to complement mine. There was always something, usually more than one thing, that was useful. So while I wasn't having any massive revelations in the first few weeks/months with Julia, it still felt beneficial from the outset.

The sessions were hard, and I would come out of them emotionally wrought and exhausted. I got into the habit of having them late on Friday afternoons, leaving work early for my appointment and taking my tear-stained cheeks home to hibernate for the night. But despite the rawness of the sessions, with a tissue in hand I would text my mum on the walk home (knowing she was already in bed), just to tell her what a great session it was. Every single time.

I started seeing Julia at the end of September, and within a few months, I felt like my divorce stuff had been processed. It no longer seemed surprising that my self-worth got shot to pieces, that my trust in people was shaken, of that my experience of love, in practice, got warped. We did a lot of work to start repairing those wounds, and although it felt like slow progress, there was progress; and for that I was thankful.

Eventually, we started digging into my parents' divorce, which still haunted me in its own way, not least because I no longer had a relationship with my father. Our relationship had ended when my father chose to act in the poorest way possible, after years of cheating om my mum. He told Mum on New Year's Eve (at the dawn of the new Millennium) that he wanted a divorce; then he proceeded to treat her like garbage during their divorce and for the next few years. I'd had plenty to say on the situation, as a scorned fifteen-year-old. He moved to New Zealand once it was all over, heeding my petulant suggestion not to contact me again, hence our relationship was frozen in time.

It's true what they say: the daughters of mothers who were victims of infidelity have very different experiences than sons, because the daughter often puts herself in her mother's shoes, experiencing the moment as if it were her who'd been cheated on. Sons are often more capable of willfully keeping a realistic distance between themselves and the parental relationship—for whatever, complicated reasons—and that's what happened with my brother and me. He maintained a relationship with my father, but I'd removed every trace of him from my life. His actions were too abhorrent for me to ever forgive and apparently challenging to forget as well. As I understand, there were always issues with their marriage, and now, as an adult, I don't think it's my place to comment extensively on them.

But my father's actions after announcing that he was leaving (news that he made my mum deliver, while he drove home from being with his new partner), and all the way through the separation, didn't improve. He started to introduce this new woman to his social circle, who commented to my mum that he'd treated her the same as he'd treated my mum). His behavior didn't improve after the divorce, when he bought the same breed of dog as our family dog with his new partner—it all just felt so unnecessarily disrespectful. Disrespectful to my mum and disrespectful to our family (and at a time when I expected his actions to bring him humility, but no dice).

I happily told people that I was divorced, but I would generally just omit my father from my life stories. Often I wondered if people presumed he was dead, or if they simply assumed that I belonged to a single mother. The latter part wasn't exactly untrue in practice, at this point in time. In one very anguished session with Julia, I articulated that I felt guilty about being difficult to deal with when my parents divorced, but on the other hand, I felt taken advantage of for never having a chance to be a child in the situation. I had to deal with things without the support of either parent, because my mum was doing all that she could just to keep herself above water. And my dad? Well, he didn't want to deal with a difficult teenager giving him grief about a decision for which he carried no remorse.

My mother is one of the strongest, most resilient people I know, but in that strength and resilience, a battle is waged against never allowing oneself a moment to pause, feel, or grieve. As a family, we had never properly addressed what happened between my parents. We just kept on trucking. I think we were all aware of the widening gap between my mother, my brother, and me, but we weren't equipped to talk about it. I'd never wanted to blame my mother for not providing the support I needed at the time: she'd done the best she could and we all knew it. I worried that in sharing my feelings, I would ultimately lay partial responsibility at her door, and I never felt okay with that idea, even in the cosy confines of Julia's office.

Staring out the window at the metal fire escape, winding down the building across the street like a serpent, I'd attempt to find the words. In time, Julia taught me that admitting to myself (and to my mum) that I didn't feel supported in the situation was okay. I'd needed more support from my parents back then, and I had a right to experience and voice my feelings about that now, but I could also forgive the situation. Forgiving the situation with softness for my loved ones didn't equate to minimizing my experience, but it might make things easier to process and move through as a family. I'd had some difficult conversations with both my mum and brother back in the day, separately, but never did I make myself as raw and open as I did in my discussions with Julia.

When we finally did find time to share our experiences from all those years ago, both mutual ones and those entirely independent from each other, it felt good to get things out. And you know what? No one died. We talked like mature adults; we owned how we felt; we made space for each other and we didn't try to justify things. It just was. What happened had happened. It couldn't be changed. No one was more right than anyone else; no one was wrong; they were all just our own experiences of the same situation. It was truly eye-opening to see how even just in one family, people can have such different interactions during the same moments in time.

After I'd addressed the situation with my closest family members, Julia suggested that I do it with the one person I'd worked so hard to make non-existent. In a cliché but brilliant therapist move, she asked me to write a letter to my dad—not to send—just to get all my feelings down on paper.

The task was not hard. I still had a letter to my dad from five years ago, in fact. My mum had insisted that I write him a thank you letter after he sent me some money, via my brother, as a wedding gift. My mum literally cannot forgo manners, even when someone doesn't deserve it. For whatever reason, it pissed me off that the money had come through my brother. Actually, it went to his wife's account and got transferred to me, which somehow made it even worse. It was also a laughably small amount.

Not that I was ungrateful for my wedding gifts; but growing up, I'd always imagined that my dad would have a wedding fund waiting for me, so where the fuck had it gone? Plus, by the time I was writing the letter, my ex had already cheated on me for the first time; so it was fun to include that tidbit for my cheating father to read about as well. All the same, I hadn't sent the "thank you" letter.

When my mum asked if I'd written it, I told her yes, which wasn't a lie. If she'd asked me whether I'd sent it, I probably would have admitted that I hadn't (because I didn't think he deserved it). But I still had the letter, having kept it all those years. After my session with Julia, I read it over and realised that my feelings were entirely the same, a sure-fire testament to how little I'd moved on from what had happened.

So, I simply bookended my letter from all those years ago with more context about where I was in my life now, saying that all of the things I'd initially written were still entirely apt. Then I took the paper with me to my next appointment with Julia. I'd read this letter a hundred times, and yet reading it aloud in our session caused me physical pain. My head was throbbing and my throat felt so constricted and I could barely get the words out between sobs.

Unveiling the feelings of fifteen-year-old me in that therapy room involved more personal vulnerability than I'd ever shown to Julia. I'd explained in the letter how I couldn't understand how he'd treated my mum, nor why he'd been so callous upon leaving. The seeming ease with which he turned his back on me, upon realizing that I was less than wanting of a relationship with him, was one of the most devastating turns of my life. Admittedly, I was difficult as a teenager, but my parents were getting a divorce and if you weren't difficult as a teenager, well, were you even a teenager? *What was his excuse?* I asked. Julia sat in silence, letting me get through two whole pages of words.

We took a moment to decompress before she said: "Why wouldn't you send that?" I sat with the question while thinking of all the possible permutations that could arise if I sent the letter. Eventually, I said: "Because I don't want to give him a chance to reject me again." Julia asked me if perhaps he deserved a chance to answer that question for himself. I laughed (I didn't think he deserved anything). The fact that my brother still gave him the time of day made me angry. The very thought of him *cooing* at my niece made my skin crawl. To be honest, I felt kind of mad that Julia had even suggested I send it to him. It was supposed to be an exercise in extolling my innermost feelings—*not* making contact with my father. The latter was absolutely not on my to-do list.

By the end of the year, I'd worked through a whole host of issues with Julia: my divorce, my parent's divorce, the blow to my self-worth, the beliefs I had regarding how love showed up, my fears about getting back into dating, and the effect that fainting had on my life. In a few short months, I could see the change from our work together, like being released from years of tension and anguish, hurt and guilt. We discovered that one of my favourite pastimes had long been carrying around guilt regarding situations that I couldn't control anyways. Usually, I saw this pastime as a skill, like a Sherpa carrying a heavy load up the mountain; but the impact it had on my day-to-day life, not to mention my mental state, was rude and *huge*.

In this world of ever-changing situations, relationships, and malleable approaches to selfhood (as it should be, by definition), the ability to reflect and grow is vital to personal fulfilment. Julia provided me with the ability to do these things in my everyday life. My experience of therapy with her was hands down some of the best money I'd ever spent (and no, Julia's counselling center is neither sponsoring nor aware of this "message"). We need to do more to remove the stigma around mental health, and accept the fact that we don't need to be manic or depressed to benefit from therapy. Life is hard, everyone's life is hard—yes, even for those who seemingly have it easy. I am now a massive advocate for therapy, and these days I'm the one making therapist recommendations for friends! In time, *the student [always] becomes the teacher.*

While I'm super happy to talk with my friends about stuff (my issues, their issues), just talking about them isn't the same. It's a great start, but a professional therapist has years of training and, crucially, no bias. As friends or acquaintances, we all have biases, mostly unconscious; but even if we truly want the best for someone, our biases live on. Dealing with our shit before projecting it onto other people or breeding it into our children should be, like, mandatory.

As I worked on my mental health, my neuro and cardio teams were meanwhile trying to figure out the puzzle of my physical health. When my neuro doctor called to announce that all their tests had come back clear, I experienced the real-life meaning of a double-edged sword. There was nothing else that they could reasonably test me for after a while, so they recommended that I just live this way for now and let them know if it got worse. *Worse! How much fucking worse could it get?* Did I need to pass out twice a week? Three times? Was it not a big enough impediment that I couldn't do anything physically exerting?

As life would have it, the call from the neuro doctor came through as I was on my way to see the cardio doctor for an update at the university hospital. I presumed that if it wasn't a neuro thing, maybe it was a cardio thing and maybe help was still on its way. But naturally, the cardio doctor also reported that my tests had come back clear. Oh great, so my brain's fine and my heart's fine; I'm obviously in perfect health and otherwise just making shit up?

Thankfully, he stopped short of telling me there was nothing else he could do. It appeared to be simple over-stimulation of my vasovagal nerve, which causes my blood pressure to drop and then faint. It's the most common cause of fainting, actually, but mine was being triggered more often than most people, for some unknown reason. My blood pressure was normal, but he suggested that I try a new medication, one that hadn't been fully tested...Before he could even finish his sentence, I practically shouted at him: "Give me the drugs!" It was the first time throughout the whole process that someone even hinted at an elixir for Lou.

My doctor explained how the drug worked, reiterating that there'd been no extensive testing for my condition but they'd nonetheless seen some success with the drug. He suggested that I try it under fairly close attention from him. I didn't even care about its unproven nature; I was just happy to leave with a prescription for something, anything, that might make a difference. When faced with a physical condition that nobody can explain, and that includes modern medicine itself (if Modern Medicine were an Oz like figure behind a curtain), the relief of knowing that someone is at least conscious of and working on your problem goes a long way. And sometimes that relief comes in the form of a prescription—any prescription. In this case, I also hoped that the medication would keep me both conscious and vertical.

It was perfect timing. I saw the doctor in early December and my mum was coming out for her first ever Canadian Christmas in a matter of days. I'd been worried that she may never leave me alone again, if she thought my fainting was still severe and with no solution on the horizon. But I had to be under supervision when I started the tablets, so this way my mum could oversee me and also satisfy her motherly need to be a caregiver. It's weird, but sometimes the universe works it magic and we end up with exactly what we need at the right time. This might take shape as an unexplained fainting condition prescribing couch time to a mother-daughter duo in Canada at Christmastime—but hey, my universe, at least, is far from perfect.

Eleven

On Progress

After a picture-perfect Christmas with my mum on Vancouver Island, afternoon tea in the Fairmont Empress on Christmas Eve, and Christmas Dinner overlooking Victoria Harbour, on December twenty-eighth, two days before my mum left to fly home, I started taking the drugs. What better way to bring in the new year, right? 2016, here I come.

Midodrine increases your blood pressure even when you're at rest. Basically, when my vasovagal nerve became overstimulated and my blood pressure dropped, the drug worked to elevate it enough that I could still keep conscious and upright. *Well, doesn't that sound nice!?* There were some side effects from taking it, but what's so bad about a racing heart if it absolves the death sentence affecting your head? It felt like somebody was using a "head scratcher" in the most soothing, fuzziness-inducing way I'd ever experienced. Literally, I had to keep touching the top of my head, entirely to know if it was still there, but otherwise it was absolutely fine!

I started 2016 with a sense of excitement. The work I'd done the previous year felt like a great foundation for progress—my keyword for the year! Yes, I was now setting intentions for calendar years, yet another thing I could add to my list of "Things I Never Thought I'd Do." Edinburgh and Vancouver might be similar as city backdrops, but as cultures, they were worlds apart, which explained the epic changes to my personal outlook after three years of living in British Columbia. It's an experience unto itself, living here in Vancouver, *the city that never plays itself*—not just in the movies, as the titular "Hollywood North," but in a larger thematic sense as well.

The culture of self-care, mindfulness, healthy-living cafes, and connecting with the outdoors creates a progressive cultural bubble. Going for a run in Vancouver is often a first class experience, provided you pick your stretch of seawall well. You can go skiing and sailing all in the same day and still leave time for a five-star meal in the city. The connection that locals have to the land itself, to caring for their bodies as they walk and think and breath upon it, reaches back further in time than most Vancouver "transplants" might know (and sometimes it feels like this city is all transplants, from all corners of the world.) The city that never plays itself, in essence, struggles to define just what or why it is for the world.

But at that point in my life, Vancouver and I had a few things in common, as far as self-identity goes. Living here would teach me how to grow into a place while also growing into myself, because the culture seemed not to care very much who anyone decided to be. It was different from Edinburgh in that way. As an urban metropolis, Vancouver is hardly more than one hundred years old. Settlers started arriving from the UK and Eastern Canada in greater numbers around the turn of the century, taking advantage of the lumber and fishing opportunities in the area. What followed was a booming real estate industry that proceeded to erect all the skyscrapers we see on the skyline today. Yet before settlers arrived and developed the local land, Vancouver took the shape of what today we'd consider a storybook, in the form of an Aboriginal fishing village.

Today, local events in Vancouver almost always begin with the host making some version of the following statement: *We'd like to begin by acknowledging that we are lucky to gather here today, on the traditional, ancestral and unceded territory of the Coast Salish peoples, including the Sḵwx̱wú7mesh (Squamish), Stó:lō and Səl̓ílwətaʔ/Selilwitulh (Tsleil-Waututh) and x̱ʷməθkʷəy̓əm (Musqueam) Nations.*

This is history that I feel is important to include, because I understand that the policies faced by Aboriginal groups in Canada have created certain systems of oppression across the entire country. The Aboriginal groups in America faced a genocide and nobody tried to call it something else; in Canada, Aboriginal groups faced *at least* cultural genocide and continue to face environmental genocide today. Moreover, Canadian consciousness is still working on calling it what it is. When White settlers arrived in this country, many of them from Scotland like me, and British Columbia joined the new Confederation, the Aboriginal population came up against the drooling teeth of Canada's "assimilatory" policies, ones that in time would separate

Aboriginal children and families from the spirit and history of who they've always been.

I was blessed that the one major rupture I'd faced in my life had sent me away into another country, where many aspects of "home" were still present, given that people like me had settled this land 150 years ago. Before the turn of the Twentieth Century, this place was not called Vancouver, and its history went back in time for thousands of years. Some of this history is captured in the book, *Legends of Vancouver*, which just so happens to be written by a woman named Pauline Johnson (no relation, I assume—but one of the assimilatory policies of Canada's Indian Act included renaming Aboriginal people with common, English names). One of these legends is about a mythical sea-serpent that once swam in the water around Stanley Park, which does have a few striking things in common with Scotland's Loch Ness Monster.

Pauline Johnson was the daughter of a Mohawk Chief and an English mother—making her a "half-breed" Aboriginal woman, as they say, a term you might also recognise from Harry Potter. At the turn of the Twentieth Century, Pauline Johnson was a popular writer, entertainer, and storyteller in Canada, having a knack for connecting with Aboriginal and settler populations alike. As far as I know, *Legends of Vancouver* is the only English-account that we have of the stories and legends of Chief Capilano, as told to Pauline Johnson, who translated them from his native tongue. The ancestral stories of this land capture a history so different from Vancouver's history today that sometime Vancouverites struggle to believe in their own past.

Pauline Johnson translated legends about natural fixtures left behind as symbols on the land, like Deadman's Island, The Lions mountains, or Siwash Rock, that cool rocky fixture off Stanley Park with the tree growing out of it; and these legends were actually stories containing history and character and wisdom, just as literature contains this same detail about our world and its culture today. For all we know, our current world could change so drastically that one day it shows up only as a hidden world, one with a new backdrop, and the people will read Harry Potter as if it holds the secrets and magic previously known to a suddenly lost world. (Full disclosure: I've never read, nor watched, Harry Potter, but the analogy works!)

All things considered, the culture of Vancouver is contagious, sometimes cult-like, which might explain why I found myself doing so many things I'd never expected to do! With the spirit of excitement that I'd carried into

2016, I decided to join a kickboxing gym with a Groupon promo. Even as I completed the purchase, I laughed and thought to myself: "What the fuck am I doing? I'm never going to use this." I was eager to get started with my new fitness resolutions, but they called to set up a time for my first class immediately! *Shit. Ugh.* Okay, I decided to do that thing where you go along with everything, setting up an appointment and planning to call back later to cancel, or perhaps rescheduling after checking your calendar. I usually reserve this tactic for the dentist, but in this situation, it seemed like a good idea.

Except that I didn't end up cancelling my first class. On the 11th of January, I found myself putting on a pair of gloves in a brightly-lit box of a gym, adorned with pictures of (mostly) women with toned as fuck arms, and abs that looked like they'd ping right off (that is, if you simply removed the skin). It was a brand new gym and all they did was kickboxing.

After almost two weeks of taking it, I was hopeful that my wonder drug would keep me upright throughout the hour long class. I'd heard multiple times that the warm up was intense, but if you survived the first fifteen minutes, you were good to go. That said, this sentiment came from the trainers, who were super perky without being super annoying. And despite twelve days of drugs, I barely survived the warmup. The multiple rounds of burpees, high knees, jump squats, push ups, Russian twists, lunges, and froggies (what the fuck even are they!) really took their toll. My heart did not appreciate changing proximity to the ground in quick succession, especially at an already elevated rate.

From the fifteen minute warm up, we moved onto six, three-minute rounds of punching/kicking combos. I made it through Round Two before thinking I was going to hurl. I figured that I had my general unfitness to thank for that, despite having recently pushed through another half-marathon in Vegas, but months had passed since I'd done any high-intensity training. When I felt the fog starting to creep up from my toes, I told the trainer that I needed to stop. It was embarrassing to say the least. Part of me thought: *Well, that was a waste of twenty dollars,* as I lay on the mat trying to regulate my heart, my ego bruised like a golden apple. But I knew I could up the dosage of my medication, having started with the lowest dose, per the doctor's recommendation.

So, the next day, I took ten milligrams of my wonder drug and resolved to try class again in three days time. When I returned for the second class, it still kicked my ass, but I made it the whole way through completely upright!

At certain moments, I wondered whether a fainting spell was about to get the best of me, but I only had my unfitness to blame. Despite the struggle, I finished that second class and practically shouted: *TAKE MY MONEY, TAKE ALL MY MONEY,* before signing up for a full membership. With a girls' trip to Vegas upcoming in July, I was determined to get bikini ready. I'd never had a goal like that before, not really, except maybe before my wedding. But I hadn't taken good care of my body during the fainting episodes, telling myself the story that it was incapable and useless. But that was going to change now.

I continued seeing Julia, which made for some interesting conversations with my mum over Christmas. It was always so difficult to find a time to address what came up for me in therapy with my mum, because we were usually on Skype and it just never felt like the right time. I toyed with the excuse of not wanting to "ruin" her trip to Vancouver and I certainly could have stayed silent about it all, but having difficult conversations in person was far more liberating than talking through a screen.

I found it most productive to approach things from a calm place, not looking to place blame but owning how I felt. My words may not be received the way I wanted, but I would be open to giving the other participant enough time to process and/or reply. Oftentimes, people just don't know how to find the words, or it's easier not to say anything at all. These days, I was learning the importance of making space for words to be found. It probably wouldn't be entirely comfortable, but hopefully the outcome would pay off.

I'm pretty sure that my family and friends back home were thinking: *What in hell's name has gotten into her? Why is she coming at us with all of this straight talk?* It was new for all of us, but the difference it made was huge. Who knew that being honest about your feelings was good for you?! Evidently, they need to teach this lesson more in school; in fact, I bet they already are. In the spirit of honesty and owning my feelings, I also decided to take Julia up on her suggestion of sending the letter to my dad. I didn't edit a single word of the letter. I just texted my brother, asking for Dad's email address with the assurance that I wasn't going to send him digital dog shit, and then I sent him the letter.

It was a bizarre feeling, forwarding my feelings to my dad. I'd just sent a particularly raw piece of writing to a man whom I didn't know. Fifteen years had passed since I'd last seen him. I didn't know who he was and he certainly didn't know me. Yet we were endlessly and inextricably entwined, by blood and chromosome, so maybe sending him my innermost thoughts was okay. I know, family is fucking weird.

As I'd told Julia, my biggest fear was that he'd reject me again, not to mention that I'd given him the opportunity to do so. It reminded me of how Mum had let him return to our family after he left for the first time. I was nine years old and blamed my mother and brother for years. Having since repeated that same decision with my ex-husband, the act of giving second chances was a delicate subject for me.

Before I sent the email, I walked through all the possible outcomes of how sending it might make me feel. No reply? *Not surprised.* Shitty reply denying all responsibility? *Not surprised.* Half-assed apology? *Not worth my time.* The response that I actually got, in less than twenty-four hours? *Surprising as shit.*

My dad wrote an initial reply saying that he was delighted to receive my email. My reaching out had been a shock but he appreciated me sharing my feelings. He dove right into apologizing for his actions, taking full blame for everything that had happened, while asking for an extra few days to reply in full to my email. The next email arrived in less than twenty-four hours, however. I saw it come in on the way to kickboxing, so I made a pit stop in a coffee shop to sit down and read properly.

It was a lot. He'd certainly put together a thoughtful response, addressing every gripe, complaint, and memory I'd included in my email. I definitely wasn't prepared for his words. They seemed genuine and heartfelt; and he probably hadn't loved putting his sentiments down in black and white. He himself had admitted that they were his "demons and weaknesses."

To have anyone lay themselves bare like that will always be emotional, especially when it comes from a parent. It was everything that I never expected to know about my dad, back when I was young and he was authoritative and in control. To have my dad admit that he isn't perfect, that he'd made mistakes, that he has regrets and his biggest regret is his (lack of a) relationship with me? My perception did a 180-degree turn.

He said one thing that we both agreed on, however: *Your mother is the most thoughtful, smart, driven and level-headed woman I have ever met.* In reading that line, I realised how much I needed to hear it from him. I was so hurt and offended on my mother's behalf, which arguably wasn't my battle to fight, but to finally hear him say something, anything, nice about my mum was sorely needed by yours truly.

When I was done reading the letter (for the fifth time), my two over-riding feelings were: surprise at my dad's openness and honesty, plus a huge and heavy-hearted sadness. It was such a waste—of family and the years of emotional trauma that had scarred us all. Every family has its own little nucleus of emotional wounds, just as every city has its own nucleus of emotional baggage (or *experiences*, in the lovely words of Julia). The goal is no longer to act as if we're all scar free, sweeping our feelings under the universe rug in turn, but rather to honor them as experiences. Baggage is something heavy that we carry, while experiences carry lessons that we must learn.

It was clear from my dad's letter that, if we'd been better equipped to deal with the emotions, relationships, and hard conversations back then, we'd have managed to salvage something greater than we had. As it was, everything had gone up in flames; the only task left was to pick through the embers. But I made it clear in my email that I wasn't looking to re-establish a relationship. I didn't want to offer my dad any false hope. I wanted to reassess my feel-ings before deciding on communicating further with him. I responded to his email after reading, thanking him for his honesty and acknowledging how sad it made me feel, just the situation in general. But it allowed me to accept my past without expecting it to transform, and I hoped to move forward without enduring that burden.

Selfishly, when considering a relationship with him, I realised that rekin-dling a father-daughter relationship would be of greater benefit to him than to me. I'd addressed what had happened and received what I needed in turn. There wasn't a gaping, father-shaped hole in my life; I hadn't had one since I was sixteen. It's funny what you can get used to—most of us can get used to just about anything, if left with no other choice. I no longer yearned for a father-daughter bond.

Having my dad around would've been helpful during my marriage, in particular considering the nature of my husband's habits. I would have loved a protector, someone to stand up for me and prevent my ex from getting away with his actions. Yet my family was incredibly supportive throughout all my hardships, so maybe I didn't need to add a father into the mix. I didn't want regular reminders of how much someone could fuck up their life, not when I was working so hard to nurture the best parts of mine; and I knew interacting with my dad would be draining.

Mostly through circumstance, and now also choice, I was moving away from the traditional, patriarchal frameworks that watched over me as a girl. I made the choice not to re-establish a relationship with my father, and I made the choice to leave my cheating husband. Meanwhile, my mother remained a strong presence in my life, and my connection to Mother Nature had increased beyond anything I could've ever imagined. I was now living on unceded, Aboriginal territory, lands that had long provided homes for largely matriarchal cultures. Coincidence? *Possibly*. But it's interesting how life threads itself together behind your back, usually when nobody is looking, and I wondered if that's what they meant when they talked about the *rich tapestry of life*.

For now, I was grateful to get closure for my lingering "Daddy-issues," moving on from that chapter at long last. The time had come for me to flip to a random page in the book of life, or perhaps pick up a "Choose Your Own Adventure" story in a local bookstore, and begin reading where sixteen-year-old Lou had left off.

Twelve

First Dates

In the midst of all of this, kickboxing had become a regular fixture in my life. The classes at the studio in Gastown were an excellent form of stress release, especially on that day I got my dad's email. It all just seemed so fucking pointless, but landing a good roundhouse kick was massively satisfying. The warm-ups were no longer killing me and I could actually do a push up! Managing my first one felt like winning an Olympic Gold.

The trainers were as supportive as competitive-yet-motivational brothers and sisters, and while I could have been cynical about their rah-rah attitudes, instead I started accepting their high fives after crushing a combo and actually listening when they told me to speed up. I also swore. A lot. At them. At myself. At the mat. At the bag. All of my classes were punctuated with obscenities. I think new members thought I had Tourette's. But I was okay with it and my trainers thought it was hilarious. Either way it got me through.

I also made a couple of friends, a surprising outcome since I hadn't been convinced that any of these people were "my people." As it turned out, the girl who looked hard as nails, and the girl who danced with abandon on the mat before class started, were in fact "my people." My pre-class chats with Colette and Charms were some of my favourite times, and I enjoyed them shouting back at me when I was yelling in pain during class.

In one of my earliest chats with Colette, I was reminded that our initial assumptions about people are often incomplete at best and completely wrong at worst. Colette looked like she could have kicked my ass down an alleyway (of which Vancouver had plenty) in thirty seconds flat. I presumed she was married to a tatted biker and had nerves of steel, but I came to find out that she had a similar relationship history as me.

She'd also moved to Vancouver alone and was currently trying to navigate dating apps. I admitted that I'd been too scared to go on the apps, that the idea of Tinder and Plenty of Fish (this was before Bumble and Hinge were the go-to apps) made me want to throw up. But listening to her and hearing how she'd met a couple of really nice guys and was going on a second date that coming week, I started to think that maybe I should give it a go.

Other than a couple of sexual encounters over my first few years in the city, I'd still been more inclined to stay away from men. The relative celibacy wasn't even a conscious choice nor a consideration for me. But Colette made it all sound less daunting than I'd built it up to be in my head, and hearing from someone else who'd got back into it after divorce assured me all the more. By the beginning of March, I was going on my first date.

Now, when I say going on my first date, I mean being practically thrown together and escorted to the bar by a friend (the only thing she didn't do was come on the date for me). Such was my Bambi-on-Ice impression that night, while trying to wrap my head around going on a date. He was a guy I'd met online, and it turned out that he'd lived in Edinburgh for a while. Super randomly, he had actually socialised in the same circle as my brother, even spending time in my brother's university apartment! The world is but a tiny little ball we're all on, no matter the separation we might sometimes feel.

So there was at least some common ground before we met. He'd also called me, like, on the phone (as Alexander Graham Bell always intended), and I'd read that was a good sign in the online dating world. I'd read a lot about dating before going on the date. *Be interesting! Be funny! Offer to pay! But don't pay! Ask questions! But not too many questions! Dress up! But don't be slutty!* I was exhausted before the date had even started.

Nervous, however, isn't a fair description of how I felt. It was more like an out-of-body experience. Even all this time after my divorce, two-and-a-half years later, I was still baffled by the fact that I was in a position to go on a date. What the actual fuck. As much as I didn't want to be married to that prick, I also kinda' woulda' liked to not be doing this.... So, I was relieved when it didn't turn out to be horrendously awkward. We had as much to talk about as I'd hoped, and it was actually fun, a possibility that I hadn't really considered.

It was all going swimmingly until he started to do something that I've been guilty of myself: being too much of an open book.

Was the story of a sink falling on him at work supposed to be funny? My internal reaction was: *How are you that dumb?* However, this story did give way to his eventual nickname of Crazy Canadian Sink Guy, which would become the first in a long string of nicknames that I'd give to every guy I dated from then on. The nicknames typically took the form of where the guy was from in the world, sometimes a noticeable feature or a story, perhaps their career, where they lived, a hobby of theirs, or a mixture of those things. I would come to date a variety of nationalities and ethnicities—and such is Vancouver's culturally-diverse population—so often their nationality was used as a distinguisher for my friends. There were far too many Matts and Nabeels to count, and given that myself and many of my friends were also from elsewhere, it was just an easy way to keep track—something that we all had in common, despite the backstory being different for each of us.

Crazy Canadian Sink Guy started to tell me about being turfed out of his old apartment (rightly or wrongly by the landlord) and refusing to give back his key, and I thought: *Are these details meant to impress me? Because I think they have the opposite effect.* Did I need to know that he'd just gotten into a physical altercation with a neighbour, one whom he thought was having a domestic dispute? Probably not, but it's nice to know how strongly he feels about domestic violence, *I guess?!* Was I really supposed to agree with him when he told me he'd been stabbed three times while living in my home city, *but you know, that's what happens there?* Um buddy, I lived there a lot longer than you did and I never got stabbed. I think this says more about you than the place. Also, rude.

On this first date, I realised how utterly loud my inner thoughts were in my head. We all think, like, all the time (unless you're some Zen master, in which case you think, like, *almost* all the time) and sometimes we're thinking about doing a million other things. What I discovered on dates was that my thoughts would raise above their usual "inside voice" and start screaming in my head. I wasn't sure if this was to warn or entertain me, but I often found myself asking and answering questions, or making jokes about the situation and finding them funny (all the while remaining an engaged and entertaining date... of course).

All this to say that the night was a bit of a mixed bag. Thinking back on it now, I laugh at myself for letting all those red flags slide while listening to his stories. But at that time, I was just so enamoured by the fact that someone appeared to like me, or at least wanted to spend time with me, because lord knows it had been a while. So, I ignored the red flags and continued to enjoy his company for a few more dates.

Alas, on top of his wildly inappropriate stories, he also got pretty clingy. It all became a bit much, and eventually I figured out that it was the idea of those seemingly "nice" things—someone paying me attention, giving me compliments, wanting my company—that I was enjoying and not necessarily him.... Chatting it through with my friends, bouncing my sense of the situation off them, it became clear that past experiences were making me question my own decision-making ability, something that probably needed to be nipped in the bud. So, with my girlfriends' assistance (I was the epitome of "team dating" at this point), I sent my very first (maybe ever?) brush off text. Under adult supervision, of course.

I was desperate to be honest and tell him that I didn't want to date anymore, but I was told, in no uncertain terms, that this wouldn't work. Instead we came up with a polite but curt text, which cut the burgeoning relationship off in its tracks. It didn't allow for much debate, but it left everyone with their dignity intact. This was the beginning of my conflict re: honesty being my only policy, but sometimes you just need to make things easier on yourself. He took it well, and overall I thought it was a good first foray into dating.

When I was still chatting to Crazy Canadian Sink Guy, I found myself troubled by what to do about all the pings from dating apps on my phone. I was old school in my way of thinking, to the point that I found it inappropriate to message people while "seeing" Crazy Canadian Sink Guy. It didn't sit right with me, but whenever I said thank you and goodbye to Crazy Canadian Sink Guy, there was this whole list of men, seemingly waiting for me to return their messages.

Having had my confidence boosted by the first-date experience, but still like a newborn foal taking its first steps after breaking with the amniotic sack, I wanted to keep the ball rolling. Hence how I ended up planning two first dates in one day. *Like, how the hell did I get here?* I could barely get myself out the house for one date a few weeks prior and now I was planning two in one day. *Bold? Stupid? Both?* It wasn't my intention to double book myself, but

I'd been chatting to both guys for a little while and simply hadn't managed to meet up with either of them yet, at least until this particular Saturday. So, when one of them wanted to do daytime and the other evening, it just seemed efficient to fit in both. And who doesn't love efficiency?

"The Day of Two Dates" started off on a coffee date with a twenty-nine-year-old Brazilian who worked in the film industry. He was friendly, soft spoken, passionate about many different things, including coffee (hence the coffee date) and I went along with his suggestion of activities because…I'm agreeable, I guess? Plus, I figured that midday drinks might have been a little too aggressive to suggest. All in all, Canada's drinking culture was a little different from the UK. In Vancouver, they love their craft beers and micro breweries; and East Vancouver is affectionately nicknamed Yeast Vancouver, for its plethora of trendy craft brew halls. So it's not that the locals don't drink—just that, opposed to getting drunk, Vancouver appreciates quality over quantity.

The one thing I didn't mention to my date, however, was that I don't actually drink coffee. I never have. I love coffee-flavoured everything, apart from coffee itself. But coffee shops don't just serve coffee so I figured it'd be fine. And it would have been fine, if I hadn't gotten distracted when I arrived and had him order me a double macchiato. The distraction was my fault; well, maybe my girlfriends' faults…. To explain, every chat, online match, or potential date was being poured over by my gorgeously witty girlfriends (Classic, AnnaB, and Quyeneth – yes even though the latter two were now back in the UK) in a freestyle form of team dating. They offered their opinions, questions, and warnings before I agreed to any in-person meetings.

In the case of the Brazilian, AnnaB had pointed out his double, full-arm sleeve tattoos, while carefully studying his profile pics from the app. Despite the eight-hour time difference between half of our group chat, a ridiculously quick message arrived from the other side of the pond: *um, I don't think those are tattoos, I think that's hair.* Hence his nickname, Hairy Tattoo Guy, was born. Leading up to our date, the nature of his arms were talked about extensively, and upon arriving at Small Victory, the stylish neighbourhood coffee place where we'd met, all I could do was try to sneak a peek at his (admittedly very hairy and definitely not tattooed) forearm. Trying desperately not to stare, while stifling a laugh and resisting the urge not to text my dating team, meant that all I could do was glance up at the menu and order the first thing I saw.

Double macchiato.

Why I ordered a *second* one of these, about forty-five minutes later when he suggested that we get another one, is beyond me. Maybe it has something to do with an aversion to feeling flustered. I hate not knowing where I'm going or what to order, or that feeling when you walk into a restaurant and spend the first thirty seconds searching aimlessly for whomever you're there to meet. I hate that whole routine. So I've always just employed a strategy of: *Don't hesitate and just sound/look/act like you know what you're doing.* It doesn't always work out, however, like in this instance.

But the coffee was good and there was a buzzy atmosphere that suited me perfectly. We covered a huge range of topics. He was a good conversationalist which is the least you can hope for when first meeting someone. The date ended with him walking me home and attempting to kiss me on the street across from my apartment in broad daylight, which horrified me. In part because PDA was something that I had forgotten all about. I'm not a teenager anymore and I wasn't really attracted to him (nothing to do with his arms, tattooed or otherwise, although a good set of arms definitely gets my attention).

I headed back upstairs for what was supposed to be a quiet couple of hours, watching some TV, filing my date report in the group chat (obviously), and then prepping for the next date. But it turns out the caffeine I'd thrown back earlier had other ideas. Almost as soon as I sat down on the sofa, I started to feel pretty unwell. My heart was racing, my stomach was cramping, and my head was pounding. At first, it didn't click with me that it might be the caffeine. I just figured that my fainting had returned. Turns out that *no,* this is just what happens when you drink two double macchiato. Did I mention that I had also been running on a pretty empty stomach? *Yah, fun times.*

I won't go into the gory details—let's just say that I now understand when people say, *that coffee went straight through me.* It was grim. And this, people, is what they call *KARMA.* Who the hell did I think I was, planning two dates in one day, friggin' Wonder Woman herself?

By the time I'd figured out that cancelling my second date was definitely the best move, he was already on his way to meet me. *Shit. Literally?* Rather than telling him to turn around, or arrive to a sweating, jittery, loose-bellied mess, I figured the polite move was to suck it up and get on with things. That's when my bigger *how-the-hell-did-I-get-here* thought occurred. Not only did

I have to go on a first date feeling like this, I had to go on a first date to a Mexican restaurant feeling like this. Now, I love Mexican food, and ordinarily I can't get enough of guac', jalapenos, fried beans, and carnitas. The restaurant, Patron Tacos & Cantina, was one block from my apartment—but on that day, the thought of it literally made my stomach wobble.

It was a tough date, but that was all on me. He was a thirty-four-year-old Canadian who worked in insurance and lived in a basement suite in a suburb of Vancouver, with ginger hair and lots of freckles on his light skin. He was nice, maybe a little nervous, but engaging and funny. Meanwhile, I was attempting to keep the sweat from my top lip and my toilet trips to a minimum. When my food arrived, I became one of those horrible dates who pushes their food around their plate without really eating. Usually, when I don't feel like my stomach is going to fall out of my ass, I'm not shy about eating on a first date, or otherwise. I find myself almost constantly able to eat, the words "I can't, I'm full" very rarely pass my lips, and I'm not ashamed of it. I wanted to address with him the fact that I wasn't at my best during the date, but I didn't want to answer too many questions.

Barely an hour later, I'd managed to hide some of my steak, rice and beans under the tortilla that came with them. He'd gotten the cheque and I was heading for the hills, aka my own bathroom. I barely even stopped to hug him properly; in fact, I might have broken into a slight run, as I crossed the road back to my building.

Later that evening, once all the water and Imodium had taken effect, I texted him to say thanks for dinner. I admitted that I hadn't been feeling my best, but that I'd love to see him again if he was keen. He replied that he hadn't noticed anything—if that wasn't even me at my best, he'd definitely love to see me again. I wasn't sure whether to believe him. (Hi there, trust issues! But also, I was a mess, how could he have not noticed?) Still, I wasn't about to question things. I took the compliment and vowed to never plan two dates with different guys in the same day ever again.

As with chatting to multiple people, going on multiple dates at a time just didn't sit well with me. Who knew that dating could leave you wondering whether you'd crossed the boundary of human decency? Was I just too naive or is this *just how dating is in [insert current year here]?* This was definitely one of those moments. I'd never dated multiple people at the same time. I'd been with one person for the entirety of my twenties and prior to that I'd had a couple of high-school boyfriends, with whom I'd chatted or flirted, but dating multiple people at a time was new territory for me. It wasn't something I was comfortable with right away.

From then on, I decided to employ the gauge scale of *how-would-I-feel-if-the-shoe-were-on-the-other-foot?* I can't say that I'd mind if someone had gone on another date earlier in the day, or perhaps after leaving my company; but at the end of the day, no one's going anywhere. There's plenty of time to have dates on different days, so why even put myself in a position where I question my morals and karma comes back round to kick my ass?

I never did see Hairy Tattoo Guy again, although he did enquire about a second date. I just didn't feel as if we had very much in common, apart from having moved to the city from somewhere else, but the same goes for about seventy-five percent of Vancouver's population, and I'm not about to date them all. *Or was I?* And despite the mess, I'd made it through my second date of the day, and I actually did go out with date number two again. Being that a hot mess didn't seem to put him off, it bode well for me.

However, as Easter Weekend rolled around and he headed for British Columbia's interior to visit family, I saw the first red flag. It had to do with the app Dubsmash which was big in 2016, where you could record yourself lip-synching to songs or movie quotes, before sending it around or posting it on social media. Receiving five of these videos from him over the course of one weekend, always increasing in their cringe-worthiness, was too much. One video started with him lip-synching to Jim Carey's lines in the police road-stop scene from the film *Liar Liar* (Google it, or don't), another showed him introducing his family members (all adults), and in the last one, he, his step-dad, and his brother-in-law were singing "The Boys Are Back In Town" from their garage, with matching outfits and real-life instruments.

I received the last video while at a Jillian's sister's party (she of the Julia recommendation). By the reaction on my face, my friends were expecting to see an unsolicited dick pic (of which I'd already received many, since setting up my dating-app profiles). It turns out that a choreographed "family" Dubsmash routine from someone whom I've only just met gets the same reaction as a dick pic. Thus his nickname of Dubsmash Dude was born. Damien and I, in our drunkenness, even downloaded the app to see if we could send him a video back as a joke—but (maybe also in our drunkenness?) we couldn't work out how to use the app.

After Easter Weekend, I wasn't that excited about seeing him again. What can I say? Watching him "rocking out" in a white vest and lip-synching (badly) just didn't do it for me. Don't get me wrong, I love people who know how to have a good time, people who aren't afraid to make fools of themselves entirely but make other people smile, but I'd need to know somebody way better before I'd ever find that funny. It's unlikely to make someone more attractive to me. I have a thing about non-professionals singing. Open-mic nights, karaoke, The X Factor—they all make me want to die.

But the next time I saw him, he drove the final nails into our dating coffin. He invited me to his place for dinner, which made me uncomfortable in plenty of ways. These days I would never agree to it. I had since learned more lessons regarding respecting my own boundaries and avoiding situations that made me uncomfortable—but at the time, I thought it was nice that he'd offered to cook, so I accepted his offer.

While I thought about saying: *That would be lovely and, just FYI, I don't eat fish,* for some reason I didn't. I just figured that he would check if he was cooking anything slightly "controversial." When the day came, he messaged me late that morning to confirm the time and address details, concluding with, *I take it you're okay with tuna?* I politely said, *sorry, no.* Let's just say his reaction was less than stellar. He made a fuss about having to return to the supermarket and finished with a big moan, announcing: "I'll just get another protein and hope it works in the recipe, unless there's anything else that you don't eat." Okay then! Now I was really looking forward to dinner!

Later that day, I took a thirty dollar cab ride out to his place. (Did I mention that he lives in the suburbs, and the burbs and I are strangers to each other?) His place was dark and a bit dingy; considering that he'd been expecting company, it wasn't particularly clean. All this to say that I was uncomfortable from the moment I arrived. As he cooked us dinner (now being made with ground chicken rather than tuna.... What the fuck is ground chicken? Not the culinary substitution I would have made, but oh well...). We chatted a bit, and over dinner I learned about one of my biggest turnoffs.

I'd never come across it before, given my newness to dating, not to mention that everyone I'd previously dated sounded just like me. You know in *Friends,* when they talk about the words that make Chandler's balls jump back up into his body? Like Janice saying *oh-h-h-h-h my-y-y-y-y god.* Well, it would appear that someone trying to do a Scottish accent was my female equivalent.

I tried to laugh it off, taking the *wow, that was terrible, haha, never do it again hahaha, lol, lol, lol* route, to which his response was to continue doing it. So, more sternly this time, I asked him to please not do that. He proceeded to tell me (still in a "Scottish" accent) that he looked Scottish (he was ginger) so he could pull it off. Um, not so my friend. The only thought in my head was: *you will never kiss me with that mouth* and I knew right then and there that I wouldn't be seeing Dubsmash Dude again.

The thing is, I would never attempt to do someone's accent: a) because I'd be shit at it, and b) because it's offensive. What if I did it to a Chinese person? An Indian person? But somehow it's cute because it's Scottish? *Get the fuck out.* Since moving to another country, I've had to get used to the whole accent conversation. Some of my immigrant friends really hate it when people comment on their accents. I don't mind—it comes with the territory of being an immigrant, and I'm blessed enough to have a country to go back to— but I'm also told often that I don't have an accent. My reply is always: *That's impossible; everyone has an accent, regardless of whether you sound like everyone around you.*

I know what people mean, however: I don't have the accent that they expect. I don't sound like the female version of those guys in Trainspotting, and I'm certainly no Gerard Butler. I had a fairly soft Scottish accent in the first place, and growing up in Cairo gave it an interesting International-School coating. Most people in Canada take a while to hear my accent at all. When they don't recognise it, they think it's Irish or Australian. Mostly, this happens because they can't really differentiate between certain accents, and less because I actually sound Australian or Irish. I have found myself getting slightly offended when people comment on my accent, as if they were somehow saying that I don't sound Scottish and am thus less Scottish somehow.

I'm an incredibly proud Scot, especially this far away from home, so it gets under my skin a little. We are resilient and bold people, heart and honour are in our DNA, and we're known for being friendly, hospitable, and with a dry, self deprecating sense of humour. We're also incredibly sentimental, hence why I don't think my connection to Scotland will wane regardless of how long I live on other shores. Like Canada, Scotland had Aboriginal people of its own as well. In the early days of Scottish history, the native people were called the Picts. The name translates to "Painted People, in reference to their custom of painting and tattooing their bodies. This was a warlike Celtic tribe descended from this area's Indigenous Iron Age inhabitants. The Picts were conquered by the first invaders to land on their shores—the Irish Celts, but Pictish culture left no written records, only some eerily impressive stone monuments and carvings.

Regardless of how strong (or not) my accent sounds, someone trying to imitate it for comic effect? *No.* Please God, *no.* It's as bad as (maybe worse than) someone shouting "Freedom!" at me, using their best Scottish-Mel-Gibson impression. *Just get out. Get in the bin.* I tried to be jokey about it with Dubsmash Dude; and honestly, if someone repeatedly suggested that I stopped doing something on a second date, I would have taken heed of their request. This guy clearly felt differently. The rest of the evening was peppered with him sporadically switching into a "Scottish" accent and me slowly losing all will to live.

After finishing our dinner—which I hope, for his sake, was crap because of the last-minute ingredient switch and not his cooking skills—I couldn't wait to leave and get my thirty dollar return cab ride home, feeling sure that I'd never see him again. If the Dubsmash vids were the initial straws on the camel's back, then his repeated attempts at imitating my accent was certainly the straw that broke this camel's back. I just hoped that all the different sides of myself had learned something from this.

Thirteen

Play That Funky Music White Boy

The dating continued during March and April and in amongst all the dodgy dates and crap conversations, I actually met someone offline—organically, "normally!" He was my friend's stepbrother whom, for some reason, she'd never thought to mention to me. Jessica is now one of my closest friends, but we first met while working together. She'd taken me under her wing, hence the Vegas-promoter introduction for my thirtieth birthday trip, and then become an incredible confidant at the tech company we both worked at, and she was fully in support of me getting back into dating.

She and I went out on the Friday night of the Easter Long Weekend, planning to see a film about Renoir later in the evening (because we're just so cultured), but that plan got nixed when her step-dad called to announce that he was in town, and thus was she interested in having drinks with him? When we met him at Parlour, an upscale pizza joint and bar in Yaletown, he told us that his son/Jessica's stepbrother would be joining us as well. When he arrived, it was one of those times when I felt myself physically "sit up and take note." Partly because she'd barely mentioned even having a stepbrother, never mind an incredibly funny and charming stepbrother. My head was officially turned. When he started talking about his current divorce and having just moved into a new place, it was clear that we had something in common. Plus, if he was married until recently, it made sense that Jess hadn't mentioned him before.

He was Canadian and a DJ. His nickname would become "Canadian DJ" (the intent was *not* to be creative). He was funny and engaging and chatty, and

I felt a sort of spark as we sat together at dinner, like a proper frisson of electricity between us. But I was a few drinks in and still rusty with this stuff, so I tried not to get too far ahead of myself. Plus, he was related (by his parents' marriage, if not birth) to one of my best girlfriends—so I wanted to get her take on it first.

I presumed she could tell that I was quietly losing my mind when my schoolgirl-esque giggling took hold. Literally, when he was telling us about the real fireplace in his new apartment, I asked him: "Where do you get your wood?" The innuendo was unintentional; I was just trying to act interested. Thankfully, he responded with a suitably innuendo-laden answer[3], and I was even more convinced that something between us was catching flame. (And who needs a "real" fireplace with such fire in the loins?)

It's fair to say that Jess was surprised when I brought it up at the end of the night. "What?! You like him? Really?! I never even thought of him for you." While surprised, she wasn't against the idea. We spent the weekend together at her Granny's place, where he naturally came up in conversation more than once—including once when her mom called. It turns out that Jess' mom had been speaking to her husband (Canadian DJ's dad) who mentioned our drinks out the night before. Apparently his son had said (about me): *She's exactly the sort of person I should date.* Needless to say, it's not something I was expecting to hear. It put a smile on my face and left a flutter in my stomach, all while sending my mind into overdrive. *Did I mention that I'm an over-thinker?*

After that weekend, I decided to be brave and bold and send him a message on Facebook, being encouraged by Jess to add him as a friend. I crafted the perfect first message—you know, the kind that is meant to sound really easy and breezy and casual but in reality took a good hour and a half of rewrites to perfect. I sent it and then panicked. For a whole twenty-one hours. It took almost a day to get a response...WTF. I felt close to a stroke the entire time. How can sending one little message do that to you? I'm an adult, for god's sake.

I'd included my phone number in the Facebook message, as well as a reference to my embarrassing wood comment. When I got a text the following day from an unknown Vancouver number that just said *Go-o-o-o-o-d morning!* I so wanted it to be from him and not some wrong number. Google was able to confirm the former for me, as it was the number he had on his website

---

[3] His answer: *A couple of places, but I usually get it in the morning.*

for his business; and I may have let out a whoop of excitement. *Um, hi, am I fifteen again?*

By the twelfth message (yes, I may have been keeping count), he mentioned going for a drink, though it seemed as if it might be difficult to plan, given that we both had a lot of stuff on the go, and he was leaving to his dad's place in Mexico for two weeks the following Monday. We decided to catch up once he was back, but there was this feeling, on my side anyway, that the impetus might dissipate by then. So, when he messaged me on the Thursday confirming that I was definitely busy that Friday night (because he had a spare ticket to a concert), I had to make a snap decision. Was I the type of girl who ditched plans with her friends to go on a date? *Death Cab for Cutie* with a boy or Ellie Goulding with my girlfriends....

Is it you and a group of friends or is this a potential "date...?"; I wrote to him over text. He responded with: *hahahahaha, not a group of friends, so let's go with "date."* Let's just say that team dating came back into play in a big way; the girls came to life in our group chat and it got pretty heated. There were those of us in the 'chicks before dicks' camp and those who simply couldn't turn down the prospect of a great date. Ultimately, it was decided that I should change my initial plans and go on the date. I checked with the friend I'd made plans with and her emphatic text response back was: *GO GET IT GIRL.* I bloody love my friends.

So the plans were made: drinks and dinner Downtown before *Death Cab for Cutie* at the UBC Thunderbird Stadium, on the Endowment Lands, just a couple blocks from the Pacific Spirit Park. We both noted how we'd gone from maybe not having time for a drink before his trip to now executing a full on first date. This would be the first of many escalations. I loved it yet was overcome with anxiety at the same time.

Feeling all the fun nerves about what I was going to wear, how to do my hair, and whether there would be a kiss (all subjects discussed in a stream of group texts with my friends), I was an anxiety-ridden mess. My anxiety was partly due to not hearing from him until three pm that day, by which time I'd convinced myself that he'd changed his mind, or else hadn't been serious about the date in the first place. After all, it was April Fools Day. *Hi there, self-doubt, you've been silent for a whole week, I missed you.* It's incredible how you can be sailing along, feeling great, almost on top of the world, winning at life and then BAM! The takedown of your self-worth and self-confidence, inflicted by a previous partner, comes crawling back like a crappy disease.

But just after three pm, he confirmed our plans and told me he was really looking forward to it, so I tried my best to extinguish my self-doubt and get myself to the bar. I ordered a double gin and ginger ale before he even arrived. But as soon as he did, I was instantly calmer, albeit with a flutter of excitement in my stomach, as we fell back into the funny, easy banter from the night we'd met.

We had a quick dinner with drinks and got a cab out to the venue. We talked constantly; it was so easy. We talked family and music, travel and TV shows, working out and drinking, plans for summer and plans for life. There were no silences nor uncertainties; we both were there to listen and share. He was funny, he was engaging, he was confident, he was gregarious. If anyone had asked me what my type was, I would have used those descriptors. I always went for the joker, the comedian, the guy who would be center of any social circle, the one everyone knew, the one who had to get the biggest laugh. Both my father and my ex-husband were those sorts of men. So, in some ways, it didn't thrill me that I was still attracted to that archetype, but you love what you know. And I certainly knew it.

At some point during the process of showing our tickets, getting drinks, and finding a spot that we both agreed seemed like the perfect place to stand, I realised that I'd have to decide how to play this, given that we were standing in General Admission. Did I dance? Or try to, while holding a cider in each hand? Should I do the over exaggerated head bob, to appear into it but blasé all the same? Should I sing? I'd given myself a crash course in *Death Cab for Cutie* songs over the last seventy-two hours. I'd known some of their stuff in the past, but I wasn't sure I could confidently nail the words anymore.

During the warm up act, we did some people watching together as an icebreaker. Needing one seemed weird at that stage, having already been together for almost two hours, but the change of environment had admittedly put me on edge. *Was I the only one of us feeling this way?* By the time that Death Cab started, the drinks with dinner and now the ciders were taking effect. We quickly found an easy balance between singing, chatting, and laughing throughout the show, as my self-consciousness slowly slipped away. We'd been standing pretty close throughout the concert, and as one of our favourite songs (well, it was his favourite song and in my "listening to nothing but Cutie" phase over the last few days, it had also become one of mine) came on, there was a line that went: "I need you so much closer," and I remember thinking: *yeah, like, fuck, just kiss me already—also, if this wasn't a first date, I would so be having sex with you later....* I guess you could say that I was having a good time.

We cabbed back Downtown, but neither of us seemed ready to finish the night, so we went for a few cocktails randomly at a Sushi place in Yaletown. After drinks with dinner and more during the gig, we probably could have done with some more food at that point, but it didn't seem like a priority for either of us and I don't eat sushi (shock horror to all Vancouverites, I know). The conversation got a little more in-depth over drinks, chats about our divorces (or separations, as his was at the time), our parents' divorces, and our own struggles. There was a lot that we had in common, and I liked that for once I didn't feel like my divorce was this weird life anomaly that nobody from my generation could identify with thus far.

His separation was still fairly fresh, but he was sure it was definitely over. Barring some back and forth about pet custody (which seemed almost as contentious to navigate as child custody), there was nothing left for them to discuss. I recognised the sadness still in him, the same sadness I'd felt myself: that sense of not quite believing it had come to an end, that you were now without the one person you thought you'd be with forever. I marveled internally at how much quicker he seemingly was able to come out on the other side in comparison to me. He was on a date only months afterwards, while I'd taken years. Actual years. I was both envious of and impressed by his resilience.

The bar was closing and he insisted on walking me back to my place. All night I had been floored by his manners. Doors were opened for me, seats pulled out, jackets put on, everything paid for—I wasn't used to it but jeez, I could definitely adjust. Every little gesture made my stomach flip just a little. Knowing his family, I wasn't surprised that he was like that; they had strong values and morals. I'm all for equality and women doing things for themselves, but there's something about chivalry that gets me, and I do believe both can exist simultaneously.

On the walk home, in the crisp night air with the most recent intake of alcohol filtering into my bloodstream, I made another bold decision and asked whether he wanted to come up to my apartment. Earlier that night, we'd discussed our love for whisky and I just so happened to have a great bottle that I thought he'd like to try. For some reason, people tend to think that Scottish people know what they're talking about when it comes to Scotch, as if we're somehow taught about it in school. Let's just say it's rare that people turn down my whisky—I guess it comes with my ethnic territory.

Ten minutes later, whiskies in hand, random YouTube videos on Apple TV, and the sofa bed pulled out for *full* comfort (I promise it was for comfort!), it felt like I was hanging out with an old friend. But an old friend who I really *really* wanted to kiss. As we got progressively closer video after video, I was clearly feeling further emboldened by the whisky and straight out asked him if he intended to kiss me. He was a little taken aback and said: "I've really wanted to but it's the first time I've kissed someone since...and I didn't know I'd be so excited about it..."; before finally, FINALLY, he leaned forward and kissed me.

I was sitting down, but there was still a definite weakening in my knees. He was a great kisser and we proceeded to make out like teenagers. At some point during our make out, YouTube, and whisky session, the fact that he was having a sofa delivered at nine am came up (it was close to four am). *What?! How the fuck had that happened?* Time had passed in a flash. We both reiterated, out loud this time, that we still weren't ready for the night to end; so after not that long of a discussion, I packed a bag and we cabbed out to where he lived, half an hour out of Vancouver...*How did this happen?* I barely left downtown during daylight hours, never mind for a four am cab ride to some far off suburb on a first date.

Following a grand tour of his new pride and joy of a house, an introduction to the cat and the dog, followed by more whisky (Japanese this time) and then things got fuzzy. As we sat by the fire (but seriously, where did he get his wood?) I just remember him saying, "Don't look behind you, but it's getting light outside." It was seven am. So, we got into bed, with him leaving the bedroom for me to change into my PJs—again, manners—and after some fairly heavy petting (we were definitely fifteen again) with an unspoken understanding that we definitely weren't going to have sex, we fell soundly asleep.

For an hour and a half, anyway. Remember that sofa delivery? Yah, nine am. Bang on time. *Why?! They never come at the beginning of the delivery window when you want them to be there.* We barely woke up to let them in, and when I say "we" I mean "he." I stayed put in bed. Afterwards, he had to take the dog out (sucks to have responsibility), but still I stayed put. We spent the morning in bed, feeling more than a little worse for wear but entirely comfortable. We chatted about the previous night, how we'd both had a better time than either of us were expecting, again sharing more stories about our marriages and respective marriage breakdowns. It was a strange thing to bond over so early, but we seemed to have very similar experiences. He was still navigating how to discuss the experience with people, so I'd like to think that I was making things easier.

Finally, we dragged our asses out of bed and wandered up the street for food. I complimented his newly delivered couch—velvet teal was a bold choice, but he wasn't exactly a shy nor retiring guy. Lunch was followed by another nap, making our time together feel like one of those cosy, lovely, and lazy Saturdays that I'd so missed sharing with someone. I had been loving my time to myself, but having no plans with someone is much better than having no plans by yourself. When someone who lives alone says, "I have no plans, I'm headed home," they're generally going home to do nothing and be with no one. But when someone who lives with people or their partner says, "I have no plans, I'm headed home," they'll likely still be spending time with someone. Very different meanings emerge for the same activity, and I truly had enjoyed living alone more than I'd ever thought possible—but chilling with someone? Well, that was almost always preferable.

As I came alive over lunch, I remembered that I had a birthday to attend that night. I'd need to get myself together for a big night out, as was always the case when celebrating the twins' birthdays. Thus his insistence on driving me home was in no way a problem, because I sure as hell wasn't getting on the SkyTrain. A whole twenty-three hours after our essentially "epic" first date started, he drove me back along the highway, which was much busier now than it had been twelve hours earlier. He dropped me off at exactly four pm, of course getting out to open my door and helping me down from his SUV. There was one last kiss, okay maybe many last kisses, before I tore myself away to get ready for early drinks with friends before the birthday celebrations. Despite my hangover and severe lack of sleep, I'm pretty sure that I could have floated up to the tenth floor, high on life, no elevator needed.

At 4:12pm, as I was jumping in the shower, my phone buzzed: *I think I'm going through Louise withdrawal.* Heart melt. Knees weak. Stomach flipped. I'd truly forgotten what this felt like. Albeit there had been a couple of dates and even some sex since my marriage, but nothing felt like this. I had entirely forgotten the giddiness, the excitement, the butterflies. The last time I'd felt them had been at nineteen when I was starting to date the man I would end up marrying. I wondered if I would ever not compare relationships, people, or feelings to him. The birthday celebrations that night were a riot of fun, as expected, and I had a severe pep in my step. (Fun-fact: this was the same night I received the offending video from Dubsmash Dude.) Even my hangover the next day was eased by having spent time with him.

When we said goodbye on Saturday afternoon, it seemed as if that would be it until he came back from Mexico, but having accidentally left my jacket at his place (I really didn't do it on purpose but I was super fucking happy that I had), I ended up seeing him that Sunday evening when he returned it. This led to an impromptu second date with dinner at the izakaya place next to my building. Again, there was an ease between us, like no subject was off topic and neither one of us was guarding ourselves unnecessarily. He left for Mexico the next morning and I felt like the next two weeks could feel like a long ass time. I know, pass me the bucket.... And where had this even come from? It was outrageous and disorientating, but only in the best way.

What followed was an unexpected, battery-draining, heart-fluttering, stom-ach-flipping two weeks of all day texts and middle of the night calls. We texted every day, and most nights we'd end up on the phone for hours. I was incred-ibly sleep deprived, but it was unbelievably lovely having someone checking in and telling me about their day (mostly beach related), asking me about my day (mostly work related), and telling me they missed me. It was enough to get me through the workday and any subsequent social engagements or workouts, before I'd climb into bed again knowing that sleep wouldn't follow for at least another couple of hours, due to texts and long distance calls. We talked about everything: our childhoods, passions and bugbears, our careers, our friends, trips we'd taken, trips we wanted to take, relationships, love and sex.

That last topic led us down a tricky path. No one wants to be over two-thousand miles away from each other with a severe sexual attraction developing while talking about what you'd like to do to each other. Or, worse still, sending those types of messages when one of you isn't on vacation and trying to concentrate on work. Maybe the no sex on the first date thing was foolish, or maybe it would have made it worse if we'd gone there already. All I knew was that the remaining days of his trip couldn't pass quick enough.

Maybe as a result of that growing frustration, and the fact that he was getting restless staying with his parents, he came up with a crazy idea. In the midst of one of our evening text sessions, after I'd jokingly responded to one of his texts re: why I wasn't there to keep him entertained with: *oh yeah I'll just get on a plane to Mexico.* He fired back with: *Why don't you?* I laughed it off, his daily tequila intake was going to his head. But when he brought it up again later that night and started proposing road trips we could take and offering to pay, I realised that he wasn't joking.

High on late-night chats and the knowledge that someone wanted me to fly to another continent to see them, I started to seriously consider the possibility. I mean, I had vacation days to take and my boss was pretty flexible, so I took a quick look at possible flights, if only to prove that it was an insane idea. Turns out that it had the opposite effect. But this was Thursday night and we were talking about me flying there on the Saturday. *Insane.* I don't do things like that. But I was conflicted...

It sounded like crazy fun and sometimes you need that in your life. However, it was also plain crazy. We'd been on two dates (if you count the impromptu dinner) and while, yes, I knew his family and was pretty sure that he wasn't about to kill me in some Mexican hacienda, it was still pretty early in the game to take a trip together.

There was also this part of me, as Laura pointed out (team dating to the rescue again), that knew I hadn't been on a vacation with a guy since my ex-husband. In fact, the longest I'd spent with a guy since my ex was in fact the twenty-three hours of my first date with Canadian DJ. And now he wanted me to go to Mexico and spend four days with him! What if I got there and freaked the hell out? How could I be sure that we wouldn't get sick of each other after two nights? Maybe twenty-three hours was our max, our peak, just the right amount of time for us to spend together at that point?

To appease him and essentially take the decision out of my hands, I asked my boss for the time off—if he okayed the whole shebang, I'd go for it. If he said no, it'd be a moot point. So I emailed my boss and told him about the crazy idea (avoiding the crucial part about the trip being with a guy I had just met) and waited. His reply on the Friday morning was: *sure. Mexico for four days is crazy but sure.* Well, he wasn't wrong.

I decided not to pass on the good(?) news to Canadian DJ quite yet. I was still mulling it over. The general consensus amongst my friends was *are you crazy?!* with a couple defectors who took the side of, *fuck it! just do it!* including, unbelievably, my mum. My mother, who is usually so sensible and level-headed, told me that, "sometimes, you just have to say "life is too short" and go for it." I was gobsmacked, all the more so by the unexpected source of this staggering advice. She must have been on the gin.

As the working day drew to a close, the sunny, patio happy hour I'd planned with friends approached as well, and I knew my crazy idea would be the main topic of conversation. We'd gossip about something that perhaps wouldn't happen anyways and sip wine in the sun. Michelle was first to arrive and she was all for it. "Think how romantic it would be, what a great story! And seriously, it's sunny here, but think how hot it will be in Mexico." She knew I had a weakness for the heat.

Laura arrived next, but she was less into the idea. She'd always been more level-headed than me, and I appreciated her ability to make non-emotional decisions. "Mexico isn't going anywhere. Let him have his trip and go on more dates once he's back. Then if it's all going well, you can go to Mexico anytime you want. You don't need to go now, after two dates, it's just too much." Her opinion, while appreciated, was definitely less exciting to hear.

This was my first experience of having to decide between pumping the breaks, not rushing things, and being generally "sensible"; or the alternative which was an exciting, romantic and altogether epic opportunity to have an experience with someone whom I had overwhelming feelings for so naturally. You get such conflicting advice on both sides of the spectrum. *Don't ruin it by rushing it! Life's too short! Make him wait! You do you! He's not going anywhere! If it feels right, do it!*

That last one was the one that got me. There was something that didn't feel right. It was just slightly off and I couldn't put my finger on it. Maybe it was my ongoing battle with spontaneity, another favourite entry point for my anxiety. Maybe it was my fear of rapid escalation in a new "relationship" (I use that term loosely), given that I was a little out of practice and didn't want to ruin things by bolstering along. For whatever reason, I just couldn't pull the trigger. Flight routes were open on my computer (and my phone) and all day I was ready to book. As I sat drinking Viognier while looking out over False Creek from The Wicklow patio, I decided to close the Skyscanner app and open WhatsApp instead. Then I wrote Canadian DJ a message:

So good news and bad news. Good news—my boss approved the days off. The bad news—despite that I don't think I should come. I think you should enjoy the rest of your trip like you'd planned and when you come back we can spend more time together before we take our first trip. You have no idea how close I was to booking those flights, and come tomorrow morning when I would have otherwise been heading to the airport and instead will be going for a run, I'll regret my decision—but I do think it's for the best. TL; DR; my boss is great, I suck.

The reply that came back was what I expected: *I understand.* When I pressed him about the slightly short response, he said: *I'm not upset; I'm just disappointed.* Ugh, great. Who doesn't like to be called disappointing on a Friday afternoon? Server, I'll take another glass of Viognier.

We texted about it throughout the evening. He admitted that he really did understand, while trying to convince me that the trip wouldn't mean anything. It wasn't a big deal, so why not think of it as a really long, far away, third date? He was a pretty smooth talker and I almost caved at a number of points. He was your typical impulsive, spontaneous, live-life-to-the-fullest type of guy, so I could understand why my reluctance to throw caution to the wind wasn't something he could accept easily. He could have found it unattractive, for all I knew, but then that was his problem.

At the end of the day, I didn't want to rush things before I was sure what the flames between us meant. I wasn't asking for any commitment from him, but given our past relationship situations, I didn't think either of us should be in a position where we might get hurt for nothing. Turns out, sometimes it doesn't matter what you do to try and prevent hurt feelings. They find their way into our lives either way.

We endured the final seven days of Canadian DJ's trip away with lots of: *if-you'd-come-to-Mexico-we'd-be-doing [insert fun/drunk/sexual activity here]* texts; but thankfully there were more *when-you're-home-we're-going-to [insert fun/drunk/sexual activity here]* chats. The tension and excitement in the days prior to his return were intense; and by that Friday we were both like kids at Christmas. We attempted to make it as quick of a turnaround as possible that afternoon—him from the airport, me from work. Heading back out to the 'burbs, my head started to wander towards the question: *how would this feel as a commute?* Um, okay, so you won't go to Mexico cause that's too fast, but you'll think about moving in with him because that makes total sense?

Seeing him again was fun. It was always fun. From the moment I got in the car, the spark between us was clearly present and the flames had a life of their own. So much so that the first part of our night felt like a distraction. At least for me, there was just a sense of really needing to get the sex monkey off our backs. I hadn't had sex with a guy I properly liked in thirteen years, apart from my ex-husband and those who came before him. No disrespect to the three men I'd slept with since my divorce, but they were never more than one-night stands, drunken sex. This was going to be (mostly) sober sex with someone I had compounding feelings for everyday.

But whose idea was it to have Mexican food before sex? *His.* In his defense, he'd suggested the idea so that it'd be "like [I'd] been there," which was sweet. At least this time I wasn't shitting my pants, lest we forget my last date in a Mexican restaurant.

The sex itself? Well, it was pretty great, despite both of us having "first time" nerves. My overriding memory was that it was funny—not in a weird way, but rather a *we-were-totally-at ease-and-laughed-a lot* way. I've always said that you can laugh me into bed, hence my recurring type of man, but it turns out that you can laugh me through sex too. And I loved it. The previous times had felt so unfamiliar. They'd been with practical strangers and that's how it felt. But with Canadian DJ, it felt far more comfortable, which is maybe not the first thing you want from sex, but more than anything else at the time, I'd have chosen sex that felt comfortable.

The next few days were everything I thought they'd be. We hung out and talked (at normal times of the day, for which my sleep schedule was thankful). We talked about all the things we were going to do and all the places we wanted to go. He also mentioned, in passing, that it was coming into the busy season again with work, but that we'd figure it out.

While I knew that the level of contact would change (it had to), he was no longer lying on a beach with nothing to do. What I hadn't expected was that, come that Monday, he would almost instantly start to pull away. Texts would go unanswered for ten, twelve hours at a time; any suggestion of meeting up was met with him having a potential client meeting or an event. He'd always say that he'd let me know, but he never did. All the while, Instagram and Facebook (goddamn you social media, constantly providing far more than we need to know about people) were telling me that he was looking for someone to go on a bike ride with that day, or perhaps that he'd been to the beach with his dog.

At the time, all I could think about was: *Well he's not that fucking busy, is he?* But as I heard someone say recently, it isn't that he wasn't busy. He *was* busy—busy with things that he was prioritising over me, and that can be a hard fact to swallow. At this point, perhaps it's helpful to point out that I'm fully aware that I shouldn't expect someone to prioritise me over their shit at this early stage of a "relationship" (again I use that term loosely). But the speed at which it had escalated, and all the things we'd talked about, had understandably elevated my expectations. I can rush things in my head, but I don't usually expect this level of commitment nor contact after three weeks of dating. I'm not that out of touch with the nature of relationships in the age of online dating.

This was when I came to understand that consistency is probably one of the key things that I look for in someone. Having had so much uncertainty in my life, particularly with relationships, knowing what to expect from someone had become hugely important. It helps with the fabulous anxiety that I developed in the midst of my divorce. The only issue with having this need for consistency is that I believe you should accept people and not expect things from them. You can't expect anything of anyone. You just need to decide whether you can accept them for who they are. It's a tricky balance between that and needing consistency, but all it really takes is someone's actions meeting their words, which apparently is more complicated than it sounds.

In the midst of the growing weirdness, we finally arranged a dinner, which felt like pulling teeth—especially after he bailed the first time, approximately one hour beforehand, right when I texted him for the final plans. I let it slide. But having finally arranged another time, we had a great meal on a gorgeous rooftop patio, sadly without the fun or the ease we'd experienced previously. When he dropped me off after dinner, I couldn't tell if he just hadn't wanted to kiss me for longer, or if he was simply worried about the traffic we were blocking (per his own comment). The result was that I was left feeling confused. What previously appeared to be a distant red flag, fluttering lamely on the horizon, had turned into a thriving sea of red flags.

We texted the next morning, again with a lot of talk about him being super busy and thus unsure of when he'd see me next. I tried to maintain some dignity (let's pretend that I wasn't checking Facebook multiple times a day, okay?) and decided that I wasn't going to reach out to him first. Well, I got to Sunday and by then I was seething. I won't even lie, I had the rage. You know, the kind that makes you send texts to your friends in FULL CAPS? Or that requires a pint of gin to spill your guts to the girls? Yup, that kind.

By now, it was early May of 2016. As I headed out to Laura's birthday brunch, I decided to call him. Nothing like a Sunday morning call to put someone on the spot; and we know how comfortable I was getting with uncomfortable conversations. I was fully expecting the phone to ring out, followed by a *sorry-was-busy-will-call-later* text, but surprisingly he answered. That said, before we'd even finished exchanging pleasantries, he cut in with, "I'm just about to go into Mother's Day brunch, can I call you later, as soon as I'm done?" Well, shit, what was I going to say? *No, make your mother wait and talk to me?* Obviously not. (Side note: Why can't Mother's Day be celebrated on the same day everywhere to make it easier to keep track?!)

I spent the day with friends, but even as we enjoyed post-brunch afternoon beers in the park, I was struggling with thoughts like, *well his brunch sure is taking a while....* Cut to seven pm and my rage was bubbling to the surface, fuelled by a morning of mimosas and a long afternoon of beers. No good could come of this day. I picked up the phone to text him, deciding to lull him into a false sense of security, so I started with an easy, *how was brunch?*, to which he responded casually. Okay, so his phone wasn't broken, and unless he's dictating to Siri, he hasn't lost his opposable thumbs. Time for a call. (Actually, he had an Android, not an iPhone, but I'm not the type of person to know the Siri equivalent on Android...sorry.)

Despite a slight delay when he took the dog out for a walk and his phone allegedly stopped working (really, how many more ways would he try to dodge talking to me?), I finally got my chance. "Tell me if I'm wrong, but it seems like something's changed, and it feels like you don't want to talk about it." It was such a stark sentence for me to say out loud, and it kind of hung there for a moment in the silence, before he made a joke about me being "very percep-tive." Very good, jackass, just give me an answer.

Finally, after many pauses, deep breaths, ifs, ands, and buts, he admitted that when we'd gone out for dinner last time, it had felt forced, as if he were putting on an act. *Ouch.* He was feeling like his last relationship (his marriage) had just continued. *Double ouch.* He concluded that he didn't think he could give me what I wanted—apparently, it was too much, which was funny because we'd both escalated things together. Then when he got cold feet, it was me who'd gone too far too fast. I told him that I needed consistency, which he obviously couldn't offer, so all I wanted now was closure. And with that, the conversation was done.

Pursuing that final conversation, knowing that it might amount to him agreeing that things had changed, is something that I'm proud of myself for doing. I could have buried my head in the sand and appreciated the few texts I did receive, otherwise letting things fizzle out. But I had to get clarity, despite how painful it might be. I cannot let things like that lie. I always want an explanation, a chance at that final conversation or perhaps just to call them out on their shit. Actions have consequences, and if the only consequence is them having to squirm during a five-minute phone call, then so be it.

But the confusion for me was the highest mountain I'd climb that year (and I was about to get seriously passionate about scaling the faces of the local mountains). Canadian DJ had been a genuine ray of light. He made me laugh like I'd never laughed in years, and he made me feel incredibly wanted. Still, I couldn't connect my feelings in the aftermath of our fling to my feelings in its early days—their proximity in time made it almost impossible to understand. Did he never really feel like that in the first place? Can those sorts of feelings really change that quickly? Is that just who he is, talking a big game and then running the other direction?

Nonetheless, I'd known going in that anything with someone as fresh into divorce proceedings as him could make for slightly tricky times. As long as he was okay with the situation, I'd decided that so was I. But it turns out that he wasn't okay with it, and as much as that hurts, I wanted him to make the best decisions for himself. In the end, I also had to make the best decision for myself though, and pushing to have that conversation was key. If he couldn't provide the consistency I needed in a relationship, clarity and closure were the next best things.

His comment about having to "act" on our last date, or that it felt like a continuation of his marriage, well, those things stung. Like, really stung. Knowing that he was feeling overwhelmed and couldn't get his head together is one thing, but feeling as if he'd been inauthentic with me was harder to hear. I'd made it clear that honesty was my only policy, but I didn't want to go looking for answers when he already had them to give.

Whether he was struggling with life stuff or not, he acted in some ways that just weren't right or proper. Of course, he had a lot going on, and perhaps he was coming at everything from a shitty place, but the same goes for practically everyone. It doesn't make him special nor afford him any special allowances. They say that hurt people *hurt* people, and this was the personification of that. I'd love to say that I came off the call, threw back a gin, and chalked it up to an experience—but this was the first time I'd actually had feelings for anyone besides my ex-husband.

This had been huge for me. There were tears before bedtime, during bedtime, and the next day. I was questioning everything—all of our interactions, my own self-worth (again), whether Vancouver was the right place for me to live, if I could have done something differently—all the unhealthy stuff that you hope to feel confident about as a grown woman. Naively, I might have believed that I just needed to meet one person I clicked with and that would be it, my next long term relationship. But there were so many unknowns, so many other things that had to align, and this one hadn't.

Four days later, I finally had a realization: nothing will ever feel like my divorce. Nothing will be that harrowing or traumatising ever again, at least when it comes to relationships. Not to say that terrible things wouldn't happen in my life—presumably they would. Yes, things with Canadian DJ had hit me hard, but I'd approached the situation with my eyes open and plenty of emotional intelligence. To feel those feelings again, to come alive in that way for a while, like a darkness had lifted, was the real gift of this experience. Weeks, maybe months, would pass before this truly dawned on me, but dawn would come and the sun would rise again.

Fourteen

Thirty-Two

In an attempt to heal my heart from Canadian DJ, I had my first experience of: *get over someone by getting under someone else.* I was quite comfortable with my decision, except that Bearded Lumbersexual (lumbersexual: *a male hipster who affects a rugged, outdoorsy look, typified by plaid shirts and a full beard...*but also the chosen partner for this form of therapy), was now the third guy I'd slept with from the same rugby club.

Vancouver is small at the best of times, without sleeping with teammates. While it's always fun and handy to choose from a fit pool of men, I decided soon after to cut off that supply chain. I didn't want to be *that* girl, and three was quite enough from one club. Dark-bearded men though...I could really get on board with that. Especially when he was so big. Spooning in bed the next morning, I felt practically tiny enveloped in his arms.

Part of me was also starting to wonder if coming off my contraceptive pill at the beginning of the year was the smartest idea, now that I was having more sex. In the midst of taking my wonder drug (which still kept me entirely upright at kickboxing) and thinking more about how I treated my body, I decided to stop putting hormones in my body—especially if I didn't need the pills. I wasn't exactly having sex at the beginning of the year, and I hadn't foreseen it in the near future.

I'd been on the pill since I was fifteen, a total of seventeen years. Like, *holy shit.* I'd started taking birth control to regulate my entirely unpredictable periods, but then it just became the default method of contraception with my ex. We only had one small scare, the year before we got married, and otherwise it always worked. However, I'd been mostly celibate for almost four years, so it just seemed like an unnecessary, unnatural thing to keep taking. Had I not thought about it myself, I imagine nobody would've questioned my taking it forevermore.

Why, as women, are we made to feel like this is something we should be doing, like it's somehow our responsibility to put whatever form of hormones, coated in baby-pink sugar, into our bodies until we or our partner jointly decide to have a baby? Name one thing that men experience in a similar way? I won't wait for an answer, because there isn't one.

I'm not against contraception. I am here for anything that saves women from dealing with unintended pregnancies, and who doesn't love the ability to have sex with the added comfort of contraception already in place? All the same, at what point did I accept the norm and never think about it again? Plus, the pill I'd always taken wasn't available in Canada. Upon being subscribed a substitute, I decided to nix it from my life altogether.

It was always entertaining to witness the moment when my soon-to-be-sexual partner learned that I wasn't on the pill so protection was all on them. There was usually a flicker of hesitation, like, *shit this is riskier than I'd like,* almost instantly followed by the natural male reaction of, *but fuck it, I'm not passing up the opportunity for sex.* And so I was absolved of all responsibility, unless of course I ended up pregnant, in which case the joke was on me. But touch wood, I wouldn't have to deal with that. (Wait, no, that's what gets you in trouble in the first place...).

As well as the Lumbersexual therapy, I was still doing the more conventional therapy with Julia to help me deal with the upsurge in emotions post-Canadian DJ. After I'd regaled her with the details, including my *to-Mexico-or-not-to-Mexico* decision, we talked about the lessons and "looked for the bright sides," but we also went hard into why it wasn't the beginning of a fairy tale relationship. She told me I shouldn't be looking for fireworks, which is what it sounded like when I told the story. Fireworks end. Fireworks always fizzle. Small sparks? Sure, the kind that can light a fire, that get you interested, keep you engaged, they are a great foundation. Fireworks? It won't just be the dogs that end up needing comfort.

The perfect antidote to all of it was a trip back to the UK for my birthday at the end of the May, where I spent some of the most precious time with my family. Having my niece "help" me open my presents, spending my birthday at a kids swimming pool and eating Nando's was beautiful in its simplicity.

I realised how much I yearned for these moments; how much I was missing time with my family; how quickly my niece was growing up and learning to become a proper little person, and I was missing it. I know this was a test, and I'd have to sit with it every time I went home. As much as I loved my time at home, it always came down to how I felt when I got back on the plane. Fainting and anxiety aside (which were now under control with my medication), every single time I'd flown back to Vancouver, I'd been more than excited to get on that plane.

It was the same feeling I'd always had when boarding a plane to go on holiday, except now it was every time I was getting on a plane to go home. (I use "home" interchangeably about Scotland and Vancouver. *Confusing*, I know.) Despite how much I loved family time, I still wanted to go home to Vancouver. Always. It was hard to say goodbye all the time, watching ZIJ's face as she couldn't understand at two years old why everyone was crying yet also cheerily waving goodbye; but it's true what they say: *you will never be completely at home again, because part of your heart always will be elsewhere; that's the price you pay for the richness of loving and knowing people in more than one place.*

I was sure it would be a transformative year for me. There was something about thirty-two—as a number, it rolled off my tongue. I delighted in telling people I was thirty-two. I was feeling emotionally more equipped for whatever might come at me, and physically I was in the best shape of my life. I was an active child until about fourteen years old when we moved back to Scotland from Egypt, where I was told by my boarding-school headmaster that: "At this school, girls don't play football or basketball or volleyball. They play netball, hockey and rounders [sort of like baseball]." Well, you can stick those up your arse, Mr. McPhail, was my thought at the time. Yah, I was a delightful fourteen-year-old.

I would in fact take up netball, but only to enable me to take the team trip to Barbados at the end of the following year. After that, I became what I like to refer to as a "sedentary teenager." During summer term athletics, I gave up high jump (too much like hard work) for shot putt (much easier, though not at all sexy) and after that I always had too many "knee issues" to do any other sports. There was also depression and chronic fatigue in the mix, so it was fairly easy to duck out of our game sessions three times a week. This preference for inactivity continued into my twenties, when I'd only run for a bus if

I really *really* had to run for a bus. At no point was I happy with the resulting body shape that the "sedentary" lifestyle provided; in fact, it would be the source of a lot of self critique and insecurity.

Now at thirty-two years old I found myself looking in the mirror thinking: *Well shit, that's not the worst thing I've ever seen.* I'm aware that this isn't quite the glowing self-love I'd like to teach my daughter, if I had one, but it was a start. Whether coming off the pill had any effect, I'll never know. What I knew for sure was that having my ass kicked at kickboxing five times a week was taking a positive toll. I had finally found a workout that I loved. The fact that I was also learning a skill was a huge part of that. Is the ability to kick someone's ass considered a skill?

As part of a six-week challenge at the gym, I'd had before-and-after pics taken and while the visible results were incredibly satisfying, the bigger win was the strength and endurance I'd built up. I was killing sets of push-ups, froggies were my bitch, and I didn't bat an eyelid at burpees. When I'd started going to classes, the walk home from the gym had been taking me thirty minutes, such was the physical pain and muscle fatigue I'd experienced after the hour-long workout, but now I was making it home in less than twenty minutes. Six am classes, seven pm classes, Friday nights, Saturday mornings— all were times when I would likely be kickboxing.

Kickboxing also meant that my drinking took a bit of a backseat. Part of the deal with my cardiologist when I was starting to take the wonder drug was that I had to make sure not to give my body more work than it already had. So minimising dehydration was super important—and you know what makes you really dehydrated? Drinking. With my overactive vasovagal nerve, I unfortunately wasn't one of those people who could just "sweat out a hangover" with a workout. Working out five days a week, I really only had one night of the week when I wasn't working out that day or the next day, and so only one opportunity to drink. My mum would tell you this was a very good thing.

The trip to Vegas was a perfect reward for all the hard work. Hell, a trip to Vegas is a perfect reward for any and everything. With those girls, it was a riot of drinks by the pool, drinks in the room, free drinks at bars…Obviously the working out was paused momentarily. I wasn't mad that since I'd moved to Vancouver I was averaging one trip a year to Vegas. The two-and-a-half-hour flight from YVR was a dream compared to the ten-hour flight from London I'd taken previously. I always joke that it's one of the reasons I moved to Vancouver, though I'm not actually sure how much of that statement is a joke.... Spending a weekend with fun-loving, funny women was a joy and feeling physically great as I did it was a huge change for me. Did I need Canadian DJ liking my Instagram pictures? No. Was it a confidence boost? Yes. Was it a head fuck? Also yes.

That summer was filled with beach days, food festivals, hiking, camping, and my first Canadian wedding. For almost all those occasions, I was accompanied by Damien, my now trusty sidekick whom I like to describe as my straight, Irish best friend, while Keith was my gay, Irish best friend. Damien was friends with Laura and Sam, and when I'd first met him back in 2013, he was dating a Canadian girl, but they'd split up and now he and I were enjoying *singledom* together. By that I mean, we were each being single apart but discussing it together.

After one very drunken night at Laura and Sam's, shortly after he'd become single, I clearly lost my inhibitions and may have hinted at something happening between us, which thankfully Damien shut down really quick. Instead we became firm friends, validating my thought that guys and girls could be platonic friends, but only once the could-it-be-more bridge had been crossed. (As in, the matter needs to be considered and taken off the table, or else explored and dismissed.) If it hasn't been taken off the table then it's still the centerpiece, as far as I'm concerned, and that's when shit can get tricky.

Damien was Irish, but otherwise he was a good guy. I'm kidding! The Irish are great, when they're not gloating about rugby. He and I had similar interests, mostly eating and drinking balanced out with outdoor activity. He would happily give his opinions on the men I chose to date and I, in turn, would berate him for his lack of creativity when it came to planning first dates. Coffee and a seawall walk *EVERY* time? I guess it was tried and tested, and to his point "cheap." It would be Damien who'd stick up for his countrymen after one of my dates earned the nickname Teeny Irish Peen, and he'd fight for his industry colleagues' reputation after The Boring American Engineer left me wishing I was watching paint dry.

That summer, we both dated a lot. We both made some questionable choices. We both appreciated getting the opinion of the opposite sex around our experiences when we were unable to read a situation. Though Damien would tell me that he couldn't keep up as I made my way through Vietnamese Cat Guy *(no, I didn't poison his cat that died after it watched us have sex)*, English

Tourist *(yes, I'm aware going on a date with a tourist was only ever going to lead to one thing, that was kinda' the point)*, Pretty But Dumb *(sometimes you don't need to talk)*, Chinese Weightlifting Firefighter *(yes, I was in it for the muscles)*, Welsh Rugby Playing Lawyer *(having the UK in common seemed like a good idea at the time)*, Maori Arms *(despite me going into that for wholly unrighteous reasons, I made a great friend)* and Ukrainian Nigerian Engineer *(his BMW didn't make up for the lack of chat)*. Like I said, it was a busy summer, not that any of them went anywhere but the breadth of nationalities and ethnicities earned me the nickname of The United Nations of Dating from my friends. What can I say, I'm all for equal opportunities.

During that time, my comfort level with dating had exponentially increased, kind of in line with my comfort level in myself. If I'm honest, it also aligned with the level of hotness in the men I was dating. Jillian would ask me, towards the end of summer, "So are you only dating personal trainers now or...?" I didn't hate it, but I was surprised by it. Despite my growing self-confidence, there were times when I'd look at the guy lying next to me in bed or perhaps show a friend their profile pictures and think "how did this happen?!"

I was feeling confident, and maybe more surprisingly, I was enjoying dating. I was meeting some super interesting people and that was how I'd learnt to look at things. After the Canadian DJ situation, I'd realised that my rose-tinted view of, "you meet someone, you click with and that's it" was a little naive. It would have been easy to be disheartened when that didn't happen with any of the initial guys I'd met who I thought were nice and attractive. Instead I'd taken to looking at dating as a way of meeting people whom I may never have met otherwise, even if only to hear their stories. If anything was to come of it, that would just be a bonus. I was aware going into each date that hoping for something more would only lead to disappointments.

Something had shifted in me in regards to my comfort level with my sexuality also. I wouldn't say I'd been a prude, or that I'd thought sex was wrong, but it just wasn't something I'd spent time considering in my life. I'd only slept with one person before my ex-husband, then with my ex from ages nineteen to twenty-eight, followed by five years of celibacy due to the trauma. Sex in my marriage had been good—well, actually, sex before our marriage had been good, but the infidelity post-wedding kind of fucked with my head and I couldn't enjoy it much after that. So, maybe that's what it was, maybe it was just that my most recent memories were tarnished. The last time that I'd slept

with my ex-husband, I'd been wishing I was anywhere else. Hardly a great way
to view sex.

But in recent months, there had been a change, a shift as I realised that
I was enjoying my body more—so too were the men I was dating, perhaps?
I was also just more present, more open to asking for what I wanted and
exploring things, with nothing really to lose. I was discovering more about
what I liked (there was a lot), and what I didn't (there wasn't much of that).
I was finally enjoying sex and actively seeking it out. And, most importantly,
not feeling bad about that. In society, women are expected to be sexy but not
sexual. *Why,* you might ask?

Because sex is power, and not because of the sex part; sex is power because
of the ability that women have to carry and give birth to new human life. If
women alone are in control of their bodies, then women alone are in control
of bringing life into this world, and that scares the foundations of the Western
system more than anything in the world. Men love the sexy part, if it caters to
their comfort level, but sexuality itself is a whole different concept to embrace.
Being sexual is the personal expression of the unique relationship one has to
their sexuality, which embodies their spirit or vibe or soul, while being sexy is
the projected expression of sex as a patriarchal ideal.

As women, I hate that we can feel so ashamed by our sex lives. As I shared
my innocent "getting back into dating" stories with friends, they were really
becoming more like "sex stories," and I realised that so often we don't talk
about the real details of sex. Yes, we'll share details of "was it good?" or "how
many times?" but talking about our own preferences, wondering out loud
about how to do certain things or whether something he did or that you liked
was "normal".... There wasn't enough of that going on for my liking. I'd soon
come to find that certain friends were comfortable with this level of chat and
certain friends were not. One friend in particular, Charms (of pre-kickboxing
trance-dance antics), would become my chat buddy for all-things-anal-sex.
We used to joke that if anal sex were a company, her and I would get commission for doing such a good job promoting it to other women.

As a side note about anal sex (did I ever think I'd write that in a publicly
published book? *Ha, no*), most women's concerns around it are based on either
hearing horror stories from other women, or experiencing those horror stories
for themselves when a man doesn't know what he's doing. Like, maybe he
gets over excited about the chance to have anal sex and bangs it inside like

it's actually a vagina, scaring the bejeesus out of her. I'm here to tell you that if men got it right more often then there would be more willing participants. Even starting to chat with men about subjects like that was interesting.

Why aren't we helping our buddies out with tips and tricks from our side? Or having the conversations with gay friends about their experiences? Keith and I love nothing more than a good sex chat. The number of men (friends, not partners) who have laughed nervously when I've started talking about anal sex, and then once the initial jokes had died down have asked: "But seriously, what's the advice?" *Seriously,* where can I go for my commission?

There was something to be said for casual dating and casual sex. It gets a bad rep, but it played a huge part in me discovering more about myself than getting into a long term relationship likely would have. I had less inhibitions when I was with someone whom I already knew I wasn't going to date. I got to have more fun, not trying to impress anyone and being a tad more selfish. Arguably, I should have been able to do that even if I was getting into a long term relationship, but the variety of men was also an upside. It wasn't something I'd planned, but it was happening and I didn't hate it.

A friend would ask me if I cared that my "number" was climbing? *Um. No.* If I was a man, I'd have been applauded. I didn't want applause but I sure as hell wasn't about to feel bad about the fact that I was discovering, and enjoying, my sexuality. If anyone felt differently then that sounded like a "them" problem. Everybody has a right to think or feel whatever they choose regarding sex for themselves, and that totally includes me.

Part 3

Fifteen

All Coupled Up and Nowhere to Go

Remember back in the day, how our parents taught us not to take sweets from strangers and our schools held sessions about not getting into cars with strange men? Well, when did I start living my life based on the exact opposite rules of engagement, without a care nor concern in the world? How did it happen that, one random Sunday in October, I decided that it was a good idea for a strange guy to pick me up and take me to the woods for a walk? It's funny how things change; at eight I would have been shouting *STRANGER DANGER* to ward him off, but at thirty-two I was hoping it'd be romantic.

We'd met on Bumble, chatted a little a few months back, and then he ghosted me mid-conversation. I never thought anything of it, because it happens so frequently on dating apps. Him reappearing was actually more surprising. In fact, it was just nice that the message had come in at nine am on a Sunday instead of two am on a Saturday, so I didn't need to work out whether it was the dating-app equivalent of a drunk text. Such is the sad state of affairs in which I found myself dating.

Before it was even lunchtime, we'd made the quickest date arrangement I've maybe ever experienced. He invited me to go for a walk with him and his dog out at Deep Cove, a cute little bay in North Vancouver that had a trail up a rock with a lookout at the top, and I'd been desperate to do it ever since I'd moved here. While I was mulling over in my head whether this hastily arranged date seemed like a good idea, he called me to confirm. I was impressed, given people's apprehension about using the phone nowadays.

He offered to come pick me up (which also impressed me, because it was entirely out of his way) then drop me off again afterwards, but he thought maybe I'd want to hear his voice before a strange guy came and picked me up. It was a fair point and I appreciated that he'd had the foresight to realise it on his own. In my head, I knew that agreeing to let a random guy pick me up in his car and take me to the woods didn't seem like the most sensible thing in the world, but I was trying to listen to my gut. Apparently my gut thought it was okay. Even writing that now, I know it sounds nuts. If a friend had told me a story like this or mentioned that they were intending to do something similar, I'd have been like, "wtf, don't be ridiculous." Normally, I was such a stickler for being sensible.

I texted Laura all the information on him that I had—his full name, where he worked, his phone number, screenshots of his Bumble profile—and hoped that if my body was found in the woods, the cops would know whom I'd been with last and how we'd met. Isn't that a romantic first date thought? After the sobering experience of having to decide what to wear for my first ever "active first date" (seriously, who am I? I'm that person going on a hiking first date. *Ugh.* Get out) and despite the seeming insanity of the situation, I was actually feeling pretty good about it. The summer had been filled with a lot of hookups and while I wasn't complaining, my preference really was for something more substantial. The fact that we were going on a wholesome Sunday dog walk suggested that he wasn't looking for just a hookup.

However, as I crossed the road to his car, he got out to hug me, even opening the passenger door. Rather than be impressed by his manners, all I could think was, *Where's the dog?* The dog we were supposed to be walking. The dog he'd said was pretty big. So big that surely I couldn't miss her in his Audi hatchback. Where was the damn dog?! *Oh my god, he's going to kill me...*

I tried not to let the panic rise too quickly, even as I slid into the passenger seat. But just as I resisted him closing my door (on the off chance that I needed to make a run for it), I saw the sweet relief of a dog ear pop up behind the back seat. *Thank God.* She was a gorgeous five-year-old Rottweiler/Rhodesian Ridgeback mix and he was a thirty-eight year old Filipino Canadian who worked in sales and lived on the North Shore.

The chat in the car was easy. We hadn't covered much ground in our messages, so we had plenty to talk about on the twenty-five minute or so drive to Deep Cove. Neither did the conversation stop while we were walking up through the woods to the lookout point over the cove. I was again thankful for my improved fitness and the fact that I was able to hold a conversation while walking uphill. It continued on the way back down as the rain randomly started and continued during our drive back downtown. Actually, he also drove around the block a couple of times so that we could finish our conversation.

Arriving back to my apartment building, all I could think was, *I'd really like it if he kissed me.* Since he'd picked me up earlier that afternoon, he'd opened and closed every (car) door for me, so I figured that behavior would likely present a pretty good opportunity for him to make a move, should he so desire. Well, it probably would have happened if it weren't for my over-eager concierge coming to open my door as we pulled up to my building.

Why is it that when I was struggling home with shopping bags or luggage, they were never anywhere to be found; but when I would have liked to be left alone, hopefully to invoke the perfect end to a date, they came rushing out, blabbering, "Hi, how are you? Do you have anything in the trunk?" *No, fuck off!* (Jokes, I'm actually very appreciative of the service they offer and understand that it's a huge luxury. But still, *sigh*.) And so a big romantic end-of-date kiss didn't happen, but a peck on the cheek and a pretty tight hug wasn't the worst alternative, even if the concierge was only a few feet away.

Closing the door behind me as I got back into my apartment, I remember having an incredibly gleeful moment of, *WTF, that was so lovely,* which made for a nice change from the usual, *WTF, I want to kill myself* moments induced by previous dates. The whole thing had been such a surprise, both in its spontaneity and in its success. I texted him as I was getting into bed that night and thanked him for including me in their walk (he'd made it very clear: *he and the dog came as a pair*) and for going out of his way to pick me up and drop me off. He responded by saying that they don't normally let outsiders crash their Sunday walks, but they were both incredibly happy that they'd made an exception for me. They couldn't decide which one of them liked me more.

Four days later, we were meeting for our second date. After the outdoorsy nature of the first date, he suggested that we go the other direction and do dinner and drinks downtown—much more my natural habitat and far easier to get dressed for than a hike. He messaged me that night to say: *I'm running late so do you mind if I don't pick you up. I'll meet you there but I promise I'll walk you home?* The place we were meeting at was literally four blocks from my house, which he knew, and he was using transit to get Downtown, so it wasn't like he could just swing by in his car. At no point had I imagined he'd be coming to "pick me up." His manners were a huge plus. Again, there's just something about chivalry that gets me riled up, in the best possible way.

In a similar fashion to our first date, our second date followed suit but with more time to talk about ourselves. Over multiple drinks (we discovered a mutual love of gin) and some food, we managed to cover a variety of conversation topics. On our first date, we'd talked about our parents' divorces, our past relationships, sibling relationships, how he was open to a relationship but would want to take anything slowly and the reasons for that sentiment. But on our second date, things became lighter and more random—favourite trips, food-and-drink preferences, friends, home décor, etc.

As he walked me home, just like he'd promised (it also gave us time to finish our conversation) he made a comment about my apartment. I decided that a nightcap at my place would give us the perfect opportunity for more time together, in addition to letting him see the apartment he was enquiring about so curiously. We headed up in the elevator, and I had hopes that he would kiss me at some point. His tactile taking of my arm on the walk home had seemed like a good sign. But I was also happy with the likelihood that a kiss was as far as it would go. Nothing that I'd learnt about him so far gave me the impression that he would sleep with someone on a second date. Given what he'd said about wanting to take things really slow, which he'd again re-iterated over dinner that night, it really wasn't even a consideration.

Back in my apartment, I made each of us a gin—and meanwhile he moved up behind me, just close enough that I could feel his clothes brushing mine. Taken a bit by surprise (he really wasn't even waiting for drinks before making a move?), I tried to carry on measuring out the gin. But as I poured the tonic, he slipped his hand around my waist, turned me to face him; and right there, with the tonic can in my hand, we had our first kiss.

He was sweet and gentle and as far as first kisses go, it was pretty great. It led to a whole lot of kissing on my couch, interspersed with more chatting and drinking the gins I eventually finished pouring. I'd been hopeful for a kiss, but it got hot and heavy pretty fast and I definitely could've been more prepared. Especially when, during our teenage-like make-out session, he made a comment along the lines of, "I would love to sleep with you." Now, don't get me wrong, I was kind of having the same thought, but he'd made it so clear, so absolutely crystal clear, that he wanted any new relationship to go slowly. I'd presumed that meant longer than two dates before he slept with someone. Or is that not what that means?

It turns out, two dates was exactly the amount of time he needed before sleeping with me. I was surprised, but not unpleasantly so. Much like the first date, it took me by surprise but it also felt right. I did stop and ask him if he was sure. I didn't want the fun of the night, or the gin, to cloud anyone's judgment. He barely let the question leave my lips before reassuring me into submission. I went with it and was not disappointed. Neither was he.

He stayed over until the morning, allowing for more great chatting, plenty of incredible sex, and an abundance of snuggling. The snuggling may have been my favourite part—being single, there were plenty of things that I missed about being in a relationship, but snuggles? They were at the top of my list.

After this surprising, but pretty great, turn of events in our dating dynamic, my girlfriends did their usual interrogation. *Did he pay for dinner? Will we like him? How was his penis?* Like I said, the usual. I didn't give up too many details, there was something very private about him, so his nickname was built from the two things my friends did know: his ethnicity (Canadian Filipino); and the fact that we'd already slept together (thus I had seen his penis, even if I wasn't giving them a full review). Thereby, he was christened Filipeen.

After our first two dates, my mum came into town for her annual visit and road trip. This time, we were headed for the US to drive the Oregon Coast. It was a good distraction from what otherwise could have been an escalating situation with Filipeen; and after the situation with Canadian DJ, I severely wanted to avoid that. Whenever my mum came to town, part of me always longed to introduce her to someone special. I'd shown her my apartment, she knew about my job, she'd met my friends; the next thing for me to show her, like, as an accomplishment, was surely a man, right? But when had that become something I was looking to show off like a trophy? As proof that I was doing life right? At least when I told her about Filipeen, his age (thirty-eight) made him entirely more appropriate than some of the twenty-seven-year-olds I'd been dating that summer.

As always, Mum and I had a great time together. She'd found her favourite parts of the city and I loved that. My friends were always so excited for our now traditional brunch, not to mention how great the road trips Mum and I took together were. The Oregon Coast was by far one of the most stunning coastlines I've ever seen. It was yet another trip of making new memories, not least when we stayed at a cabin in the middle of nowhere in Forks (a town made famous by its use in Twilight), and we felt convinced we were going to die there.

Thankfully, we survived Forks and after Mum returned to Edinburgh, Filipeen and I found ourselves seeing each other multiple times a week. We went out for dinners, enjoyed more walks with the dog, and cooked together, a lot – I believe it's a Filipino thing. We went to watch a movie (yes, singular, I'm not a big movie-goer and he was delighted to get me to one), while I was just delighted that I didn't fall asleep. Mostly I'd go over to his place across the water in North Van. He worked later than I did and had the dog, so it made sense. It was the first time that I'd "travelled" for dates. My friends used to mock me for not going over bridges for guys, but now I was doing it on a regular basis—they knew I must like this guy.

From talking about upcoming Halloween plans on our first date to entering full Christmas mode in December, I remembered a dream date that I'd longed for since I'd started dating again: the Christmas lights in Stanley Park. Filipeen planned it to perfection without any prompting from me: on a crystal clear winter night, we took in the display of over three million lights. It was cheesy and romantic and I loved it. Especially since we finished off with a great steak dinner in a fancy restaurant. Over dinner, we got pretty deep into conversation about our life goals, and he asked me how I felt about children. *Yeesh...this minefield.*

My feelings about having kids were that, when I got married the first time, I'd been in my mid-twenties and neither of us had even thought about kids. It wasn't a top priority on my list, nor did I have super strong feelings about it one way or another. With my ex-husband, I'd always assumed that as we grew older, we'd likely just slide into the feeling that we were ready for kids. As it turned out, six weeks after we got married, I knew that I could never have children with my husband, because I wouldn't bring my children into a situation with someone I didn't trust (probably a good indicator that I shouldn't have stayed with him).

While trying to repair my marriage, I also made peace with the fact that I might remain childless. It wasn't a huge issue for me, but it was bundled up with all the other grieving I'd done back then—how handy, right? When you're newly single at thirty years old, bringing children into the world no longer feels like a choice you make actively. These days, I can picture my life without children and I've made peace with that possibility, but I'd love to meet someone who makes me want to have their babies. Not in a gun-to-the-head way, but perhaps something more aligned with the sentiment: *He is an incredible person with whom I would be lucky to procreate.* Often, I picture myself as a grandmother surrounded by a big family, so perhaps there's a blank somewhere in the middle, one I must fill in to make my vision come true.

I explained all this to Filipeen, but as I finished talking, he sat back in his chair and just looked at me. He didn't say anything. It was a habit that I'd started to notice with him, a technique people used to make others feel uncomfortable enough that they'd start filling in the silence with further information. I dutifully fell for it, tripping over my words as I gave him far more context than necessary. Finally, he spoke, stating without a doubt that he absolutely wanted a family, which aligned for me as well. I wanted to meet someone whom I liked/respected/trusted enough to have kids, and Filipeen wanted kids—there were no red flags. The conversation changed directions and I never bothered thinking about it again.

By then, holiday social invites were abundant. Charms, she of kickboxing, dancing and also the Philippines, insisted that I invite Filipeen to her annual Christmas Pie Night (literally exactly what it sounds like—just a night with a tonne of home-baked pies). I dutifully agreed to invite him, thinking that he'd politely decline. However, he informed me that it was rude for Filipinos to turn down an invite from another Filipino, especially when it involved food. At this point, I'm pretty sure they were both just winding me up; but the following week, I found myself in the car with Filipeen, headed to pie night, where he would meet some of my closest friends, including Laura, Sam and Damien.

What struck me was that I'd never done "meet the friends" before in my life. As I mentioned, my ex-husband and I had known each other since childhood. All my friends knew him long before we got together, so we simply had to announce that we were dating. Prior to my ex-husband, all my boyfriends were high school romances, so we all knew each other from class—but this? This was a whole different ball game and it stressed the hell out of me, more than I could have imagined, but I couldn't work out why. It got to the point where, over the course of that night, I was so nervous and quiet that nearly all my friends started asking what was wrong with me. I was definitely out of sorts.

I'd asked my friends to play nice with Filipeen, which they did, while taking the piss out of me and ensuring I was thoroughly embarrassed. (What are friends for, right?) Despite my personal anxiety, it went incredibly well, especially when he asked my friends which one of them had given him his nickname, which I'd told him about a few weeks earlier. At the end of a seemingly successful night, we headed back to his place with my friends commenting again on how much time I was spending on the North Shore.

As we started down the road to his place, out of nowhere he asked, "Have you ever slept with any of your guy friends?" Without even hesitating I said, "My guy friends here? No." Then I thought about it and clarified that I'd never slept with my guy friends at home either. The question was abrupt, so I figured some other thought had prompted him to ask. In return, I asked him the same question. He had a lot of female friends; in fact, it seemed like most of his best friends were female. As soon as the question left my mouth, I kind of wished that I hadn't asked. I didn't know whether I needed the information. He also said no, but that people have presumed that in the past. (Who knows why, I didn't ask.)

Then he asked me whether Damien was single. I said yes, adding that his ex was kind of on the scene, so I couldn't be sure. With that, I wondered if we might have a problem. With those two questions—*have you ever slept with one of your guy friends* and *is your specific guy friend single*—his mind started racing with other questions/assumptions. I tried to pre-empt things by voicing that it was actually possible to have platonic relationships (exactly as he'd just said). He then commented on an earlier moment in the night when Damien was furiously shaking his leg at the table—an incredibly annoying habit of his—and I grabbed a hold of his thigh and held it down. We'd asked him to stop a few times, but he wasn't listening and I was sitting beside him anyways. Filipeen was sat on my other side, but I never thought anything of it. It was obvious why I'd touched Damien's leg, and I was hardly fondling or groping him. Nonetheless, Filipeen had filed the moment away in his memory bank for later.

I laughed off his comment, all the while trying to reassure him. I never wanted to make anyone feel uneasy or disrespected. I've been there myself way too many times, so I try to keep aware of situations that make other people insecure. However, it didn't sit well with me that upon meeting my friends for the first time, Filipeen had created what I could only imagine was a warped backstory in his head. But I decided to take the route of underplaying it entirely, attempting not to add more fuel to the fire by protesting too much.

With Christmas only a few weeks away, plans for the day came up between us. As a devout Catholic, I figured he'd be all family all day. "I go to church every Sunday; I hope you don't have a problem with that," he'd told me a several weeks earlier, to which I'd replied, "I don't have a problem with you going as long as you don't have a problem with me staying in bed while you do." And we were both happy.

Despite his religious inclinations, he decided to spend the day with family and Christmas night with me. It worked out with my plans to see friends during the day; and for the first time in quite a few years, I would be dating someone over Christmas, someone who had included me in their Christmas plans. There was a spring in my step, a flutter of snow in the air, and more than just a little excitement in my heart.

However, Filipeen's query about my friendship with Damien kept coming up. I got more frustrated every time I had to defend my platonic relationship. He'd started asking me more pointed questions about my life goals, perhaps furthering the conversation about kids from dinner. Every time, he'd sit in silence and wait for me to fill it with justifications for whatever I'd just said. He'd been so warm and kind when we met, but that same warmth was now interspersed with "off" moments, and winter was getting chillier.

One particularly frosty night, we spent an inordinate amount of time discussing cannabis in the Walmart parking lot (I don't want to say arguing). I remember feeling very Canadian. The "discussion" wasn't actually about weed itself, but it factored into the equation nonetheless. If you're not already aware, smoking pot is an incredibly common occurrence in Vancouver. I always say that you're more likely to smell weed than cigarette smoke here; and Filipeen smoked to help with his muscle pain from an old snowboarding accident. Personally, I don't smoke weed. My ex did, so I have some residual feelings about the substance that stem from our relationship. But mostly I avoid it for myself. For Filipeen, or anyone else? *Knock yourself out; in general, I have no judgment about it.*

But as we left the house that night, heading to Walmart for another set of lights to decorate his place (yes, we were decorating his apartment together), he made a comment about being tired. As we drove, he suggested that I roll him a joint at home and he'd make us dinner. I laughed at the suggestion and fired back with, "Um no, we'll do it the other way around." I wasn't about to roll him a joint—not that I knew how anyways—but I would happily cook dinner. Thus started the weirdest/most disproportionately reactive "discussion" I've ever had with Filipeen.

According to him, I was being judgmental and projecting shit about my ex onto him. Both were statements I could have shrugged off, if he hadn't proceeded to call me a hypocrite for not liking weed (you know, since I drank so much). *Wow.* Where the hell had that come from? I remember him reciting numerous unhealthy aspects of my life, as I gazed at the rain bouncing off the windshield, thinking: *What the fuck is going on? Am I losing my mind? Why am I having to justify my lifestyle?*

It became clear that we wouldn't reach a consensus. In an effort to get out of the car, which was practically closing in on me, we agreed to disagree and walked around Walmart pretending that everything was fine. But in fact, I had no clue what had just happened and couldn't help but question my own sanity. The following week, the Walmart debacle was still very much alive in my head. By the week before Christmas, we both felt the underlying tension re: the increased charge in our conversations. At least we were on the same page about needing to discuss things. We made plans to go out for dinner that Friday, with the unspoken understanding that we'd try to work things out.

By the end of that week, I was sick as a dog with a cold. I should have been in bed. Instead I drugged myself up, helped myself to a nip of whisky, and steeled myself for what I assumed wouldn't be a fun night. When did I cease looking forward to seeing him? We started with the usual "how was your day" chit-chat, but as the starters arrived, we got round to talking about the massive elephant in the room. We started by agreeing that doing the couple-y things, like walking the dog or getting groceries or decorating his house with Christmas lights, were great and all, but we weren't there yet. Those things, if anything, shouldn't have been all we did. We also didn't have enough famil- iarity with each other to be running errands or dealing with stress together.

I explained that his hot-and-cold nature was difficult for me. It had started in the last few weeks and ultimately left me feeling rejected, which is kind of my biggest fear. Of course, I'm not alone in that regard. I'd actively sought to avoid any situation where rejection could arise—at least since my divorce.

In part, I could blame my fear of rejection for how long it took me to start dating again.

Filipeen admitted that he wasn't sure how he felt about me/us. He said: "Sometimes I look at you and think, *I am not in the same place as her and I need to tell her.*" I asked him why he hadn't put some distance between us then, perhaps opting out of ridiculously couple-y scenarios or declining my offers to play the girlfriend role and do shit like walk his dog. All he could say was: "Because sometimes I think I am in the same place as you, but then most of the time I don't think I am."

I let his words hang in the air, feeling the tears sting behind my eyes. I wanted to put them down to my cold, but that admission from him weighed heavily on me. It would prove to haunt me for a long while afterwards. He did follow it up by saying that he hoped to be in the same place as me, but that for now I was "*much further down the road.*" I wasn't even sure what road we were walking, and did being further down mean closer to the destination or the beginning? Or was the road actually a circle?

My head was already cloudy as shit with the cold, but this conversation was really fogging it up and while I had gone into the night hoping it would bring me clarity, I was getting the distinct impression that it might do the opposite. The chat lasted for most of dinner so between the topic of conversation, my inability to taste the difference between gumbo and mac and cheese (we were at Chewies, a NOLA-inspired restaurant), and only being able to breathe out of my mouth, it wasn't the most fun Friday I've ever had.

We finished the night discussing how we would try to resolve things, both acknowledging that we did want to try. We decided to get back to proper dates—dinners and drinks and walks (not me walking his dog for him) and other fun stuff. We knew that we needed to spend time getting to know each other, doing fun random stuff, not errands or chores at someone's house (I'd like to note that they'd all been at his house, not mine) and no more friend intros until we'd figured stuff out.

While I was totally on board with all of that, I needed to be okay with feeling as if things were going into retrograde a bit and not take it as a negative, especially when I hadn't been the only one pushing it forward. I would have to stop offering to do things out of kindness and set some boundaries for myself. He clearly wouldn't say no if I offered; and why would you, when someone is game to walk your dog when it's shitting snow outside while you stay indoors and cook? I let go of my disgruntlement about his comment that meeting my friends happened too soon, but it was definitely his decision to come that night. Apparently I was too far down the road, yet he'd made no vocal objections about our pace until now.

We called it a night after main courses. Thankfully, he didn't want dessert and all I wanted was my bed. As I went home, alone (he didn't stay…I was that sick), Laura called to ask how the dinner had gone. After I told her the tale of the night and how confusing it all was, she accurately stated that "it shouldn't really be feeling this difficult this early on; you really shouldn't be this confused."

She was entirely right. The confusion was overwhelming and only compounded the next day when, driven by what I can only imagine as guilt (he's Catholic, after all) about some of what he'd said the previous night, Filipeen messaged me early in the morning to see how I was feeling and apologise that last night hadn't been a tonne of fun. That bit wasn't confusing, that bit was nice.

What's confusing was that a mere twelve hours prior, we'd decided not to do couple-y things until we both felt ready; but the next thing he did was insist that I go over to his house, so that he could take care of me while I was sick. He said that he would have come to my place to look after me, but he had work to do from home. If I could get over there, he'd do the rest.

Now, ordinarily, in the cold light of a good health day, I wouldn't have thought twice about saying no. Not least because a) I've found myself to be fiercely independent when it comes to taking care of myself since getting divorced, and also because b) it was the exact opposite of what we'd planned to do! However, feeling like such a bag of shit and so ridiculously sorry for myself, I took him up on it.

I packed a bag, plus my self-pity, and went over to his place. Cue the confusion rising…. He'd changed the sheets on his bed to make them extra fresh for me. He was making chicken soup and had the air purifier on in his bedroom to help clear my head. The kettle was boiled to make me a honey and lemon drink, and there was a table moved next to the bed for me to put all my tissues, drinks, phone etc on. Not to mention, there was a bath running with lavender Epsom salts for me to relax in before I got into bed.

Don't get me wrong, you can be kind to someone that you're dating when they're sick—heat them some soup or pick up some meds—but all of that?

I'd died and gone to heaven, but there was a voice somewhere, really far back in my head, voicelessly screaming: *What in the actual fuck happened to what we talked about last night?!* At another time, I would have tried to make sense of it all, but not then. I took a long hot soak in the bath followed by an afternoon spent watching Netflix, as he periodically checked in on me, got me fresh water, made me more hot drinks and then made us dinner.

The next day, as he drove me home on Sunday morning before he went to church, we mused on the fact that in a week it would be Christmas. Since we both had pretty busy weeks coming up, we'd agreed to see each other the following Friday, after we'd finished work for Christmas and could do something fun. That felt a little better, a bit more "normal," a little bit more like what we'd talked about at dinner two nights ago.

Within that time, I was aware of a shift in things. We didn't text as much; and when we did it was generally at night, with him saying he was tired and going to bed. When the end of the week rolled around, he offered to cook dinner. We could stay in together, since we'd both had such busy weeks. While that did sound like bliss, I couldn't help but feel as if it weren't quite what we'd agreed on at dinner (again). I also know that I'm a stickler for the rules and need to loosen up at times, so I just went with it. Still, there was a sense of internal conflict that I didn't love.

I went with his suggestion, seemingly not able to set my own boundaries, and we had a super chilled, super relaxed evening followed by plenty of great sex. Have I mentioned the sex? I don't think I have. We had incredible sex. Throughout it all, even when that underlying tension was bubbling to the surface, the sex was always amazing. Plus, there was always a lot of it. I'm pretty sure his shower had been designed specifically for us.

We woke up on Christmas Eve, starting the day off with a run with the dog, before heading to buy food and drinks for the Boxing Day dinner he'd be hosting for friends. I know what you're thinking: *If that doesn't sound like a couple-y Christmas Eve, I don't know what does.* Yah, you and me both. He dropped me off at home early that afternoon, after all our errands, and he made mention of the Boxing Day dinner for which we'd been shopping. We'd previously discussed it, and he'd hinted at me going; but that was before all the confusion and weirdness of him saying that we shouldn't do friends again until things got a little better. He spoke about the dinner in a way that presumed I would be there, and I couldn't just let it slide.

I told him that I'd presumed I wouldn't be there and I was absolutely okay with that. He was having his best friends around and I didn't want to add a layer of complication to the evening, while also trying to be respectful of his boundaries. Just over a week prior, he didn't know how he felt about me. If he'd said no to "doing the friends thing," was it really wise for me to go? *He'd love for me to be there, but it was up to me.* Way to pass the buck. I told him that I'd think about it, but I knew not to give the matter any more space in my head. Still, it would have been easier if I wasn't going to Filipeen's on Christmas Night, hence I'd be waking up there on Boxing Day.

Christmas night itself was...difficult. I went to a friend's place for Christmas dinner. My friends were also friends with Welsh Rugby Playing Lawyer, whom I'd dated that summer until he ghosted me. It turned out that he was coming for dinner as well, so the four of us sat around and ate turkey together. It was difficult to enjoy my sprouts when I couldn't stop wondering what the fuck had happened with Welsh boy, not to mention why he'd ghosted me. But really, Vancouver was too small. My friends were aware that we'd been on a few dates, so you can imagine the tension and awkwardness when he barely acknowledged knowing me the entire night. When Filipeen picked me up, I was glad to have survived that ordeal, but his demeanour was not that of someone who'd spent a happy Christmas Day with his family. Or maybe it was, I mean, families can be stressful. But as someone who was spending another Christmas away from their family, it kind of grated on me.

Either way, he wasn't what I'd describe as "cheery." I'd spent a lovely day with friends (apart from the Welsh awkwardness), yet I found myself in a car wash at nine pm on Christmas night, still heading back to his place, because his car needed a clean. That's not a Christmas Day activity! I thought he was a Catholic! He did admit, amidst the soap suds, that Christmas had been hard for him because he wasn't where he wanted to be in life. He'd been with his brother and family, but he'd thought by now, at thirty-eight, he'd have a family of his own to be with on Christmas.

Now I heard him, loud and clear. Did I really expect to be where I was? *FUCK NO.* But here I was. Yes, there were times when it got me down, and there were times when I wondered why, but they were fairly few and far between. If I knew that I was doing everything I could to get myself where I wanted to be in life, and hopefully spending time with good people in the process, then I was able to manage my mood a bit better than Filipeen.

After the very solemn Christmas Night car wash (honestly, this story, wtf),
the rest of the night wasn't about cosying up on the sofa and enjoying each
other's company. Instead we started prep for the feast he'd be hosting the next
day. There were about fifteen people invited and he wanted three main courses,
four side dishes, two desserts and tons of appetisers. Let's just say there was
a lot to do. However, Filipeen insisted that I not do anything, apart from
enjoy a gin from the bottle of Botanist I'd bought for us to share at Christmas.
We'd decided not to do presents for each other, having agreed it was too early,
but it wasn't too early for domesticated bliss on Christmas Night, apparently.
Confused much?

So instead I got drunk, perhaps even a little belligerent. (I'd started my
Christmas Day at a bottomless mimosa brunch with Keith.) If belligerent
looks like telling Filipeen that he's boring and taking myself to bed? Then
yup, I was belligerent! *Merry Christmas, folks!* The next morning brought no
mention of last night, apart from my horrific hangover, more food prep, and
me playing sous chef and runner. There was a long list of things he'd forgotten
from the supermarket, so I drove his car to Safeway and picked them up. So,
now I'm driving his car, his pride and joy, to do grocery shopping for the dinner
party he's having with friends later, which I'm not even planning on attending.

My girlfriends got a running commentary of it all via text; and by this point,
they were all just like "GO HOME!" I, of course, did not go home. I couldn't
find the opportune time to just leave and let him finish the prep himself. I
knew it would've left him in the shit. There was no way he'd get everything
done by himself, and I couldn't leave him; I'm not that person. I'm too nice.
As dinnertime rolled around and people were due to arrive, I resigned to the
reality that I was obviously about to meet his closest friends. *I should probably
change out of my sweatpants,* I thought.

Despite the stress in the build up, the night was good, if a little awkward
when I was introduced and nobody even knew that Filipeen was dating
someone. This wasn't helped by the fact that he'd disappeared into the kitchen
when everyone arrived, so I ended up greeting people for him. You know, like
a good girlfriend does. *Oh, that's right, I'm not his girlfriend! He introduced me
a couple of times as his "friend." Right, got it. Fuck. My. Life.*

I desperately wanted to go home, but I couldn't drive, because my coping
mechanism was the wine. The wine he and I had chosen on Christmas Eve,
while shopping together, *LIKE A COUPLE.* I got drunk again that night, but

after everyone had left, he took himself to bed almost instantly. And again I got a little more belligerent. After helping him all day and being the perfect hostess for a dinner I wasn't even hosting, with people I didn't even know (they were all lovely though, thankfully) and clearing up the kitchen afterwards, he'd barely thanked me. Instead, he got into bed after "such a tiring day."

I was angry, hurt, confused, drunk. The behavior of drunk me is always a great indicator of what else is happening in my life. If drunk me is a nutcase, I'm dealing with unresolved issues. If drunk me is laughing and having a great time, my life is all roses. Let's just say that drunk me wasn't laughing nor having a great time. Luckily, Filipeen was asleep, or at least trying to sleep— so he was entirely unresponsive when I announced that I didn't want to be a housewife, or that he'd treated me like a slave all day. It was perhaps a little over dramatic, but this was obviously my underlying feeling.

Sure, I'd allowed it all to happen; it's not like he held me captive. Eventually, I joined him in bed and fell asleep in a drunken stupor of misery and confusion. How did my first Christmas dating someone again turn into such a shit show? Why was I so confused and edgy all the time? I'd felt as if I needed to prove to Filipeen that I was worthy of him dating me, worthy of being introduced to his friends, all by playing *hostess-with-the-mostess*. Why the hell wasn't I calling him out on the fact that his actions and words could not be more mismatched if they tried?

The next day, Filipeen was back at work, but I had an extra day off. So, in my "I can't help but be nice" state of mind, I finished tidying up the rest of his place. We'd done a lot of it the night before, but there were still piles of dishes, boxes of drinks, and generally stuff all over the place. So, I let my cleanliness OCD take over and fixed everything up. I also walked the dog, and for the second day in a row, he'd given me the keys to his pride and joy of a car. I drove the rental plates and glasses back to the hire place, as you do for someone who'd been introducing you the night prior as their *friend*, right?

I did all of that with a hangover and major brain fog, trying to work out what in hell's name was happening. After dropping the keys off at his office, I made my way back downtown. The thank you and minimal kiss he'd offered on the side of the street outside his office weren't reward enough for the bitch of a morning I'd had. But had he asked me to do all those chores, or had I offered and he'd simply taken me up on it?

Did it matter? Well, yeah, because I can't really be mad if I offered and then got pissed off because I didn't get a big enough pat on the back. But it was more than that. He probably shouldn't have let me do those things without understanding the nature of his feelings for me. But again, can you blame him? Who would decline the offer of a free housemaid for the morning? Especially one you could have shower sex with before work. Throughout it all, the sex was an unwavering constant. Maybe the only one. It was always great. Sex was the one activity during which I wasn't second guessing myself. By this point, I felt fairly confident in my own sexuality. I was sure that there were no complaints from his side; there was talk about it being some of the best sex he'd had, rather than being another source of disconnect for us.

Post-Boxing Day dinner party, post-Christmas Night weirdness, post-Christmas Eve domesticity, I still couldn't get a grip on what in fuck's name was happening. I couldn't understand how we'd arrived in a place of so much confusion and tension. Ultimately, I was feeling worse about myself, not better. Just to add to the trials of The Holidays, New Year's Eve was coming up. We definitely shouldn't have spent it together, but we'd already made plans for him to be my plus one at a friend's engagement party. After everything that had happened, we probably should have rethought the decision and taken the night to ourselves. But why try and keep things simple when you can add more confusion to the mix, right?

With the way I felt, I'd need to address certain issues with him before NYE. I hate taking negativity into a new year, but if there were underlying issues and I got drunk, all hell could break loose.

So, on the thirtieth of December, I went over to his place. He cooked us dinner and we had another chat about our relationship—a mere two weeks since the last one. I started by saying that we should slow down and focus on spending time just the two of us. Christmas had gotten in the way of that plan the first time around, but why not forgive ourselves? Come January, we'd try to start fresh again. I just thought that we needed to slow down like we talked about, and I needed to stop giving away so much power by doing things like walking the dog and being domesticated at his house. (Talk about deja-vu from the conversation two weeks ago—had I learnt nothing?)

I presumed that he would agree: that we would try (again) to make some changes and things would get better. End of story. But his reaction left me speechless. He told me right off the bat that he felt like something was missing. He wasn't sure that our life goals aligned. The way he trailed off at the end of the sentence ("...You tick all the boxes on paper but something feels off, I mean you should be everything I want but...") was hardly something a grown woman wanted to hear.

He felt like something was missing with me, but he was pointed in articulating that it was ME with something missing and not him. Still, the part that got me the most, the thing that shattered a little piece of my heart was when he looked me in the eye and said: "I don't have butterflies about you." Not to be melodramatic, but it felt like a stab—the quickest insertion of the finest blade deep inside me. My biggest fear—rejection—was staring me squarely in the face.

As I fought back my tears, he declared that he didn't think I wanted to give up my downtown party lifestyle and that, despite what I'd said, I probably didn't want to have kids. The want to cry quickly turned into the want to punch him in the throat. At what point had all of my trips across the Lions Gate Bridge—the main access point to the suburban North Shore—to walk his dog in the shitting snow before our cosy quiet nights together, did it seem like I wouldn't want to change my *downtown party lifestyle?* Even that phrase was ridiculous! I am practically a GRANNY! I hardly ever go out, and my drinking had only increased during our relationship because of the ensuing mental anguish. Also, why did either one of us need to give up our lifestyles this early, or at all?

And don't get me started on how insulting it was for him to question my sincerity, honesty, and vulnerability when opening up about how I felt about having kids. Who the fuck was he to decide that I wasn't being honest about my priorities and desires? I was sitting on my hands, entirely to stop myself from reaching out and strangling him. What I thought was rock bottom disappeared and sent me free falling through time. He'd finished up his character assassination with: "But look, I'm hoping all those feelings about you change, because I would really love for this to work. I'm happy to give it time, to work on it, and see if those feelings develop and maybe if our life goals can align. If you are? But I understand you've been hurt in the past and the last thing I want to do is hurt you anymore, so I'll understand if you want to walk away. I'll let you make the decision."

If it hadn't been for my ex-husband's incredible displays of psychological manipulation years before, this would have been the most exquisite example of gaslighting I'd ever seen. I hadn't wanted to go this fast. Yes, it was fun and ultimately domesticated bliss was the long term goal, but it was scaring the shit out of me. The confusion it brought was not worth it. But for some reason, I sat on that sofa and actually weighed the options. Now, with a clear head and better hindsight, all I can scream as I type these words is: "RUN, YOU DUMB BITCH." Trust me, reader, I feel your frustration.

I was so torn and feeling incredibly alone in that moment. Again, in hindsight, I could have reached out to any of my friends, and they'd have uttered the exact same sentiment as my subconscious (also in all caps), but at the time, I felt pretty stuck making the decision all by myself. My mind was racing but kind of in slow motion: surely we needed to be together longer for those feelings to develop, for him to realise that we were on the same page re: life goals. (In other words, spending time apart wouldn't convince him of those things, so taking a break wouldn't exactly help.)

If those feelings weren't present already, would they show up in time for happiness? Did I really want to feel as if I needed to convince him that we were right for each other? Does any of this matter right now? It's still so early in the relationship. Do we even need to have these conversations? Is walking away sensible as self-preservation, or does that amount to running off scared at the first hint of trouble? I tried to calm my mind enough to move or talk or do something, anything—ideally to get up and go home. But he outdid himself by coming out with the line: "Look, I can see you're upset. This wasn't a fun conversation and you shouldn't be alone tonight, so why don't you stay?"

Again, in hindsight, it should have been a no brainer; I should have been halfway across that mother fucking bridge already. But still I was there on the couch, and ultimately I ended up staying. I felt so paralysed by the fear of making the wrong decision, as if it'd all be over if I went home that night. Despite everything, I really didn't know if I wanted that.

At the time, I just knew that I didn't *not* want him in my life. Amidst all the bullshit, he did make me laugh, he was generally sweet and caring; he seemed like such a good person, with good values. He made me want to be better with his motivation and drive, and I loved how he was so family and friends orientated. (Plus, you know, the sex was incredible.) As we climbed into his bed, as I had so many times before, it felt like I was drowning in uncertainty and fear. Fear that I'd make the wrong choice, namely fear of facing rejection again. Once more, I might have to walk away from something, even though walking away wasn't entirely what I wanted. What I *needed*, however, was a different story.

He tried to initiate sex, which shocked me. Calmly, I explained that I couldn't be enough for him in the bedroom if I wasn't enough elsewhere. While he turned over and went to sleep, I replayed everything he'd said to me, every untruth he'd told me about myself; and then on the last morning of the year, I cried myself to a restless few hours of sleep. The best part (note the sarcasm) was how he'd left the conversation entirely on my shoulders. The decision was mine to make; I'd be the ref to make the call—and despite the mass of billowing red flags hitting me across the face from all directions, I genuinely didn't know what to do. So what would you do in this situation? I bet the answer isn't, "still go to your friend's NYE engagement party with him." But it was for me?

Yup, having told him that I wanted to put the whole thing out of my mind, we got all dressed up and tried to enjoy the night. Off we went, planning for him to meet more of my friends. We'd bring in the new year, celebrating love, and I'd reflect on having fully lost my mind. I remembered this feeling all too well: knowing a situation was monumentally fucked up but not totally knowing how to extricate myself from it.

Surprisingly, the night itself was not a complete wash. At moments, I'd catch myself ruminating on shit and actively change my train of thought. He'd make comments about how he hoped for an invite to the wedding, or that he'd love to hang with my friends again. *You don't even know that you like me; why do you think we'll be together in nine months for the wedding?* Otherwise, we did pretty good. None of my friends in attendance had met him before, thus they had no clue that anything was wrong. They thought he was great, of course. Why did I always choose men that could charm the pants off people?

We toasted the upcoming nuptials and I remained sensibly semi-sober. Afterwards, I dutifully headed back over Burrard Inlet, despite the fact that my place was just ten minutes away from the party, but Filipeen had to go home for his dog. Always the damn dog! I loved that dog; she was a sweetheart. But fuck me, that bitch was an annoying excuse and he always had her up his sleeve.

On January 1st, he dropped me back at home. I was doing the annual New Year's Day ocean swim with some friends, including Keith—he was always up for crazy events. Before leaving, Filipeen suggested that we do dinner the next night. It'd be our last night of the festive period before returning to work. At that point, I didn't have another trip across the bridge in me, so I insisted that he come downtown and we could go somewhere convenient for me. To this, he happily agreed.

A few hours later, I was in a bar with Keith and another guy friend, trying to warm ourselves up by a heater, with a whisky each. We'd already shocked our systems by diving into freezing water, so I told them the story of Filipeen. They'd known I was dating someone, but they hadn't heard any of the rest of the story. I actually hadn't told anyone about the pre-NYE chat. I couldn't bring myself to talk about it, because it was just so…*embarrassing.* Did I feel ashamed of how he spoke to me, or did I feel ashamed of myself? They were uniquely intertwined, because his speech sought to influence how I felt about myself.

Naturally, my friends' reactions reflected absolute horror—that I'd spent NYE with him and moreover that I was still considering my next move. They were incredibly kind and they said some very lovely things. (You know, that I deserved better and he sounded "like a nutter," as one of them so eloquently put it). I figured everyone would say that, but he'd done an excellent job of normalizing the nature of his communication. He had a way of turning things around on me, and with his less-than-stellar review of my character weighing on my mind, I'd started to wonder if maybe those things were wrong with me. Maybe I should just be happy, if he was willing to make things work? Yes, my self-worth was entirely MIA by this point.

The lesson? Let your friends "sense check" the shit a guy says about you, because gaslighting is real. This wasn't the first time I'd experienced it in a relationship. The following day, I prepared myself for dinner with Filipeen, wondering whether I should cut things off that night. I was all too aware that he was my first serious "relationship" since getting divorced, and I wasn't sure if I was running scared or self sabotaging. I wanted to be sure that I made the right decision. Of course, that night, we had to get in just a bit of domesticity and buy him a laundry basket—just how every girl wants a dinner date to start— before heading to the restaurant.

Dinner was fine and we kept the conversation light. It did feel like a nice way to finish the holiday season. We'd started them together, and in some capacity, we were finishing them together. But when he came back upstairs to mine for a bit before going home, things changed. He sat away from me on the sofa—in fact, he sat on the *only* other chair in my apartment—and declared that he felt like "the decision" had been on my mind all night. He said that we wouldn't get anywhere if I couldn't let it go.

If I couldn't let it go? IF I COULDN'T LET IT GO?! I'm sorry, it's kinda hard to forget that the person you're sitting across from at dinner, following to parties and sleeping beside at night, isn't sure that you're right for them. Especially if they've actively informed you of this, along with plenty of other fucking reasons that you suck, enough to fill your new fucking laundry basket. If you don't like someone, that's fine, but what would Thumper say about the situation? *If he didn't have anything nice to say about me, he didn't need to say anything at all* (I love a Bambi reference). It was early in the relationship, and we could've just gone our separate ways without anyone trying to annihilate the other person's self-worth.

Not to mention, he had the audacity to get annoyed with me, upon asserting that I needed to start letting more shit go. Hadn't I let enough of his bullshit go? *HE* was annoyed with *ME*. I was speechless, but I did manage to tell him that I thought he should leave. I didn't want to see his face; I didn't want him near me nor in my house. He called me that night to apologise, but it was a short conversation that ended with me telling him I wanted to be alone for a week. The next day, we both went back to work, and I had an appointment to see Julia later that week. I knew she'd sort me out. I knew she'd help me get back to clarity and unpack the craziness of the last few weeks.

That Friday, as I relayed the story to Julia—in her cosy and comfortable *safe space*—I knew the answers upon hearing the words leave my mouth. I knew what I should do; I knew that walking away was the only sensible option. But for some reason, I needed this reinforced. I needed her to tell me it was okay and I was doing the right thing; because instead of just knowing I should do it, I had this feeling that me walking away was a cop out. Yes, it was mildly reminiscent of struggling to walk away from my marriage, albeit on a totally different scale. My self-worth definitely still needed some work.

Julia's role isn't to tell me what to do—that's not how counselling/therapy works. She asks me questions instead, setting me up to look at things differently, perhaps thinking a little deeper about the development of my feelings about the situation, so that I can reflect and learn new ways of being. But on this occasion, she broke with her usual "no opinions given" demeanour and pointedly said: "You know that I'm not here to tell you what to do, but you already know what you need to do. You know you need to walk away and that is absolutely the right thing to do."

And that was all I needed. I messaged him on the Saturday morning and asked if we could meet up sometime over the weekend to talk. He suggested Sunday afternoon. He would come downtown and we'd walk the seawall. So, on a bitterly cold, early January afternoon, I met him (and the dog) at Waterfront Station. We started to walk, and after a couple minutes of catching up, he said: "It seems like the woman has something on her mind...." The patronising tone, his smile, and his seemingly small understanding of my mental anguish, were perfect reminders of the rationale behind my words.

I'd gone through it in my head many times already, so I launched straight into it, ensuring that I left no breaks for him to interject. It was straightforward: "I don't want to be with someone who isn't sure about me. I don't want someone who questions whether my life goals are genuine or not. I don't want someone who thinks that I drink or date too much. I want someone who likes what they know about me and wants to know more. I need someone whose actions match their words, who gets butterflies about me the way that I get butterflies about them. I need to feel safe, loved and supported. You offer me none of these things, so I can't see you anymore."

He seemed a little taken aback by my brevity (actually, so was I). He had this way of making me stumble over my words (sometimes even my thoughts), but for once I'd managed to concisely convey the nature of my feelings, without worrying that I would upset him. He responded by saying that he'd wanted to connect on a deeper level, but the relationship had become too sexually focused—something he'd never mentioned to me before. There were barriers that had prevented him from getting to know me well, apparently, so we'd be better as friends. But he didn't not want me in his life, in some way, because I was such a great person and my friends were so fun. *Ummm....how about no?*

I disagreed with so many of his thoughts, if not all of them (other than me being such a great person and my friends being so fun, obviously), but it was hardly worth debating. No more wasting my energy on this shitty circus. But the polarised nature of our two perspectives was a perfect example of us being on different pages. After feeling my fingers go numb from the cold, followed by my brain from all the shit he was talking, I suggested that we walk back to the SeaBus station. I struggled to keep myself together on the way, but I could feel the tears rising as we neared the station. As I hugged him goodbye, he did an incredible job of leaving me with the perfect reminder of his *shit-bagness*, posing the serious question of: "Do you want to feel my arms one last time?"

I had a thing for arms—and he knew it. But in that moment, all I wanted to do was tell him that there were already[4] ones in my life that far exceeded his, and they were attached to a far better human. Instead, I took the high road and politely declined, bursting into tears as he disappeared from sight and sobbing all the way home. Whether the tears were out of heartbreak or relief, I wasn't entirely sure, but my heart was definitely hurting.

Having cried all the way home, I actually felt better than I expected, upon settling myself into the sofa and eating my feelings in leftover Christmas chocolate. I absolutely knew that I'd done the right thing. It was over; I didn't have to deal with him again—what a fucking relief. But I couldn't help but wonder how I'd got myself into the mess to begin with...Why hadn't I been quicker to walk away? Why had I let things go so far, to the point of letting him diminish my self-worth? Why did I honestly think that he was the only person who wanted to date me? From where did that scarcity fear, as Julia calls it, come?

They weren't questions I had answers for right then, but as I pondered them more, my thoughts were interrupted by a text. From *him*, reading: *So, I don't really know where we left it? Am I ok to contact you? Can we still be friends?*

Mother of fuck, get a clue.

I saw no future in which we were friends. He'd be a shitty friend! I hadn't been on Bumble to make friends, and when someone strips your character down to nothing, why would you keep them in your life? It made no sense to me. But he'd done a great job of making me feel guilty about it.

During our last discussion, he commented that people who can't remain friends after dating clearly aren't mature; thus setting up the narrative that if we couldn't be friends, I was obviously immature. Even now he was manipulating my thoughts. I didn't even know what to answer in reply. I was too tired to deal with it, so I just said: "I don't know right now. How about text me if you want and I'll see how I feel?"

That was the Sunday; on the Tuesday, he took it literally and texted to ask if I'd watched anymore Archer. We'd been watching it together on those nights at his place; funnily, I hadn't been tempted to remind myself of those

---

[4] Arms was a Tinder date that turned into a friendship. <3 He made for a pair of Arms in my life like none other.

by watching more episodes. I told him, "no, I've been busy seeing friends and taking care of myself", hoping my terse response would help him to realise that I wasn't interested in friendly chit chat.

I made it through the rest of the week relatively unscathed. It was the first week back after the Holidays, and I was hardly in the best of moods. To celebrate surviving, I went out with Jillian for tacos, margaritas, and Holiday catch-up time. Obviously, my festive tales were fairly exclusively focused on Filipeen; and we were knee deep in the pre-NYE assassination of my character chat when my phone buzzed. Being the terrible friend that I am, I checked it mid-sentence before stopping dead.

This moment became the latest part of my story about Filipeen, and the look on my face obviously said so. Jillian's only response was, "Tell me how exactly this story turns around to the point where he's still fucking texting you now?" She was incredulous. I insisted on finishing the story before we dived into the text. And as the story progressed, she'd interject every so often with, "And he's STILL texting you?! HOW?!" Once she was finally caught up, I read the text aloud to her: *Hey! Where was that bottomless mimosa brunch place you were saying was good?* Oh, now you want to leverage my downtown party-life-style knowledge? What am I, some fucking restaurant concierge?

Jillian asked me how I felt, and I said not good. I didn't want his name popping up on my phone and disturbing my days / nights / life. She was right when she said that I needed to tell him that. Fuck what he thinks about people who can't stay friends after dating; fuck it if he thought I wasn't coping; fuck it if he thought he'd gotten to me. She was pretty resolute about the whole thing, so we spent the next half hour crafting the perfect response.

We moved from the restaurant to Forever 21, seeking outfit pieces for an event we were attending in a few weeks. Browsing the racks, we put together a text that ultimately declared that I didn't want to be friends with him— he couldn't bring value into my life—and in addition, I'd realised that his treatment of me and his behavior in general was incredibly selfish, confusing, and unfair. I wanted to be nice but honest, firm but fair; and ultimately I wanted him to leave me the fuck alone. *Text iterated for the one-hundredth time…and sent!*

He replied later that night, with an essay-length text, saying it was unfortunate that I saw the situation this way (insinuating, of course, that it wasn't

that way at all) and he didn't think we could be friends anymore (despite that
I'd just asserted over text that I didn't want to be friends), but he wished me
nothing but the best because I really was an incredible person who deserved
to meet someone suitable for me and the life I *really wanted to lead* (another
nod to him not believing that I really wanted the things I wanted). I never
replied; instead, I deleted our entire message history.

I was grateful to be with Jillian when the brunch text arrived. Otherwise,
I probably would have sent a mindless reply. Instead we talked the whole
thing through, in that she's also a trained therapist. While she can't counsel
me professionally (instead she introduced me to the therapist love of my life,
Julia), she does an incredible job of putting her knowledge to use when chatting with friends in situations like this. She's also one of the most empathetic
people I know, which helps massively and I love her for it. Discussing things
with her, I realised that Filipeen came up with so many excuses for why things
wouldn't work between us, as if grasping for any old reason. But none of them
were reason enough for him to cut things off himself. He had to point out
everything that was wrong with me first, leaving me to decide whether I could
live with a relationship that couldn't live with me.

If anything, it was a test to see how much I'd put up with; perhaps he
wanted me to break it off instead of him, so that he wasn't the one responsible
for "knowingly" causing hurt, so that he wasn't the bad guy. Even wanting to
stay friends afterwards—this was always the sign of the good guy, right? But
it's bullshit. I wish he'd been man enough to say: "This is how I'm feeling. It's
not working for me. I'm sorry but we can't keep dating." Instead, by being a
coward (to save me from hurt, as he put it), he'd caused me more confusion. If
there's anything that causes more lasting damage than hurt, it's confusion.

Confusion breeds doubt and insecurity. It leads to mistrusting your gut
and struggling to cut through the noise. For men, it's a tactical go-to—just
confuse her, that'll really fuck her up. Because if there's one thing that's easy
to explain walking away from, it's a messed up woman. Well, fuck him. I knew
what I wanted. I'd put it out there and didn't regret that choice. How I live my
life, how I am, comes down to me.

Certainly I didn't love Filipeen, but the way I went about loving people
also didn't seem to suit him. Perhaps I'll never fully understand his reasons for
feeling and acting in certain ways. Were we really not compatible, or was he
just scared? Did he go through this cycle with all his partners? I don't know,

and it doesn't actually matter. What matters is that *I* know what I want, that I know who *I* am. I want someone to be all in with me, someone whose commitment I don't have to question or wonder about—and that wasn't him. *End of saga.* Best of luck, Filipeen, and thanks for the epic sex.

Sixteen

Casual/Multi-Dating

Having wallowed in reflection for a few weeks after Filipeen, I eventually felt better enough (aka *bored* enough) to get back on the dating apps. I'd noticed that the more connected we were becoming digitally as a society, the more our physical connections were decreasing, thus dating apps had started to accommodate the need for community on short notice (like, when all your coupled friends are otherwise focused on their relationships), in addition to desire for sex and dating.

As always, when you haven't been on Bumble for a while, you get a string of really attractive guys at first, to suggest that you've been missing out, and then slowly it fades into various faces that you've seen on there for months. You didn't swipe right then (to say that you liked them) and you won't be swiping right now. I was always convinced that those attractive bait ones were just made-up accounts—the men were just too pretty—but my theory was debunked when I matched with one the next morning. We made plans to meet up on Saturday night. What is it about Friday and Saturday night dates that feels so much more serious? Like who gives up their weekend for a first date? Apparently *us*.

He'd been fairly serious in our messaging, with only slight hints of jokes; but that Friday night, as I was getting ready to go out with friends, things got a little more *banterful* (how I prefer all my messaging) and flirty. When his plans for the night changed, he asked me whether I was free to move our date up a night and meet later that evening.

As much as I was excited to meet him, he was going to have to wait. It was Damien's birthday and I wasn't sure inviting him along would be a great basis for a first date, because a) my friends are liabilities and b) we were going to an amateur strip show in a super dingy bar on the east side of the city. Yes, you read that right. It was a strip show with only two rules: entrants couldn't be professional strippers and no sex acts on stage. Otherwise anyone and everyone could have at 'er. It was called Rent Cheque because the winner of the monthly event would win their rent. Well, not most people in Vancouver's rent, but maybe a co-op in the Downtown Eastside?

However, while having drinks at Damien's before heading out, I changed my mind about it not being a good breeding ground for a first date and asked if he wanted to join us. We'd been texting almost constantly and I realised it would be easier, and less rude, for him to be here than for me to be on my phone all night. At first he sounded keen, even after I'd provided full disclosure about where we were going, but then he changed his mind, likely as the reality sank in, and we agreed to stick to Saturday instead, as originally planned. We said goodnight but only after our texts descended into innuendo-laden comments about the nakedness I would be witnessing that night (and what I might witness the next night).

He was twenty-nine and originally from Vancouver but now living in Toronto. The fact that he didn't live here (albeit he travelled back for work about once a month) and following the joking mention of nudity on the first date, I was well aware that this likely wasn't the start of a beautiful long-term relationship. But at that point, I decided a sex date might actually be just what I needed to wash Filipeen right out of my newly-highlighted hair, once and for all.

The next day, over texts and a couple of phone calls (again, a guy who uses the phone for actual phone calls...maybe it wasn't that rare), I suggested that we meet in a bar, but he suggested that we stay in with a bottle of wine. Still feeling a bit shaky from the effects of last night's birthday antics, I was actually okay with that. So, for the first time ever, I gave a man I'd never met my address and had him turn up on my doorstep. Was this a step up or down from having Filipeen pick me up and drive me somewhere on our first date?

And I know what you're thinking: *ARE YOU FUCKING NUTS?!* Always meet in a public place, never give your address until you know them, make sure they know that you do kickboxing and can kick their ass, etc.... Like I said, it was the first time I'd ever done it and part of me was horrified at myself, but the other part of me trusted my gut; and my gut told me it was okay, he didn't seem like "that sort of guy." You know, the sort to murder a Bumble date in her apartment. (I joke, but it's a serious issue and I'm aware that women need to take care of their safety at all times, which I don't take lightly.) Just after eight pm, my buzzer went off and I apprehensively waited for the elevator to deliver him to the tenth floor, anticipating a knock on my door.

To say that I wasn't disappointed would be the understatement of the year. Things that I hadn't noticed or seen in his profile pictures: his unbelievably sexy salt-and-pepper hair, more expected on a man of forty or fifty but hugely attractive on a hot guy of twenty-nine; arms that even under his jacket I could tell were going to be my favourite part about him; and this deep dimple square in the middle of his chin that I just wanted to nestle my head in forever. Something else I couldn't have known from his profile but had picked up on in the couple of phone calls earlier in the day was his incredibly attractive accent, coming out with a maybe East Coast-ish, slightly husky voice. It was possibly the best, most pleasantly surprising WTAF (what the actual fuck) moment I'd ever experienced since I'd started dating. I did all that I could to get words out of my mouth, while simultaneously quieting the voice in the back of my head that was saying, "Well, he's going to be disappointed with you." Oh hi, self doubt!

He'd brought wine, so while I opened that and he took a look at the view from my balcony, the easy chatting we'd had over text picked up in person. He'd led a really interesting life, which made the conversation fun and wide-ranging. He was also clearly a lover of the finer things in life—the wine he brought was not a cheap bottle, and from his stories he only flew business class, not to mention that his taste in hotels sat squarely at the luxury end. He clearly knew that he was successful for his age, but in a matter of fact, *appreciative-because-he'd-made-so-many-sacrifices* kind of a way. I didn't hate any of it. Successful men that make me want to be more successful in life are a huge turn on.

With all our talking, it took me a while to realise that we'd either just have a lovely evening of wine and chit-chat, or he'd have to purposefully make a move. Because being in someone's apartment, while it did provide easy access to a bedroom, made it more difficult for something physical to happen naturally. At least at a bar, you might be huddled around a table and free to get a little closer. Or moving from a restaurant to a bar, there was the opportunity for some contact while walking. At the movies, there's always the potential for a *brushing-of-hands*. Sitting on the sectional couch in someone's house? You really had to make that shit happen for yourself. And I, for one, would not be the one to do so. No matter how much I wanted to get a little closer to that dimple.

We ended up talking about basketball, and I commented that, despite playing in high school, it wasn't the sport for me—given my short, fat fingers. He leaned forwards and took my wine glass out my hand, placed it on the table, and then took my hand to look at and said "short, fat fingers." I was simultaneously distressed because he was now examining one of the areas of my body that I hated the most—why had I brought up my goddamn chunky digits?! But I was thrilled that, other than a swift hug when he first arrived, of which I'd barely been conscious because I was so pleasantly stunned by his appearance, we were now engaging in physical contact.

The physical examination of my hand seemed to be the only "in" he needed. He briefly dropped my hand, took a sip of his wine, and in one swift movement was half standing, half kneeling on the sofa over me. It felt imposing and incredibly sexy. From his energy in that moment, I was aware that he was probably very dominant in the bedroom. Yah, this could be FUN. He was forceful but in a flirtatious, non-threatening way, so not once did I have a concern about this man whom I'd met only a couple of hours earlier and let into my apartment.

Go ahead, order me around and exert passionate force over my body! I was more than happy to comply. He took his shirt off and the delight I experienced when he first arrived was elevated by about a hundred. His arms were, as I had imagined from that first glimpse, delightful. That salt-and-pepper hair, which turned out to be outrageously long on the top of his head (once I actually ran my fingers through it), with its matching stubble and his chest hair, was ridiculously sexy. And that dimple? Good god, that dimple.

After making out and getting pretty *hands-y* on the sofa, he picked me up, carried me to the bedroom, and threw me onto the bed. I'm not just using that phrase because it sounds great, either. He actually threw me onto the mattress with such force that I remember bouncing. I was pretty sure the bounce wasn't sexy, so I attempted to steady myself, find some composure and maintain an air of grace. (Picture your childhood best friend after "double-bouncing" them on the trampoline and you're not far off.)

The sex was better than great. He knew what he was doing and obviously what he liked, but he was also suitably generous. The one thing I did notice, however, was that when we started having sex, the kissing stopped. Some men, perhaps also some women, equate kissing during sex with intimacy. In their books, if they're not looking for a relationship, avoiding kissing can minimise the intimacy. The other side of that argument, of course, is that sex in and of itself is one of the most intimate acts that humans engage in. So it seems like a futile attempt to minimise connection. I personally hate when there's no kissing during sex; it feels incredibly cold to me. I don't care if I never want to see you again; I still want you to kiss me while you're inside me. Is that too much to ask?

Even more off-putting than the no kissing was the lack of post-sex cuddles. I think I've said it before: I'm an avid *cuddler*. The closeness, the comfort, I miss it as a singleton. But similarly to the kissing, I think closeness after sex scares some people, because it feels too intimate (as if having your genitals intertwined just moments before somehow suggested more separation). So instead we lay slightly apart in bed, chatting until he had to get going. We talked about seeing each other before he left back to Toronto again, but we didn't make any firm plans.

The next morning, as I was filling in Jillian about my previous night's antics, she mentioned knowing someone professionally in the same industry as Toronto Dimple Chin (as he was now Christened). Within three minutes, she came back to me to tell me that *yep*, her friend knew him—mostly in a professional capacity, but they thought he was a good guy. We joke that she's like the FBI. Those memes you see on Instagram about giving someone a first name and five minutes later they have the whole family tree? That's Jillian—therapist and FBI agent.

As it turned out, Toronto Dimple Chin and I never caught up before he left town. Four weeks later, I was at the Rugby Sevens in BC Place Stadium (Vancouver's most fun weekend where everyone gets dressed up and incredibly drunk). The World Rugby Sevens Series is an annual series of international rugby sevens tournaments (like normal rugby but played with seven players on each team and only seven minutes per half) tournaments featuring teams from all the countries you'd probably expect (like South Africa, New Zealand, Australia) and then some more you might not (like Kenya, Argentina, and Russia). On a visit to the bar with Jillian and Damien, I happened to turn around and see Toronto Dimple Chin walking in our direction with some friends. Despite the crowds, he saw me at the same time and made a comment to his friends, who carried on walking as he headed my way.

Jeez, I'd forgotten just how attractive he was. *Was anyone else seeing this?!* Yes, Damien and Jillian were. As he and I hugged hello, they sidled up beside me with their drinks replenished in both hands. It was a quick introduction before they said their goodbyes and headed back to our seats, but I could tell by the look on their faces that there was much they wanted to say. Knowing them, I was impressed by their silence. Toronto Dimple Chin and I had a fairly quick chat. He wasn't supposed to be in town, but his plans had changed. He said it was nice to see me and we should get together while he was in town. I agreed and we had another quick goodbye hug. With another glance at the dimple, I returned to my seat as he headed off in the direction of his friends.

Before I even got within earshot of our seats, I could tell that Jillian and Damien were filling in the rest of our group on the details of our bar encounter. As I approached, Jillian stopped talking, looked straight at me and said: "He is one of the most attractive men I've seen in real life, in my entire life." And I couldn't disagree. Damien thought the same thing, having said to Jillian, "I don't know who he is, but I'd do him" and apparently he was incredulous when Jillian told him that I had in fact already "done him." So, I was glad that I hadn't dreamt up his attractiveness or remembered the cuteness of that dimple through overly rose-tinted spectacles. Not only that, but for my friends to witness this too, well, it made me sound a little less nuts after I'd insisted that he was the most attractive man I'd slept with in my entire life. *Oh god, had I peaked? Was that it? Was it all downhill from here?*

Despite the excitement of seeing him again and the pleasantries we exchanged in the stadium concourse, we didn't meet up during the rest of his time in Vancouver. We texted a couple of times, but if I'm honest: if he'd lived in closer proximity and I'd seen him more, that dimple could well have been the death of me. Instead, I got back to random dating, including an Irish guy who'd eventually admit to me, on our third date, and only when he couldn't get it up in bed, that he was going through a massive custody battle for his kid. A kid I hadn't known anything about until that moment. I wanted to be sympathetic, but he'd actively chosen not to share this small detail with me until now. I also really didn't have the capacity for that sort of drama, so instead I asked him to leave. On hearing that story, Damien said that I had turned into a guy: backing away once someone expresses emotions. *Oh god, really? But why such a double standard? Why did I have to be understanding just because I was a woman?!*

There was also an accidental night with a twenty-one-year-old, but honestly, your honour, I thought he was twenty-four. Not that three extra years made it that much better, and my mistake was hammered home when he asked to shower at mine before heading back to uni, because my shower was so much nicer than his shared bathroom. Lord, help me. Then I met a couple of twenty-five-year-old guys. There was something about younger men—it was easier, especially if I wasn't looking for a relationship. They were more eager and, as proven by Filipeen, being older doesn't necessarily equal a better person or partner.

The first young dude was a French personal trainer who'd moved to Canada as a kid (not to be confused with being Quebecois aka "French Canadian"). Frenchie was the easiest, no-strings-attached sex I'd found, and there's nothing wrong with that if you both have the same expectations. Texting was kept to organising times to meet up; and when we did meet up, it was usually to play Mario Kart and eat pizza (yah, apparently we were teenagers) and then have sex. What's not to love?

The other twenty-five-year-old I dated would prove more troublesome. Malaysian Persuasion came in hot. I got the feeling that he was used to dating younger girls, who would fawn over his good looks and seemingly mature (for his age) attitude. While we didn't have a lot in common, our sexual chemistry was like nothing I'd ever experienced. Twenty-five-year-olds are eager to please! And their endurance level is unsurpassed—it made for a lot of fun nights, and a lot of lost sleep.

The difference between Frenchie and Malaysian Persuasion was that while one was straight sex, the other was a lot more intimate. Malaysian Persuasion and I would text everyday, chatting about life and work, and we sexted. *A lot.* But when I was heading home to Scotland for almost a month in April, I figured that things would just fizzle out and that would be it. Instead, we ended up messaging daily, only breaking when the eight-hour time difference meant that one of us was sleeping. Although, with the jet lag I was suffering, I was rarely the *sleeping beauty* in this equation.

While home, I went to another one of my close friend's weddings (one of the final items on my list of "events I won't miss, despite living in Vancouver."

It was a beautiful day, and I was glad to enjoy the weather after the stress from the last wedding I'd attended. Then again, I was in a much different place now emotionally. The trip home was particularly taxing, however. I was having dental work done because in Canada it's almost as expensive as the cheese. Thankfully, work had been great about letting me work remotely, but trying to navigate the eight-hour time difference with my Vancouver colleagues, while also seeing as many friends and family members as possible, plus the traumatic dental experience, didn't make for the most fun trip.

I'd had veneers fitted at eighteen, and fourteen years later, they were overdue to be replaced. Unfortunately, having veneers removed is like having your teeth pulled off your teeth—if that even makes logical sense. I bite my lip just thinking about it. The only upside is that I could completely choose how the new ones would look, something I hadn't gotten to do the first time, resulting in my sporting short fat teeth for far too long. They had made me incredibly self-conscious about my smile, because instead of having longer, top-middle teeth, getting shorter as they go back, mine kind of went the other way.

My middle teeth were super short and then they got longer, so it looked like an upside down smile. For most of my adult life, I'd avoided giving a toothy grin. I would normally smile closed-mouth, which I also didn't love, because my top lip has a bulge from when I put my tooth through it as a toddler. My preference would have been for most pictures to include a paper bag over my head. *Hello, even more body insecurities.*

The dental work was a medical requirement and not an exercise in vanity, but still, the main outcome after multiple sessions and hours in the chair, was entirely aesthetic-related. *Holy shit, I could smile. And I liked my smile!* I'd never actually admitted my insecurities about smiling to anyone, such was the shame of the drunken night in my teens when my two front teeth broke and led to veneers. It felt like an apt punishment for a reckless teenage decision, one I would think about every time I looked at a picture of myself. How awful that I'd lived like that for so long. It gave me an understanding of why people have work done, be it dental or cosmetic. Yes, it would be great if we could just love what we've been given, but that's not always realistic; and if there's something you can do to make yourself feel better, without harming yourself, why not do it?

With that new smile, I felt like I got a whole new lease on life. Having said that, the pain and discomfort was considerable; and with the jet lag and general emotional rollercoaster of going home, it was a tough few weeks that everyone still presumed were lovely—because who wouldn't want to be on holiday for that long? Well, a holiday it was *not*. As always, it was wonderful seeing everyone, but I couldn't wait to get on that plane and go home to Vancouver.

The whole time, I'd been sharing the trials and tribulations of my trip with Malaysian Persuasion over text. He'd been great at keeping my spirits high with talk of plans for when I got back. However, in the space of the day it took me to leave Edinburgh and fly home to Vancouver, he'd all but disappeared. Like, he was suddenly busy, with plans that he somehow didn't have before. Out of nowhere, he wasn't able to see me for a while. When I pushed him on the surprising turn of these plans, he claimed to have cold sores and thus he couldn't see me. *Um… what? Are you busy or do you have cold sores? Which is it? Also, how bad are the cold sores?!*

In the next week, we texted a bit, always with me initiating and miraculously hoping his response would click back into the tone I was fond of now. But it never did. He never once asked anything about me—nothing about my trip back or the jet lag or how it felt to be home. Nothing. The complete one-eighty in his demeanour was a giant head fuck. I've said it before and I'll say it again: confusing someone is no better than hurting them. Particularly when, most likely, the person knows what they are doing. To make someone question their own sanity and, in my case, start to over-compensate for the other person and make allowances you shouldn't otherwise make, was an awful thing to do. I heard myself explaining the story to my friends and saying, "But maybe he is just busy?"; or "Maybe he is just really embarrassed about his cold sores?" *Get a clue, Lou.*

In time, I started to make peace with the fact that whatever the hell "it" had been between us, it was now well and truly over. But, as is always my way, I can't just let things go; I need to tie up loose ends. So I texted him and said that I didn't know what the hell had happened but it was shitty and he should be ashamed of himself. He didn't reply—*for four days*. Then he responded asking if we could meet up. I was beyond pissed, but my curiosity, as always, got the better of me.

When we first met up again, he claimed that he'd been busy, like actually. But I said that if he kept this bullshit going, I was going to leave right then;

so he took a pause from all the excuses and shifted in his seat. He proceeded to explain that when I'd first left for my trip, he'd been worried that I was going home to sleep with all my exes. Clearly, he hadn't understood that my only ex at home was my ex-husband, and I wouldn't go near him with a barge pole. Then, as it had gotten closer to me coming home, while realising how much we'd been chatting while I was away, he worried that I was returning expecting a relationship which he wasn't looking for. So basically, he'd been worried that I was going to go off with someone else, but next he worried that I was going to come back only wanting him? This made no sense. Especially for something that was supposed to be so casual.

This, my friends, is a classic case of someone letting their imagination run wild, failing to fact-check their projections and ruining shit. Somehow, in the midst of the conversation—with him apologizing as I clarified that his perceptions had been a) wrong and b) dick-headed—he told me that he'd missed me. At that point, I forgot about the boundaries I'd set for myself at the beginning of the night. I had vowed not to let him charm me into forgiving his behavior, and I wish that I'd made better(?), smarter(?), or more self-serving(?) decisions that night. But I hadn't. I was learning that with every boundary we set for ourselves and then break, we trust ourselves a little bit less, because the subconscious learns that our word doesn't equal an internal vow. I could set all the boundaries that I wanted, but if I wasn't going to observe them, what was the point?

The next morning, upon waking up with him in my bed, I wasn't sure what the hell had happened. Maybe more importantly, I didn't know what the hell was going to happen. I did know that, despite everything, it had been incredible to see him again. Besides, nothing had changed in terms of our sexual compatibility. If anything, the imposed hiatus had only heightened it. I had been so pissed off with him less than twenty-four hours beforehand, but I couldn't deny the massive part of me that didn't hate how things were turning out.

What does that say about me, I wonder? Could I be so easily swayed after someone was a complete dick to me? Perhaps it wasn't my finest hour. The only thing that marginally made me feel better was that I'd been explicit with him about what I expected going forward. Consistency and honesty. It didn't need to be anything more than that; I wasn't looking for a commitment or a relationship, just consistency and honesty. Easy, right?

If he hadn't asked me a few weeks later whether I was sleeping with anyone else, it all would have been fine. In all fairness, the answer was easy: Yes, I was. While Malaysian Persuasion was fucking about with his insecurities, I'd picked up my easy hookups with Frenchie again. I didn't give him the full details, but I did affirm that yes, I was sleeping with other people. Did that sound better or worse than saying it was one specific person? How was I even having this debate in my head? I'd gone from not feeling right about messaging two people at a time to now comfortably sleeping with two individuals. I, naively, thought this answer would please him, given our agreement that nothing serious would come of this. But please him it did not.

Instead, he told me that he didn't know what to do with that information. Apparently, it didn't sit well with him. When he sleeps with someone, it means something, which he'd told me the first time we slept together. Well, here's a suggestion, buddy, *don't ask questions if you don't want the fucking answer.* He didn't want anything serious with me but expected me to be exclusive with him? How was I supposed to have known that? And why was I feeling like this was my fault? Like I'd somehow disappointed him? Like I was somehow a big old ho? Let's just be grateful that I didn't tell him I was sleeping with another twenty-five-year old, one who could probably kick his ass in the gym.

Again, Damien would liken me to a guy. He wasn't necessarily wrong, but it was just another double standard in dating. If I'd been a guy, my behavior would be expected and accepted. But being a woman? *How dare I have my cake and eat another kind too! And, worst of all, I was enjoying it!* My feelings around dating and sleeping with multiple people had clearly changed, mostly out of necessity. They'd changed to accommodate the nature of dating right now. It's not that I liked it, but I wasn't about to hold out for someone if they weren't keeping themselves for me. I found it hard to believe that Malaysian Persuasion was holding himself to the same standards that he expected of me. Even if you're keeping it casual, some guys won't like the idea that you're actually out there "keeping it casual" with more partners than just them.

Malaysian Persuasion and I never really recovered from this fissure, although we'd have a couple more trysts—such was our sexual chemistry, and we couldn't seem to give it up entirely. All the same, in amongst trying to keep things casual, feelings had surfaced on both sides, making it difficult to continue without one, or both of us, getting hurt. Though I didn't hate it when he told me, months later, that I'd ruined sex with other women for him—such was the enjoyment he found in us sleeping together. *You're welcome.*

Seventeen

Friends or Dates?

By the middle of 2017, things seemed a bit uncertain, all over the place, and unanchored. They'd felt that way since I came home from my trip in April, but I'd hoped it would pass once I got back into my routine and the fun of summer. I knew a lot of it was linked to situations with other people, to which I'd assigned too much weight and importance and needed to reclaim some control for myself, but I wasn't sure how to take back my power. Once power has been given, getting it back is harder than not giving it away in the first place.

Ultimately, I felt as if something was missing from my Vancouver life. My friendship with Laura had palpably changed, Damien was back with his ex-girlfriend, Sara, and going from checking in everyday with Malaysian Persuasion to not talking to him at all, or anyone else in that way, had been a tough adjustment. I was also struggling with my financial security, or lack thereof. At this age, I'd expected to have more freedom in that sense, but I didn't. I so longed to freely go and do whatever, whenever, but I had to be more responsible than that. The feeling of guilt re: my financial situation weighed on my mind constantly. The divorce had cost me plenty, and I'd never fully gotten back on my feet. I felt indifferent towards friends and social situations that I'd once enjoyed, and I'd generally checked out of life. How was it possible that I wasn't excited about another Vegas trip? Why wasn't I looking forward to spending time with the girls?

I needed to change something or shift my focus. Should I get back on the job hunt? Stay off the dating apps for a while? Or maybe just alter where I'm spending my time, or with whom I'm spending it? I didn't want to be the person who got herself down about being single, nor the person to vent about her feelings all the time. But I knew that, ultimately, I wanted to be in a relationship. I didn't think this was a bad thing to admit, even if just to myself. However, I needed to be totally happy on my own, in order to enable a happy/healthy relationship to blossom—and I wasn't sure my existing level of confidence would get me there.

Every small glimpse of the men I'd slept with made me want more, so I worried about putting too much focus on intimacy. I wanted to be open to a relationship yet totally okay without one, knowing it would happen at the right time, with the right person. Until then, patience and self love were key. All the work I'd done the previous year, to be more carefree and less anxious, seemed to be unraveling. In part, I was less focused on it than last year. I wasn't seeing Julia as regularly and there were a few situations that had set me back. What should've been little knocks felt like massive setbacks, from which I needed a whole lot more energy to recover. I tried to remind myself that I was strong enough to deal with anything that came my way, remembering always that this too shall pass.

Amidst all these ups and downs, the most consistent part of my life became my exercise schedule. I prioritised working out, not least because I needed to keep up with the twenty-five-year-olds. In doing so, I'd found a new sense of confidence, buoyed by how I felt in a bikini and boosted by the hotness of the men I'd been dating. Was that super shallow? It wasn't the only thing I was basing my happiness on, however. I was spending a tonne of time outdoors and expanding my social circle with people who prioritised healthy lifestyles. But ultimately I was enjoying the new and improved physical version of me. I found myself drinking less frequently, albeit when I did drink, there was a lot of overindulgence. Can you say *Classic British Binge Drinker?*

When I found myself back in Vegas, this time for Jaime's (Jillian's sister) bachelorette party, there was something I couldn't entirely put my finger that made me feel totally unlike myself. I struggled with it the whole weekend. It was pretty much the same group of girls as the previous year's trip, which had been so much fun, just with a couple of additions, but I felt entirely out of place. I'd had a falling out with one of the girls a few months prior, fuelled by alcohol and miscommunication, although really my underlying problem was that everybody shared feelings and stories extensively in our friend group, apart from her. As a result of her unwillingness to share, I was left feeling vulnerable, feeling that she knew so much about me and I knew next to nothing about her. It was something I'd come to realise that I needed in relationships, both romantic and platonic—as a total open book, I need the same level of openness in return. Otherwise, an imbalance forms that causes insecurity.

I'd decided to try and put aside the underlying tension, for the sake of the bride-to-be, but on further reflection I shouldn't have asked myself to do that. The fallout created a split in the group with Laura squarely in the middle; and while it was no one's job to babysit me, I felt isolated for the whole trip. I struggled with the typical, girly bachelorette fun that these weekends so often hold. I just couldn't let myself go enough to enjoy it. In addition, I was sick as a dog with a cold that had fully taken hold in the days before we flew, to the point that I almost didn't want to go. It's fair to say that I didn't bring a whole lot of fun with me, and for that I've always felt bad. But ultimately, things were tough due to the strange sense of no longer feeling like I totally belonged in a group that included some of my closest friends from the past three years. *When had things changed so much? When had I changed so much? Had I changed too much?*

I tried to chalk up the Vegas weekend as a blip, put it down to me not feeling well and hoping things would return to normal. Once I was finally able to shake the cold, I occupied myself by again utilising dating as a filler. I met up with a guy I'd matched with on Bumble before I went away to Vegas: Hot Doctor. Yes, the nicknames were getting more literal as we went along. But the nicknames were key: there was a sense of keeping the importance of someone to a minimum by not using their name when discussing them with friends. This was in no way meant to reduce their identities to labels or stereo-types, but it helped to prevent me from getting overly attached to them, which is an important point since they weren't attached to me. The nicknames were the easiest way for my friends to keep track of my dating-and-sex life, as the numbers were building. To be honest, my friends still don't know most of the guys' real names, which if anything protects the guys' privacy.

Hot Doctor was Pakistani-Canadian, dark skinned with the most impos-sibly well-kept beard, a twenty-seven-year-old body that could melt butter and eyes that pierced the soul (in the best possible way). I'd gotten all that from just his pictures. That summer, I'd found no shortage of dates or online-dating app matches, but his dating profile pictures were almost too immaculate.

His response to my first Bumble message was too smooth, his Instagram too curated. He was either a catfish or a douchebag. But seeing as he had his Instagram linked up with his dating profile, I guessed I was going to have to presume it was the latter? Alas, that didn't seem to put me off. I was intrigued.

He texted to ask me about meeting up one Saturday. I had, unsurprisingly, spent the day at the beach for several hours of drinking with friends. The thought of getting ready to go out didn't thrill me, so instead I suggested that he come round to mine. My suggestion made it clear that it was "just a sex date," but with his chiseled good looks I had no other designs on this meet up. Isn't it funny how we can make so many assumptions based on someone's looks? Like, he's too good looking to want a relationship. But he was also training in the UK to be a doctor, and it had taken us so long to meet up that his summer trip home to Vancouver was ending the very next day. So it wasn't about to be the start of a beautiful life-long relationship. Plus, after my night with Toronto Dimple Chin, inviting a stranger over to my apartment didn't feel so risky.

I realised afterwards that the other reason I wanted him to come over to mine, rather than go out, was that I was actually intimidated by him. Annoyingly, I was intimidated by how good looking he was and how well put together he seemed. It's ridiculous to me now—he's human, no one is as perfect as they seem, and he was obviously attracted to me in some way. Why would I be nervous to meet and go out in public with him? I didn't realise it at the time, but inviting him over to mine for wine was one way to minimise any embarrassment, in the event he got there and thought: "Wow, she is not what I was hoping for tonight." (Although I like to think my profile pics were an accurate representation of me.) Given all the changes I'd made on myself, both physically and emotionally, crashes in my confidence weren't a regular occurrence anymore, but there were definitely a few men I was nervous to meet, and he was one of them.

To say his pictures were true to real life doesn't do justice to real life. If possible, he was even more attractive—as if some model had just wrapped up a photo shoot and ended up at my apartment door. I was two-for-two on having impossibly beautiful men turn up on my doorstep, in other words. He was soft-spoken and thoughtful with his words, which I hadn't expected with my harsh first judgment. From the get-go, he had a lot to say, but also a lot to ask. He wanted to know about my upbringing, my travels, and moving to

Vancouver. We covered a lot of ground while sitting on the balcony at sunset.

When I stood up to replenish our wine glasses (cause that's what I needed after my day of drinking in the sun) he followed me inside. As I turned back with the replenished glasses, he stood in my way, reached for my face, and kissed me. It was soft, almost enquiring, as if he wanted to test the waters, to see if the tide was high on us fooling around for real. Unsurprisingly, I was on the same page one-hundred percent; the glass of wine in each hand was the only thing stopping me from ripping his clothes off. We returned to the balcony for some more wine, but by that point, it was more about *when* we'd end up in bed and not *if.*

There was an intensity in the way he looked at me with those big brown eyes, probing and completely disarming. It disarmed me of my inhibitions, and I no longer felt like he might not be interested in someone like me (Instagram's a terrible thing when you can see a picture of someone's ex-girl-friend before even meeting the guy). All I really wanted was to get completely and entirely naked with him.

So that's what we did. And the fun that ensued was incredible.

Between each of our four rounds of fun (God bless the stamina of men in their twenties), we continued our chat from earlier on the balcony. We talked about our thoughts on dating and his past relationship (which broke down because he was often in the UK and generally ambivalent towards marriage). We talked about my marriage, my divorce, and forgiveness. We discovered a shared love of the poet Khalil Gibran, whom he was shocked to find out I knew. Why? Because a white girl can't know a Lebanese writer? One of Hot Doctor's favourite quotes of Gibran's was: *Out of suffering have emerged the strongest souls; the most massive characters are seared with scars.* I fell in love with the words when he said them, and I still love them now.

We both admitted that while we'd expected some of what had happened that night, neither of us imagined that we'd be having such broad and deep discussions. I'd settled into the fact that sex dates could be about just that—sex—and you could count yourself lucky if the sex at least was good, never mind getting to feel a real connection. Not only had we fit physically, like a glove, we also had a lot to say to each other. He'd even made a posi-tive comment on my body, one that I'd never heard from a guy. After one of the best moments in our evening, I said something about working out, and he said: "Yeah, your shoulders are super strong, I noticed that when I was behind you."

Two things about that made my heart flip. One, the thought of him checking me out while behind me was thrilling. While many moons ago, I would have preferred that *lights-off-and-eye-contact-maintained-at-all-times* kind of sex, I was now more of a *yeah-take-a-good-look-at-all-this* kind of person. Again, was that really shallow of me? But secondly, he was talking about my shoulders; boobs, ass, those were all things I was used to having men comment on. But my shoulders? Apparently they looked "strong." *Yes! Thank you!* I've been working fucking hard.

He left just after midnight, following a glorious amount of snuggling which put us both to sleep. But it was his last night in Vancouver and he needed to go home. I knew he was leaving the next day. Maybe we could fit in some afternoon fun before his evening flight, but I think we both knew it'd be unlikely to happen. Texting me from the airport the next day, he said he'd be back in December. *December?!* It was June.... Jesus, that's a wait. But the thought was still nice.

While I was enjoying the casual nature of my summer dates, it was simply my remedy to starting the year with all the Filipeen confusion. I'd started longing for something more long term again, rather than all my numerous but great sex dates. My friends said some things that were sticking in my head, particularly about the type of men I was dating. Yes, they were pretty. Yes, they had great bodies. But were any of them suitable partners? Arguably not. A suitable long-term partner was not the demographic I'd been swiping for back then.

Thinking that I *should* be looking for something else, I decided to go against my better judgment and swipe right on people whom I ordinarily wouldn't. If they weren't my typical physical type, I somehow thought that they might be a good match for me. It was the strangest logic, but that's where my head was at and I went with it.

In time, I made my way through a whole slosh of dates. There was Ukrainian Boy Racer (Eastern Europeans have never really crossed my radar, and though he was nice, his extreme interest in kink was a step too far for me, even though my own sexual journey was diversifying), Mexican EDM Festival Performer (his lifestyle of bejewelled t-shirts and bedazzled jeans kind of put me off), and Canada Day Boat Guy (he didn't have his own boat, but his friend did, and our first date was on it, along with a bunch of his friends on Canada Day when I ended up getting on better with his friends than him). None of them went past a first date, and as nice as they were as people, not only was there not a personality click, but I wasn't even attracted to them physically. So what really was the point?

Then came another tall and bearded Persian guy. I was slowly discovering a large Persian (or Iranian) community within Vancouver, and while I'd previously found myself going for clean-cut, white-boy good looks, there was something about these Middle Eastern types that I found myself drawn to. Maybe it was growing up in Egypt; maybe they felt familiar? Regardless, our first date was a pleasant surprise.

To be honest, between arranging the date and finally meeting outside my office that Friday afternoon, I wasn't sure what made me swipe right on him. His pictures were the type that didn't give you an entirely good look. He seemed a bit different in each pic and it could have gone either way upon meeting him. Perhaps he'd be super hot, or perhaps I'd be disappointed. So, meeting this incredibly athletic-looking, hot, brown guy, all 6'5" of him, with a jawline that could cut glass, albeit covered by a very well-trimmed beard, was totally welcome.

We sat on the patio of *Per Se Social Corner* in Yaletown. It was one of those dates where the server comes to take your order four times before you've even thought about what to order because you're talking so much. We seemed to have a lot in common. We talked a bit about dating and our views on it and seemed to come from a similar place. We didn't have time for games and we wanted something substantial. It was refreshing to have that clarified before our drinks had even arrived.

We shared our love of sports and good drinks, and how we both felt like old souls, who preferred chilled nights and early bedtimes. I also found out that he didn't like scheduled sex or waiting; he preferred calls to texts and not asking questions to which you didn't want the answer. The more comfortable I was with him, the more comfortable he'd be with me. He told me that he could be unemotional, as a safety mechanism, and he wouldn't want to rush into anything. I gave him the same level of detail about myself and it was a lot of information for such a short space of time, but I didn't care for surface-level bullshit. I wanted to get deep and understand if there was substance here.

I wanted to know if we aligned on the important stuff. I felt like he was being open, genuine, and I loved that.

Drinks only came to an end when I had to meet Jillian for dinner. He offered to walk me and suggested that we meet up later. I liked that he wasn't trying to "play it cool." He wanted to see me again and wasn't afraid to ask. It made for a nice change. The only negative was that a first kiss probably wouldn't take place until later on, when we weren't in the middle of Friday night Yaletown crowds.

Well, no, as we said goodbye in front of Tacofino, he leant down (there was a foot of height difference between us) and kissed me on the cheek, as if tentatively checking the response—then he went full in. A full on, tongue in, hands-on-the-face kiss. It caught me a little off guard, but Jesus! It was far from terrible and gave me total butterflies. My knees possibly went weak. It was a pretty perfect first kiss. He smiled, said goodbye, and continued walking past the restaurant. While trying to gather my composure, I turned to face the restaurant and saw Jillian standing about ten feet from where Original Persian and I had stood a moment ago. Oh, and she had taken a picture.

Initially, we just called him Persian, amending his nickname to Original Persian in later years, (OP for short) as the Persian count climbed. As it turned out, she'd walked behind us the whole way along the street, taking tons of pictures like a creeping paparazzo; but the kiss even caught her by surprise. Looking at the picture over dinner, I realised just how short I was compared to him. I barely made it to his big, brawny shoulder. As much as I love my independent, strong-woman demeanour, it can be nice to feel tiny with a big man to protect you.

OP ended up joining Jillian and me at the end of dinner. He did a great job of fending off all her questions before we headed back to his place, but not before meeting one of his best friends on the street. He'd spoken about how important his friends were to him, how he tried to surround himself with good men, mature men who were motivated but also in touch with their emotions. I liked that these were distinctions he made, that he understood "good men" weren't just guys he could have fun with, but that there was a sense of wanting to better themselves and each other.

Our first night together escalated real quick from just happy hour drinks, not least because I'd agreed to go back to his place (something I never did). There are arguments for and against whether it is safer, as a woman, to have someone come over to your apartment or to drop by theirs, but for me the bigger consideration was always simply a cleanliness and comfort thing. Plus, my place was usually most central—but in this instance, OP lived about six blocks from me, and part of me was actually interested in seeing his place. Let's just say the modern interior and cleanliness came as a relief. He asked me to dance with him in the living room, and as we navigated the height difference and I glossed over how cheesy it felt, I tried to work out whether this was a one-night thing or something that could grow legs.

Our chats over drinks had suggested the latter, but ending up in his apartment suggested the former. As a result, I was reluctant to sleep with him on that first night. Having read and heard far too many opinions about the need to abstain from sex to build a meaningful relationship, I was conflicted. Such had been my conviction that drinks wouldn't lead to anything more, at least that night, that I hadn't shaved my legs in preparation for our date. Still, I was finding that whenever I shaved my entire being to within an inch of life, no one even batted an eye at me. But on the nights when my legs were doing a good yeti impersonation? Oh yah, someone for sure would want to jump my bones. Maybe it had something to do with the way body hair catches sweat, which catches pheromones, which make me into a sex magnet. Or, maybe the universe was playing jokes on me, just to have a laugh.

We talked about having sex and we talked about not having sex; and, well, sex won out. Because I wanted it to—it was as simple as that. I had come to enjoy sex so much that if I was with someone who wanted to have sex with me and vice versa, it was beyond me as to why I wouldn't let myself have that. There was also the argument that, even if I'd wanted it to be more than just a one-night thing, was it not also important to make sure we were compatible sexually? That's how important sex had become to me. If I were to meet someone whom I clicked with in every way, but sexually we were misaligned, then I wouldn't pursue the relationship. I enjoyed sex far too much for it to remain just a functioning part of a relationship. I wanted it to be one of the most satisfying parts as well.

Thankfully, OP and I would have no problems in that department. The attraction was mutual and our bedroom preferences were very aligned. Thankfully, the height difficulties from earlier were easier to navigate in bed. As Laura always says, "We're all the same height lying down." But I have a P.S.A. for you all—showering with a 6'5" guy makes for some logistically awkward moments. Also some bloody cold moments, when he entirely blocks the water flow from reaching your skin.

In an escalation that made my dates with Canadian DJ seem tame, OP and I ended up seeing each other again on both Saturday and Sunday night. I attempted to put some distance between us, initially declining his offer to cook me dinner on the third night, not least because I like having my Sunday nights to prep for the week. But he said it was his way of apologizing for being so drunk the night beforehand. I hadn't thought he'd been that worse for the wear; I was just glad that it hadn't been me. Yet despite his want to cook for us on Sunday night, his beach day lasted a lot longer than planned. Dinner was getting later and later and my anxiety had me in a ball.

Apparently, my anxiety was obvious. As he got ready to shower, he asked why I seemed so reluctant to have dinner with him. I tried to explain my general preference for control and plans, and the fact that unexpected changes cause me anxiety, all while feeling very vulnerable sharing these deep-seated fears with someone I'd known for such a short period of time. He knelt down beside me as I was sitting on the sofa, towel wrapped around his waist, bare chest heaving, and said: "If anyone understands about anxiety, I get it. As a result of my [basketball] injuries, I suffered from depression and from that I developed anxiety, so I get where you're coming from. Just know I understand." Then he kissed me on the forehead. It was incredibly sweet and my heart skipped a beat. For being such a big, bullish guy, he was surprisingly sensitive and tender. And who doesn't love a forehead kiss?

Despite that, over a week later, we were coming up on our ninth day of seeing each other in a row since our first date, and I started to feel more than a little uncomfortable. Granted, we'd simply woken up with each other every morning, but it was still nine different days of seeing his penis. It scared the bejeesus out of me. With every date, every night of snuggling, every dinner, every incredible sex sesh, my feelings for him grew into something I wasn't sure I could control. And honestly, I like myself, but I'm not sure I'd choose to see myself for nine days straight, if I didn't have to, you know?

I told OP that my concern about things being so full on was that one of us (but I really meant him) would all of a sudden have a change of heart. What if he got freaked out and ran the other way? I told him that I just hoped there'd be a conversation rather than just a slow retreat. He agreed, claiming to be a much bigger fan of having difficult but necessary conversations, rather than people getting lost in their own heads and fucking things up by not communicating. Had he just recorded my own thoughts and played them back to me? It was like listening to *myself*.

But it sounded like his last relationship was a bit of a head fuck, with a serious lack of intimacy. I wasn't sure whether he'd fully come to terms with it yet. He was also coming off the tail end of a long injury, and dealing with the physical and mental effects of that experience was complicated, and included a constant intake of weed. He was building his business and despite surrounding himself with seemingly older friends and mentors, he was only twenty-six (did I not mention that? oops, my bad) and had already called himself unemotional. So, my expectations around anything blossoming in our relationship needed to be realistic. God, why did I need to have expectations at all?!

Also, up to this point, OP's actions hadn't entirely matched his words. He wanted to go slow, but we slept together on our first date. He claimed to be unemotional, but he'd been super open about his feelings (maybe that's different?). Since his actions were "better" than his spoken intentions, I wasn't complaining, but not complaining left me confused. I didn't want to hear one thing and wonder if he'd do something else. My head doesn't need to be messed with, and it wasn't a super pleasant reminder of how things with Filipeen had begun.

OP told me to get out of my head, claiming there was nothing to worry about and assuring me that my fears wouldn't be realised. He said: "I don't know what's going on. I never want to text someone as much as I do with you. I've been thinking about you so much during the day, and I don't know the last time I've spent this amount of time with someone.... But none of it feels weird with you. So I don't know what's happening but we'll figure it out." That same night, I met with Keith at Sunset Beach for a couple of beers, talking things through with him. He said something that he had said to me many times: "If the issue is that you don't think you deserve this sort of happiness, you do." Keith is the voice that I wish I could always use on myself—kind and forgiving. Was I self-sabotaging, though, or was it just realism?

With OP's "we'll figure it out" comment ringing in my head, I allowed myself to trust him. Things continued at the speed of a purebred racehorse, but after our tenth day of seeing each other, we physically weren't able to meet on Day Eleven. *Relief.* But I missed him. *See, I knew my feelings had gotten out of control.* We would fit in seeing each other between him working late and us both trying to prioritise workouts, so sleep was often forgone in an effort to spend time together. We even spent a day working from my bed together. He went to get us coffee while I took a call, and I made us breakfast while he dialed into a meeting. We went to the outdoor cinema in Stanley Park (another event I'd always wanted to enjoy on a date), and I was soaking up every moment.

Of course, since I was enjoying it so thoroughly, it had to break. It would crumble on its own, regardless of how grateful I felt for each moment. Similarly to Canadian DJ, it wasn't totally obvious at first, just enough of a palpable change that I knew something had shifted. But I couldn't say for sure that it was an attempt from him to end things. I so wanted it not to be that, so I gave him the benefit of the doubt. However, when I messaged to call him out for being MIA, I made it clear that I didn't want to deal with inconsistency. He couldn't go from being the *text-messenger* of the century (while always claiming that he hated texting) to essentially being completely silent for twenty-four hours.

Here's the thing with consistency of communication: I don't need 24/7 communication, but I do need 24/7 consistency. So if you only text me once every three days, that's fine, but keep doing that. If you text me once every hour (don't—I don't think anyone should text someone that much), then you better set your alarm to keep that shit going, or else I'll assume that you've died. Granted, that's an extreme example, but my point is: don't fuck with the consistency of communication. Yes, life happens. Yes, consistency is not always possible, but that's why it's important to know your limitations and not set unrealistic expectations. Numerous times already, I'd questioned OP about the likelihood of him maintaining the high bar he'd set, but he always insisted it wasn't a problem.

I spent the weekend at my adopted Canadian granny's house. I'd made some wonderful friends in Vancouver, and some of them had been kind enough to share their families. Jess wasn't just my former colleague (who'd since moved to New York) and the step-sister of Canadian DJ; she was now one of my closest friends. She'd also shared her wonderful grandmother, Carmelita, with me. If there were ever anyone I wanted to be when I grew up, it was Granny

Carmelita. She'd raised three girls by herself while becoming Canada's first female stockbroker, and now at eighty years old, she was one of the most vivacious and active woman I'd ever met.

Sitting at her patio table in the beautiful garden of her house in White Rock, summer in full bloom, I explained the OP situation to her. Afterward she said: "when you've explained to someone how inconsistency causes you anxiety, then you can't trust them when they become inconsistent and seem unconcerned for the anxiety, which they must know their actions are causing." Right there. *Bam*. If someone knows that what they're doing is causing you upset and still continues to do it, their intentions for you can't be good. It was so stark, so simple, and so right. I will never get enough of granny's wise words.

But here's where I differ from some people. For some, as soon as a new love interest backs away from them, they put up their own walls, turn the other way, and never look back. I, on the other hand, get right in amongst the shit pile and stir things up, as if I'm not done with things until I've tested them to the nth degree. Partly it's because I'm a hopeless optimist, praying that one day my gut will be wrong and someone will come running into my arms instead of backing away. I know the retort to that is: *Why would you want someone who wasn't sure about you?* Don't ask me; I'm all sorts of fucked up.

Also, if someone wants to end something with me, then I want them to say it. I want them to say the words (perhaps both for their discomfort and my closure). I'd rather be stabbed with a knife than slapped with a fish. *Does that even make sense?* No matter, I'm going with it. Like, if you're going to walk away from me, give me the brutally honest reason—don't just leave me hanging. After days of confusion, hot-and-cold environments, and one *are-you-up text* at three am, I finally got him on the phone the next day. He claimed to know that he'd been off; he'd been busy and things felt different. I was disappointed with the inconsistency and told him so, to which he apologised, saying he'd never wanted to let me down. Alas, he also knew that he didn't have space in his life for someone right now.

He didn't have space for someone in his life right now—the very thing that I'd asked him about a number of times, only to be promised that we'd figure it out. *Wow.* I guess what he meant by "we'd figure it out" was perhaps that he'd wait for the startling realisation that he couldn't make space for me while keeping up his great ghost impression, rather than actually talking to me about stuff, like he'd said he would.

To say I was disappointed is an understatement. Mostly, I was disappointed in myself. I knew that I shouldn't have allowed myself to get swept up, thus avoiding opening myself up to hurt again, because I knew things were going too fast. But he assured me; he said all the right things and convinced me that he wouldn't be leaving an OP-shaped hole in my life anytime soon. Four weeks later, I felt the hole.

Once again, the feeling of being cast adrift found a home in my heart. It had become the one thing I feared the most, the one thing I couldn't quell, for it caused me self-doubt like none other. Would any relationship ever work out? Would anyone ever live up to their promises? Was there something inherently wrong with me? I had more questions than answers and more concerns than confidences.

A while afterwards, a friend said to me: "You don't need to know why he did what he did, just know that it wasn't an accident." In struggling with the swiftness of our *zero-to-hundred-to-zero* journey, I couldn't discern what had happened on his end. What had changed in his mind? All I knew was my part and my feelings, from which I could learn, and I'd learnt enough to know that I couldn't do this anymore. Dating, perhaps, needed to take a backseat for a while.

Maybe I didn't agree with abstaining from sex to build lasting relationships, but I could see that rushing into things or seeing someone too much could have detrimental effects. Sometimes, however, this was one of my worst habits. In unpacking that less than desirable trait with a friend on a hike, I stumbled upon the fact that my want to rush into things stemmed from "losing" my husband. Not exactly surprising, I guess; at least it made sense. In a way, I thought that if you spent more time with someone, you'd be more likely to build something stable together—to lock them in, so to speak. But why would I want to "lock" someone in? Why shouldn't they make the choice to stay every day, of their own free will? Why did I feel like I had to rush into getting someone to commit in some way? As if any of it meant anything, anyways.... I'd seen with my husband, and my father, that even the most socially revered act of commitment, marriage, didn't stop men from leaving if they wanted to go.

Eighteen

When Is It My Turn?

OP had been coming and going from my bedroom, but summer brought a beautiful new group of girlfriends into my life. Serendipity is a wonderful thing. Inviting two friends who didn't know each other (one I'd met at kickboxing and the other through Damien) to the beach one day and having them each bring another friend, was a great idea. We gathered at Third Beach on the edge of Stanley Park as a group of five, building friendships that would span a number of beach days, nights out, hikes, and winter activities.

I always marveled at how varied my friend group was in Vancouver. It was one of my favourite things about the city: just how many places people had come from originally. Either directly, by moving here themselves, or indirectly, by their parents or grandparents moving here before them. For the first time, I found myself as the only white girl in our group. It was a novelty that wasn't lost on me (you know, that my whiteness was only novel in the face of their minority-in-numbers). I couldn't possibly understand the experience of being in their position, but I could get to know them and learn from their perspectives. The most beautiful part of diversity is what we can all learn from each other. Racism exists today because not all of us have learned how to *learn*, from the world and each other, and to embrace growth with every lesson, rather than fearing the unknown.

In Vancouver, I'd had the opportunity to see life through a slightly different cultural perspective, clearing a road in my mind along which to relearn certain things that I needed to teach myself in a new way. From a dating perspective, I was back in that place of not wanting anything serious but still going on dates, with varying degrees of success. *Success* simply meant someone I actually found engaging and hopefully good sex. Whitecaps Player, a twenty-eight-year-old Cameroonian who'd been traded to the local Vancouver MLS team from an American team, provided for a fun and casual arrangement for a few months, made incredibly convenient by him living just a few blocks away but less convenient by the language barrier. (Is it still a language barrier if it's because of a thick French African accent?) I would have liked to learn more about his country, his story, and how it was for him in North America, but we could hardly communicate about what he wanted to drink, realistically.

Around the same time, I got to know Alaskan Basketballer, which was an interesting lesson in dealing with someone with clear anger issues towards women. He was half-Black and half-Aboriginal, with a body frame that towered over me at 6'9". Eventually it felt safer to put some distance between us. His anger issues towards women were complex and probably systemic of his background, for he carried genes toyed with for generations by the otherwise white-faced Western World. On one side, he carried the imprint of slavery in America; on the other side, he carried the trauma of losing the freedom to celebrate his people's culture, beliefs, and their connection to the land and themselves.

To top it off, his issues were enmeshed in becoming a father at a young age, in what he called a "calculated move" by his ex-girlfriend. But he was also using his post-NBA career to inspire young men and Aboriginal youth, through talking about his personal and familial experiences with depression, abuse, alcoholism and toxic masculinity. He knew his issues were his responsibility, albeit not his fault, and he was attempting to resolve some of them for the next generation. I didn't need to be on the receiving end of his struggle to respect women, but I admired his dedication to his son, to himself, and to his people.

He was also the only Aboriginal guy I dated. Despite Vancouver's history, which still struggles not to be lost, I rarely saw any Aboriginal men on the apps. Otherwise, Vancouver's cultural and ethnic mosaic was fairly well displayed on the profiles of Tinder and Bumble. There were a lot of Asians, Persians, Europeans (I could pick the Brits and Irish out with my eyes closed), but barely any Aboriginal men. I won't pretend that I understand all the reasons for this. Was their consciousness just so far removed from mine that dating apps weren't a thing? The apps were full of White people, Asians, and Persians; I suppose that if the culture of your ancestors had been like a design on an etch-a-sketch for over 150 years, well, you might be hesitant to consider a long-term partnership with somebody "on the outside" of your culture. I don't know the answer, but I think it's important to think about sometimes.

Yes, perhaps online dating was yet another aspect of Western Civilization that didn't register as a lifestyle choice for the Aboriginal community—or perhaps we ought to consider that Aboriginal men are more often incarcerated in Canada for charges such as sexual assault (which meeting a stranger on Bumble could invite into your life); and Aboriginal women have a long and tragic history of being kidnapped, raped, and often killed. Even though my app preferences weren't set up to find women on the apps, maybe it was a vulnerable place for these women to be (simply type, "Missing and Murdered Indigenous Women and Girls" into Google, and history will answer all your questions).

I think this is important to acknowledge, because the oppression and violence faced by their people probably makes it harder to freely explore, or feel comfortable expressing, their sexuality in Vancouver. All this to say that the experiences I had were a privilege afforded to me by my cultural, national, and familial roots; even here on their unceded ancestral lands, space had been held for these aspects of who I am. The least I can do is point out that space still needs to be protected for them, too. We are blessed that their cultural history insists that protecting space for them means protecting space for the environment, because if we don't do both and fast, there will be no planet left for life to grow on.

As the weeks rolled by, I was simply going through the motions of life, with a lessening sense of satisfaction at work. I found myself becoming despondent again, which was poor timing with my trip to Palm Springs, where Jaime's wedding celebration was happening. The wedding was sure to be beautiful, and I was excited for my first trip to Palm Springs, but as with the bachelorette, I felt like I didn't fully belong to this group of girls anymore. By this time, I was entirely comfortable going to events without a plus one (alas, no one to be my sidekick); but trips like those, particularly for weddings, always bring up a sense of *I wish I had someone*. Laura and Sam were going, but it wasn't their job to always include me in their plans, so I travelled by myself. I shared a room with one of the girls at the wedding hotel and enjoyed a stunning celebration of a picture-perfect couple. Plus, any reception that serves In-N-Out Burger is always a winner.

However…let's just come out and say it: weddings are tough. Or maybe it's not even weddings but simply celebrating love. I still believe in love. I know it can happen, but there's a sense of pessimism I have around weddings that I just can't shake. On top of my own experiences, by then I'd seen relationships breakdown between some of my closest "people." It's hard to not be affected by it. Life just seems so unpredictable, so chock-full of cruelty, so how can you trust it? How does anyone ever know that making things work with somebody forever is even possible, given that as individuals we have no *real* control over the actions, needs, or choices of our partners?

Sure, we can *try* to establish control over our relationships, but there is no god powerful enough to take away our free will in relationships and our lives on earth. Marriage is just one of the ways that our societal systems encourage us to try to asset control over our partnerships; and it's an honourable thing to create a home for children and provide them with consistency as care-giver. All the same, so many parents aren't able to offer this consistency of love and attention anyways; perhaps they never had the time to give these things to themselves; and perhaps they would have figured it all out for the better soon enough, if they hadn't "tied the knot" before learning to untie their shadow from themselves. Our relationship systems are broken, which is just a symptom of what's broken in our grander political, societal, and economic systems, so I say fuck the system (but wear a condom, dear reader, or the system will just birth itself some new babies to abandon again).

The recurring theme in every relationship breakdown is problems arising from underlying personal or familial issues that go unresolved, uncommunicated or unidentified and ultimately make the partnership untenable. This was the case in my marriage, and from what my father told me, the same applied for him and my mum. By then, my best friend and my brother's marriages had also both broken down with similar undertones. Always it creates complete devastation. It ruins people's lives and could ruin their futures. Having said that, in both of those situations, their abilities to co-parent despite the devastation has been inspiring to watch. Whenever I have discussions with anyone going through those situations, my advice is always the same: *therapy*.

I wondered about a world where relationships were allowed to stop and start as they so pleased, but this reality was complicated by our feelings and the possibility of one day throwing children into the mix. Vancouver certainly had its share of polyamorous cells, but the cells were not mainstream and of course it's harder to manage multiple relationships at a time than just one. I was already living a polyamorous lifestyle, in a way, but I craved the connection that came from a committed relationship. So, while I wondered about the birth of a world where maybe, one day, we could have a bit of both, I wasn't sure how that world would come to be. Maybe, like so many things, the change would happen slowly, in the wake of a rupture that insists upon the new.

That year, going home to Edinburgh for Christmas was unsettling. I'd just started a new job at the beginning of December, at another tech company. I'd said goodbye to Don, my Canadian Hockey Dad boss, and I'd taken the new job knowing that it was a huge step up in what it would require from me. I'd gotten comfortable in my last job and kind of worked myself out of the role, what with all the hires and systems I had implemented. It was time to go, but leaving the comfort of one position for something new felt scary. It ate up a lot of brainpower, practically unleashing an entire army of Pac-Men into my prefrontal cortex. No joke, I'd taken to giving myself pep talks.

It was another time in my life when I would have loved to share my decision with someone, to bounce my ideas off them, talk things through, debate things out. Of course, my friends were super supportive, and my mum and brother were always rational and pragmatic, but it's not the same as sharing things with a partner. I couldn't help but kick myself for not feeling more comfortable making big decisions alone by now. Ultimately, if I didn't take the job, it would've been out of fear, and I don't think decisions should ever be made from that emotion. With the new job, I'd still be working in sales and marketing operations, but on a whole new level, and I knew that pushing myself was exactly what I needed. Building my life and career were good things, even if it meant enduring change.

Despite the changes I'd gone through recently, I still wasn't a massive fan of the phenomenon. To make things worse, just as I was getting started in my new role, it was time to go home for the Holidays; and back at home, I was dealing with even more changes to what I'd always known, due to those aforementioned marriage breakdowns. My best friend Lisa was no longer with her husband, and my brother was using Christmas to introduce his new girlfriend to our family. Both situations triggered me in slightly different ways: one triggered something that happened in my past (divorce), and the other triggered things that I was dealing with at present (new partners).

Lisa's situation made my heart ache, for her and her daughter. Seeing her struggle with this new reality brought back memories of when I'd been in the same place—that same dark alien hole, from which you wonder if you'll ever rise. I found myself uttering clichés in an attempt to explain the inexplicable to her, because there was no manual, no instructions, no timeline, no escape route. I toyed with not telling her anything at all, because everyone's experience is different; and I didn't see "here I am, over three years later, still struggling" as an inspirational story. Moreover, I hadn't endured my trauma with a child in the mix, so I didn't feel like I had a whole lot of advice to offer my friend.

Meanwhile, with my brother, although I hadn't personally witnessed the end of his marriage, even from afar, I had been devastated to know that he and my sister-in-law were going through the inevitable trauma of separation. Now, here he was, introducing his new girlfriend to our family. While I was pleased that this new relationship eased the hurt and depression from his separation, I was equally concerned that he'd rushed into things too quickly, without fully acknowledging the residual issues. More than anything, I was stunned that he'd found his way into this new relationship so fast at all (mostly because I was still the epitome of single).

I'm aware that comparing lives is never a good use of energy, especially not when it comes to siblings, but the difference between me and him was stark. I hadn't anticipated that it would hit me like that. On Christmas morning, as we exchanged gifts, I realised how much time had passed since someone special bought me a Christmas gift. Of course, I have friends with whom I exchange thoughtful and fun gifts, but the gift is not what I missed—it's what the gift signifies. I missed those memories of past Christmas mornings, spent in the same living room with the same fire burning, as my brother, his wife, my ex-husband, my mum, and I shared Christmas morning in our element. Things had changed almost beyond all recognition, save for the big over-stuffed sofas. Would I ever have someone special to buy gifts for again? When would I have someone to bring home at Christmas and introduce to the family? Why did it feel like not having those things made me a failure?

I became so over-emotional about the situation on that Christmas morning that I had to take myself back to bed, citing jet lag and my cold, which I was now developing on every trip home. As my family made their way outside to watch my niece ride her new bike, all I could do was climb back into bed and stifle the tears with my duvet. Otherwise I would've had a Christmas day

meltdown in front of everyone. As we all filtered out of the living room—
me to my bedroom, as everyone else went outside—my Auntie C (having a
sixth sense) squeezed my arm and whispered a word in my ear about smiling
through it. She knew it was shit for me, and I love her for that. She doesn't try
to fix nor justify things; she just calls out the crappiness of the situation.

That there was even a tiny amount of jealousy mixed in with my overriding
sadness made me feel like a shit human being. Who wants to be jealous of
somebody else's life? Who wants to let whatever they don't have override their
ability to appreciate what they *do* have? My family was together, and I could
have been out enjoying the time with them, but instead my heart was breaking
in bed. Reticent that my aunt had picked up on my feelings, I felt a duty to
be happy for my family. Knowing how awful everyone felt about what had
happened in my marriage, I wanted to prove that they didn't need to worry
about me anymore—that the life I'd chosen and was building for myself, the
one I'd left them behind to embrace, was the right thing for me. I didn't want
to be a burden nor pitied, but it was another hard trip home. Once again, I
was glad to be getting on a plane back to Vancouver.

It would be some time before I chose to go home for Christmas again;
and that decision came with its own guilty feelings. Wow, I was just carrying
around *all* the guilt and shame.... (Clearly, I had a few too many outfits in
that style.) So, I did the only thing that I could when I got back to Vancouver:
I rang in the New Year blackout drunk, alongside one of my favourite new
friends, Priscilla. With most of my Vancouver friends now in relationships, I
was delighted when a mutual friend introduced Priscilla and me. As one of
my few single friends, she understood the trials and tribulations of dating in
Vancouver. Not that she was actually dating (she had the good sense to avoid
the apps, at that point), but having someone who got it was a blessing.

She was also divorced and there's something about being divorced that
bonds women together. You've both been in the trenches and you know it, so
there's a shared sense of experience, even though the experiences themselves
are different. Divorce, in and of itself, is the kind of trauma that cannot be
understood without going through it. None of my friends were divorced (that
I knew of) while I was going through my own divorce, and I found solace
in my friendship with Priscilla. So much was understood between us, even
though it went unspoken with actual words.

That said, I wasn't so grateful for waking up on the first of January with a twenty-seven-year-old Irish guy in my bed. He'd been messaging me on and off since we'd matched on Tinder a few months ago. Waking up beside him that morning, it was clear that I was attempting to patch up parts of my life that were still broken with alcohol and men. It was a classic crutch combo. As I tried to find ways to break or understand the cycle, or at least identify the source of my decisions, I decided to start documenting the dating stories I'd been sharing for a wider audience. People often told me: *you should write a book,* upon hearing about my absurd, hysterical, and painful dating experiences.

I figured the writing could be cathartic for me, and I'd actually be creating something out of the dates, given that a lasting relationship didn't seem forthcoming. I joined a program called Damn Early Days (DED), where for twenty-one weekdays, I pledged to get up at some insanely early hour to work on something I'd otherwise been putting off—a project that I hadn't the time or perhaps the focus to accomplish. I chose to start my dating blog.

The program was run by a group called Chasing Sunrise. Primarily, they were people who did stuff in the outdoors, including some incredible hikes and seriously nutty road trips (Vancouver to Mexico, just for the weekend to eat tacos, anyone?) I'd watched from afar for about a year, always too intimidated to sign up for one of the hikes and definitely nowhere brave enough for the road trips.

Along with the DED program's early morning wake ups (and therefore time dedicated to writing), they also hosted Real Talks, early morning coffee meet ups covering topics like: "Why is it so hard for us to follow what we really want in life?" *Woah.* Chill, it's six am. I went to my first one presuming that just a few people would be there; we'd be spoken to by the guys that ran the program, and I could just slink into the background. I'd take what I needed and head to work at eight am, already having had a new experience. What I didn't anticipate was that the coffee shop in Mount Pleasant, Milano Coffee Roasters, had opened at half past five *just* for us; and it was full of twenty to thirty people, all ready to bare their soul before the sun even rose on that cold, dark January morning.

We talked about challenges and false narratives, along with why we had signed up for DED. We shared where our fears came from and what success could look like. There were frustrations and tears (not mine, at least not on this first occasion) and this deep level of vulnerability, which people stepped into because of the safe space created for them, in this innocuous coffee house at the beginning of a new year. It was a truly liberating experience; and as I drove back downtown to work that morning, I actually *whooped* aloud halfway across Cambie Bridge.

I'd come a long way from that conference room in the Pinnacle Hotel, on one of my first weekends in Vancouver. There, a coaching course had resulted in a dissociative experience as people revealed some of their innermost thoughts to me. Instead, this felt like somewhere I should be, with people who were grappling for something more like me, something different, something to help them feel more whole every day on their own. Until I found that something, alcohol and men were still very much my Band-Aid of choice, and both were in full flow that March.

During the Rugby Sevens weekend, I again ended up with an Irish guy in my bed, who was far too excited (given the number of love bites he left on my skin). Shortly thereafter, Malaysian Persuasion popped up and we went back to my place. It seemed like we hadn't fully quit each other, and Instagram is terrible when location tags reveal that you're both in the same place at the same time. The same familiarity existed with our sexual connection. Jesus, did it ever make me realise how much everyone else had paled in comparison. But it would only be a one-night thing and with that came resignation. I still wasn't exactly making one-hundred percent good decisions, but this was a thread I didn't want to pull.

The week following the Sevens, once I'd caught up on sleep and my love bites had died down, I arranged to meet a guy I'd matched with during the weekend. We hadn't had time to connect as I was "otherwise engaged." As Damien and I walked back from a night at the climbing gym (another item checked off our annual bucket list), I told him about the guy I was going on a date with and found myself saying: "I don't really know why I'm going."

In one of our earliest message exchanges, he'd agreed with something I'd said and added: "Well, now you can have my number." I disliked how he'd made it sound as if I were privileged to get it, but I'd started to over-analyse little things that guys said in app messages, in an effort to weed out the *fuck boys* early. So, I let it go, figuring that if he wanted to take me to dinner, why not let him. *Like, come on, Lou: take the free meal.*

He was Italian Lebanese (which became the entirety of his nickname), twenty-six years old, and an engineer. What was it with guys in their mid-twenties? I wasn't explicitly discounting anyone my age nor older, but I was always finding myself matching and chatting with men at least four years younger than me. He was E.S.L. (English as a Second Language) and from our messaging, I'd say that he was quirky. Like, he'd mentioned something about Lola in one of our messages, which he thought was a nickname for Louise. To him, I would forever be Lola. His quirkiness was confirmed when he texted me to say that I could find him in the dried fruit-and-nuts shop next to the tapas restaurant, where we were meeting on Denman Street—and did I want any nuts? *Was that like a Lebanese dating ritual? Who would ask that before a first date?!* I laughed, figuring that at least I wouldn't be bored.

He was dark-skinned and very well put together. He clearly liked nice clothes and visible labels, and he took pride in his appearance. The importance of physical appearance didn't just finish with himself, however; it extended to his partners, with him commenting on my eyebrows as we enjoyed patatas bravas. *Um, what?* I've never had a guy comment on my eyebrows, at least not a straight guy. If anything, I was feeling more self-conscious than pleased about meeting his eyebrow standards.

I left our first date not at all sure how I felt, but given that I'd gone in thinking I would just go through the motions and get it ticked off the list (wow, what a great mindset that was), I was more interested than I'd expected. Interested enough that we went on a few more dates, building up to sleeping with each other on our fourth date. For the first time, at least with someone with whom I'd felt things could go somewhere, the sex was less than satisfying. It was hard not to make comparisons to some of the other great experiences I'd had by then. But he made the comment that it takes him a while to reach a full level of comfort when sleeping with someone, so he felt that the first time was a good foundation for us to build on.

Unfortunately, I didn't entirely share that outlook. I need to feel as if it's at least good and can get to great, but I wasn't even sure if it met that first most basic level. I was also concerned and slightly offended by his firm stance on finding oral (on women) and anal sex dirty. He put it down to his own germaphobe OCD which had plagued his childhood, although it was now better managed. Still, not well managed enough for him to think those particular acts of intimacy were anything other than repulsive to him. Looking back, I should have seen this as a red flag, but I'd possibly been putting too much emphasis on sex lately. Letting it be a deterrent for what could otherwise have been a fulfilling relationship was maybe churlish, despite knowing my need for good, plentiful and aligned sex.

Other than the sex issues, he was kind and chivalrous, motivated towards his career and education, a good communicator, interested and interesting. After a month of dates, he asked me out to dinner to chat about something. I thought it might be about the date he'd bailed on a week beforehand, and our lack of communication while I was in Whistler for the weekend with friends. Instead, after some surface-level chat over appetisers, once the main course of pizza and pasta had arrived, he started by telling me about this girl he kept seeing in Whole Foods who had asked him out on a date two days earlier. He told me that she was funny and chatty and pretty. So, naturally, in my head I'm thinking, *Did you bring me to this Italian restaurant just to tell me you fucked a girl from Whole Foods?*

I sat silently as he said, "But it wasn't just that I didn't want to go on a date with her. I realised that the only person I want to go on dates with is you." He proceeded to say how proud he'd be to take me to a work event; I was independent, successful, driven, healthy, motivated, disciplined—everything he wanted to be and everything he was looking for in a partner. He finished by saying, "So I wanted to know if you'd be my girlfriend?"

Still I sat silently. In part because I'd been expecting another outcome entirely; but I'd also never had someone say those sorts of things to me, not since my ex-husband proposed on that fateful night in Dublin. It was slightly overwhelming to hear but incredibly lovely. To have someone so clearly express their feelings, albeit starting with a weird story about another girl, was not something I was used to these days. Eventually I stuttered a yes, but not before he had to ask me twice. It didn't feel one hundred percent right, but I knew that relationships took work. If he was willing to make that kind of a statement then it was worth exploring. *Was this the best way to enter into a relationship?* Maybe not, but life was a highway and I was looking at a big **Begin One Way** sign.

A few weeks later, my mum came out for her annual visit. It still felt kind of early to introduce Italian Lebanese to her, but if they didn't meet while she was there, it would likely be another year before the opportunity came up again. A year felt like a long time if he ended up becoming an important part of my life. So I bit the bullet and they met over happy hour after work one day. As I knew would be the case, he charmed the pants off my mum, while we enjoyed gin and tonics on the patio of the Yaletown Distillery. She commented afterwards that he reminded her a lot of a Lebanese family friend we had back home, who is also funny and irreverent and a complete gentleman.

A few nights later, the three of us attended my friend Brianna's thirtieth birthday. I played designated driver while they enjoyed bonding at the open bar. All the same, as Mum and I started our road trip the following morning, this time to BC's wine region in the Okanagan, I mused about being unsure of whether Italian Lebanese and I aligned entirely on world views. I am aware that there are couples in the world whose politics don't match, but as long as there's space for mutual respect despite the differing views, compatibility is possible. However, what I was struggling with that day was knowing whether it wasn't so much the things we didn't align on but the way in which we communicated those views.

For example, on meeting Charms and her newborn baby (she said something about allowing him to have dolls and wear a skirt if he wanted), Italian Lebanese felt it was appropriate to question why she would force gender neutrality on her child. While initially I put his almost aggressive tact down to his ESL, this was likely more of a hopeful excuse than a genuine belief. In that moment, his views on gender issues weren't really my concern. It was more the fact that he'd felt it appropriate to bring something like that up, just after meeting one of my friends, to question her choices about how to raise her own child. *Weren't we all supposed to be on our best behaviour when meeting the friends? And so it's probably best not to rail in on their life views and choices?* Thankfully, Charms loves a good debate as much as she loves dancing on the kickboxing mat. She went toe to toe with him, appearing entirely unphased when she left, but to say I was embarrassed and uncomfortable was an understatement.

If my problem on that occasion was his communication style, the next occurrence was definitely more based on content. Walking home one night after drinks, he made the comment when hearing someone playing Bhangra music in their car that, "People should leave [those cultural influences] where they came from." Again, I thought the ESL thing could have made the comment sound more aggressive, or essentially racist, than intended. But the conversation continued on the walk home and seemingly for an age back in my apartment. It went from cultural references to religious practices, and we got to the point where he essentially told me, in English that did not sound mistranslated, that anyone who had any religious belief or outward religious expression (wearing a turban or a cross, for example) was only one step away from fundamentalism. *Um, I'm sorry, what now?*

Now, I am aware and agree that religion is the source of many of the world's problems, and I myself am not what I'd consider religious. However, even I could concede that simply having a belief in religion and expressing it in whatever way someone might want did not directly make someone an extremist. An extremist is someone who expresses a belief in a way that hurts or invalidates another person or group of people. I argued that both of us, as immigrants to Canada, should be grateful of this country's cultural mosaic and the welcome that they extend to people of all cultures and religions. He, however, believed that if people want to live with parts of their culture or religion still intact, those people should go back to where they came from—a viewpoint that ignores the reality that so many immigrants are actually refugees, with no country to return to right now.

I had been stunned to the point of asking him to leave my apartment that night. I was leaving for a work trip the next day, to New York and Boston, and while I'd been looking forward to spending my last night at home with Italian Lebanese, I was so turned off by his views that I actually felt sick to my stomach. Not to mention his demeanour toward me while expressing them—I was apparently too liberal, with the inability to have a constructive debate. Really, I just needed time to process things, and for him to be far away from me.

But now, discussing these things with my mum on our four-hour drive to Kelowna weeks later, I heard what was off in everything I was saying. The gap was far too wide to be bridged. I wondered aloud if we could live with differing views, but what he believed was so fundamentally against what I believed that I questioned him as a person. Did that make me judgmental? Should I be accepting of his views, even if they weren't my own? As we continued to discuss it, I told my mum that there were plenty of things that I thought would get in the way of me having or staying in a relationship, but this wasn't one that I'd considered. Not only were we completely opposed on certain things, but I'd been on edge whenever he interacted with my friends, for fear that he'd voice his entirely-not-shared-by-me views. The last part was not something I could live with for long.

Despite knowing those things, I was still unsure what to do about the problem. I was leaving for another work trip as soon as my mum went home, this time to Montreal, and I got a speculative "how are you doing" message from Hot Doctor while across the country. In fact, I'd also received one in New York, but I hadn't even entertained it. I had a boyfriend—boundaries and respect were my utmost priority. But getting that second one with all of the other uncertainties about the relationship swirling in my head, I indulged in it for a second longer than I should have. I replied to it without shutting it down instantly, which told me everything I needed to know about where I was at personally in my relationship.

I resolved to make a change, but this was complicated by it being my birthday that Friday. I'd be flying home from Montreal on the Saturday, for dinner with Italian Lebanese and brunch with him and friends on the Sunday. My decision to end things was reaffirmed when he not only neglected to acknowledge my birthday from across the country on the actual day but was then late picking me up from the airport. I know this is where I start to sound like a super high-maintenance girlfriend, but I truly don't think I am... *Though isn't that what we all think?*

Maybe we should stop talking about how we qualify people (and when I say "people", we know it's usually mostly women) as "maintenance" at all. A house is high-maintenance if it constantly needs repairs (or maybe has ghosts or something), yet women get called high maintenance for a whole swath of other reasons, which have nothing to do with needing repairs or being haunted! If high-maintenance is hoping that your boyfriend will wish you a happy birthday or enjoying being picked up at the airport with heavy luggage, then fine, I'm high-maintenance and proud.

The birthday thing was weird. At eight pm on my birthday, as I sat at dinner in Montreal with Kim, my work colleague and friend, I asked him over text if he was planning to wish me a happy birthday. He said it "didn't count" because I'd chosen to spend my birthday away from him. Apparently he didn't celebrate birthdays anyways, but he said we'd celebrate when I came home tomorrow. *Okay, gee, thanks for the sacrifice?* That didn't sit well with me at all. I love birthdays and I'm not afraid to say that I love being celebrated, even if it's from afar. Also, it was a work trip. It wasn't like I'd actively decided against being with him on my birthday. I was still perturbed by the whole thing when, the following day, he was late to meet me at the airport.

It wouldn't have been a problem if he hadn't lost his license after a DUI anyways and thus wasn't driving to get me—hence I could have easily jumped on the SkyTrain without waiting for him. Additionally, I'd dreamed of being met at the airport by someone since moving to Vancouver. At some point, I would be flying back into YVR and someone would be there to meet me (as if that would be a significant development in my new life). This was the first time that could have happened and it got spoiled because he was late. Instead we met on the SkyTrain platform, in amongst crowds emptying and refilling the train, and what might have been a lovely moment just wasn't lovely at all.

Just before Italian Lebanese arrived, I also received my annual "happy birthday" email from my dad. He'd started sending them after I'd gotten back in touch with him, despite me explicitly saying that it wasn't about restarting our relationship. Also, I got it the day after my birthday, because he'd been "playing golf and it had slipped [his] mind."

Men. Fucking men. Honestly, don't rely on them for anything. *What was the point? Why was I even surprised?* They were all fucking useless and never did what they said. I don't have these thoughts often, because ultimately, I know they're not true. But in that moment, it was all I could do not to push all the male SkyTrain passengers off the platform. Fucking *men.*

I pushed back the tears as Italian Lebanese got off the train with a bunch of flowers (no, they didn't make up for the lateness) and kept my feelings at bay at dinner that night. The restaurant wasn't exactly downtown, which he hadn't factored in and thus I had to drive. I was still blinking back tears when he told me, the following morning, that he'd have to go home before my brunch, because he'd forgotten new clothes for the day. Thus he wouldn't be able to help me set up. (I was hosting.)

Again, I might sound like a high-maintenance bitch, but I wasn't just looking for someone to pick me up, drive me places, and help me with stuff; it was my birthday, and everything feels bigger and more emotional on your birthday, but the fact that he wasn't helping out in a helpful way irked me beyond control. The flowers, the dinner, and him coming to brunch to meet my friends were all lovely things. But ultimately, it's being in the trenches with someone, doing the mundane and helping with shit—that's what I'm looking for in a partner. When it comes to Love Languages, *acts of service* are pretty high up there for me, and that's despite me thinking I'm so independent. Essentially, I need someone who can spot when I'm struggling and offer me help, but I also need to get better about being explicit in my needs.

Up until this point, I hadn't confided in my friends about my concerns, possibly because I was embarrassed to reveal his extreme views. Maybe more importantly, I knew what their advice would be: *He's not right for you.* When one of my girlfriends arrived to help with brunch setup after a last-minute SOS text from me, I unloaded everything on her, and it became even clearer that I needed to deal with things. First things first, however, and first things meant getting through brunch—which we did (albeit with him spending an inordinate amount of time outside on his phone, and leaving early when he suddenly had a meeting out of the blue. On a Sunday, for a side business he'd never told me anything about. *Like, oka-a-a-a-a-y...*

We finally had time to catch up together a week later. In my apartment, I told him that I couldn't do it anymore; certain things weren't working for me and they outnumbered the things that were. I didn't go into our opposing views, and perhaps it was cowardly of me not to bring that up, being as it were a prominent reason for my decision—but I didn't think we could have a constructive conversation about it. To be honest, his beliefs were kind of nonsensical; they didn't seem like religious or spiritual or political beliefs but rather personal or egoic inclinations. Presumably, I'd again be told that I was too liberal, or somehow unwilling to hear viewpoints that were different from my own (which is actually the *opposite* of being liberal, but we have Jordan Petersen to thank for *being the kettle that calls* compassion, change, and understanding *black*).

It seemed like Italian Lebanese had no idea how his expression on certain issues had bothered me. Instead, he asked me whether I thought he'd been cheating on me, when actually he'd been so busy with work. I instantly replied that cheating had never crossed my mind (though of course, now I wondered). But that had been a massive sense of relief: despite that things weren't working between us, I'd managed to trust him. Trust, in that way, is not something I'd expected to ever experience again. I'd never second guessed what he was doing or with whom, nor did I have any hint of a nagging feeling that he was dishonest in any way.

I knew I was doing the right thing, but with that realisation came the momentary threat of tears. In his inimitable ESL way, to which I'd become so accustomed, he said "don't drop tears," as if somehow I could just pick them up and put them back in my leaky eyes. I wished so much that this were the case; wouldn't life be so much easier if we could do that? Then he told me that I was hoping for perfection and would never find it—and that dried those tears up real quick.

Was I hoping for perfection? I mean, if anything, the bar was set pretty low at that point. I was settling for breadcrumbs from attractive men, meaningless sex, and relationships with people whose values and morals didn't align with mine. If I had been looking for perfection, I definitely wasn't finding it. But joking aside, I don't think my head was in the clouds with images of Prince Charming entering my life and making everything better. But if by perfection he meant respect, alignment, communication, compatibility, loyalty and consistency, then yes, I was looking for that. Truly, I believed that I would find it—maybe not from nowhere, but if I'd already found those things inside myself, surely the world was big enough for me to find them in someone else as well.

All the same, I cried because the relationship I'd wanted had felt so close. Feeling secure with someone, as if he weren't out looking for something/someone else, was a sensation that I hadn't experienced in a long time. In that regard, and despite our gaping differences, Italian Lebanese was a blessing; and sometimes even blessings arrive in the disguise of difficult lessons. That is how much the energy surrounding us longs for us to grow and succeed and learn to love in ways that the world can learn from in turn—because that is how love really works. But I don't mean love, but Love, the kind you have to lose yourself in, be it in the world or art or other people, in order to grow from and learn.

Nineteen

Return to the Middle East (But Not Actually)

Coming off the tail end of turning thirty-three, I'd ended things with Italian Lebanese and begun writing regularly for my dating blog. After attending a bunch more early-morning Real Talks, I'd cried with a bunch of strangers on the beach and had my first sunrise ocean swim when summer started. It felt like another season of change. Damien and Sara were now properly back together, so our friendship felt like it had shifted a little and I wasn't sure what I should be doing; but incrementally, things felt like they were moving in the right direction, whatever direction that was.

I'd made a point of befriending Sara when she and Damien finally rekindled their relationship. Much in the same way that I hadn't wanted Filipeen concerned about my relationship with Damien, I didn't want Sara to wonder about it either. She and I had met the same night I'd first met Damien, back when they were still together, but they broke up soon afterwards. In the time since, Damien had become one of my closest friends. I wouldn't have blamed her for possibly thinking, *Who is this bitch?!* So I knew that if I wanted to remain friends with Damien, it was important that she and I also had a solid friendship. Also because, when it comes to things like this, men are dense, as proven by Damien's proclamation while we were planning a camping trip that, "I'm sure she won't mind if we share a tent." *Yah, okay buddy.*

After Damien and I completed the Vancouver Sun Run—an annual ten kilometre race through the city on each Sunday each April, with far too many people running in close proximity—we met up with Sara and some friends for brunch. At the time, I was still dating Italian Lebanese, but when Sara turned up with a dark-bearded friend of hers, who was hot and seemed like a fun guy, I briefly wondered why she hadn't introduced us when I was single. But I didn't dwell on it and instead went back to ensuring that Italian Lebanese wasn't spouting anything remotely offensive, all while some of my most socially-aware friends sat further down the table.

Fast forward a few months and I'm back on the online-dating apps. On Bumble, I happened to come across said hot, dark-bearded guy. Now that I didn't have to worry about an offensive boyfriend, I was much more aware of how attractive this familiar twenty-seven-year-old Persian really was. Not least, one of his pics in which he was bare chested on a sunny day by a lake. We matched, and I started the conversation by asking if we should tell Sara, to which he replied almost instantly by saying, "That's the million-dollar question. She'd probably tell you to run a mile." Well, at least Mutual Friend was honest.

Very quickly, he began testing my boundaries in our messages, after getting flirty on our first night of messaging and calling me at one am on his way home from work. The next day, he said that I didn't have the balls to go through with meeting him. He was right, I didn't have the balls; I had the ovaries and honestly lunchtime sex is never off the table. So, in less than twenty-four hours from when we matched, we were meeting up at my apartment.

This was by far the quickest escalation I'd ever experienced, and I knew no good could come of it. My readiness to ditch my lunch plans and meet up for sex, with someone who was essentially a stranger, was marginally frightening. Although the stranger piece was less concerning because I knew that Sara was good friends with him. How bad could he be? Plus, I'd had great sex on previous spontaneous occasions like this. We'd made a deal to limit what we did, as if somehow that meant respecting each other's emotional boundaries. Most people are like, "maybe we'll kiss on the first date, but no sex"; and we were like, "ok, we'll do everything but full penetration." Where had this girl come from? *How had I gotten here?* There was almost an inevitability about it all—like *of course we were going to do that*, like *why bother with a date, that will come later.* Which it did, with brunch that weekend at Juke Fried Chicken in Gastown. Had the attraction started over that first brunch with our friends? Was this whole affair somehow predetermined while I was still with Italian Lebanese?

We didn't tell anyone about it at first. We thought it'd be fun to secretly hook up with no one knowing, until one Saturday at Kitsilano Beach, in a neighbourhood named after the Aboriginal Squamish Nation Chief, August Jack Khatsahlano, where Mutual Friend lived, we both ended up hanging out in the same group of people, including Sara and Damien. What had felt like a fun secret suddenly became a lesson in emotions boiling over. I wasn't sure if it was my fault or his, but it was certainly one big drama fest.

First, he accused me of ignoring him via text, as we sat opposite each other in our group. Then I accused him of disrespecting me when he introduced a girl to the group, introducing me last and saying, "Oh her? Umm, whatever, just call her Bob." When I texted him to question it, he unleashed all hell on me, telling me that I wasn't special and if I was going to get jealous then I should have stayed away. None of this was helped by the copious amounts of alcohol we'd consumed in the summer sun. But why did he want to make me feel like shit? Why was he testing me like that?

I decided that I had to get it out my system before I screamed in his face and interrupted everyone's sunny drinking session—so I took Damien away from the group and told him that I'd been sleeping with Mutual Friend for a while but now he was being a total dickhead. The look Damien gave me was a mix of *why him?!* and *I'm not surprised.* Damien never tries to hide his condemnation of my choices and this time was no different. But he did offer a solution and suggested that we leave the beach, with Sara and her friend Alana, to find dinner instead.

As we were attempting to leave, Mutual Friend decided that he actually didn't hate me anymore and wanted to come along. *Hello,* mood swings. Cue a super awkward dinner of me being confused as shit by what happened that afternoon, Damien knowing more than anyone else (quietly loving it and hating it at the same time), Mutual Friend not knowing that Damien knew anything, and Sara and Alana having no idea that Mutual Friend was feeling me up under the dinner table.

Things would continue to be complex with Mutual Friend, never knowing if he was coming or going, or if I was, which I mean with regard to how much space we held for each other. (Although there's also a pun here! Our sex life had always been great, so it was more of the former, less of the latter.) But it felt a little too much like Malaysian Persuasion, this instant sexual compatibility. No matter how pissed off one of us got with the other, the sex was always phenomenal and we rarely (if ever) could turn down the orgasms. The attraction between us seemed to overcome however much we each triggered the other. We didn't date per se, instead we'd mostly spend time watching movies (yes, this was one of the few times I watched movies), watching him lose at playing video games and eating at his apartment in Kitsilano. The beachside neighbourhood had laid back vibes and stunning mountain views; it was the very neighbourhood Sara was leaving to move in with Damien. While it was never a healthy relationship between Mutual Friend and me, there was something that kept me going back to him. I just couldn't put my finger on what it was.

Around the same time that I started seeing Mutual Friend, I'd matched with another dark-bearded guy, who was also twenty-seven and also Persian, although it was on Tinder and we didn't have a friend in common. But still, a little too similar? I'd find out that he lived a block from where I worked, in addition to working as a lawyer two blocks from where I lived. *Convenient.* Persian Lawyer was everything Mutual Friend was not. He was professional, reserved, and mature. Unlike with Mutual Friend, Persian Lawyer and I had a much slower start to things, messaging back and forth for a week before we found matching breaks in our schedules. By then, we'd bonded over the Euro 2018 Football Tournament, our love of working out, and being morning people.

Upon arranging to meet, I worried it'd be one of those times when everything was great via text and then you meet in person and it's not. Those moments were always so disappointing. Like, why is it so hard for life on the screen to be translated into real life? He'd also had the type of profile pics that could have gone either way in reality, either really attractive or just a couple of good angles. Fortunately, meeting for drinks at the bar of Earls right by his apartment building, my concerns about physical attraction were instantly calmed. All I needed was one glimpse of him in his all black Blue Jays baseball cap and matching black sweater. Jesus, he was hot, in a half nerdy/half frat boy way. And what was it about dark men with beards? Maybe I was starting to have a type....

Our easy breezy messaging also translated perfectly into real life and the date flew by. It felt like both of us could have continued talking, if only we didn't have early mornings waiting for us. Being a gentleman, and acknowledging that he chosen a place for drinks that was more convenient for him than me, he walked me home. As we walked, he took my hand; and as we reached my building, he kissed me with absolutely no intimation that he was looking to come up. When I got upstairs, totally by myself, I was confused by what had just happened.... I'd gone on a date with a super hot, super intelligent guy with whom I'd had a lot of fun—who'd paid, walked me home, kissed me, and *didn't* want sex. *I'm sorry, is this a thing?* I was fully here for it.

So now I had these two guys, both in my phone and in my life, who were polar opposites, except for their shared ethnicities and ages, and somehow they existed in almost complete isolation from each other. I never saw one as a threat to the other because they were so entirely different in what they offered me and what I wanted with them.

Mutual Friend would continue to blow hot and cold, meanwhile I was setting boundaries with Persian Lawyer, like after the first time we slept together and he left right afterwards and didn't text for an entire day. Mutual Friend got away with messaging me in the middle of the night, while Persian Lawyer was told that I didn't mind being flexible in terms of scheduling, provided there was some give on his side as well. Again, the differences were stark. Anytime I remotely pushed back with Mutual Friend, his reaction was a childlike tantrum, with name calling and the silent treatment. Persian Lawyer, on the other hand, he responded, communicated, understood, and adjusted.

I'm not sure why I needed them both; it was almost like insurance, as if putting up with Mutual Friend would keep me on my toes *and* save me from putting all my eggs in another (Persian) basket. Or maybe it was that I didn't really think I deserved someone like Persian Lawyer, foreshadowing that of course it was going to go down the shitter; so it made sense to have Mutual Friend around as the runner-up prize behaviour that I *did* deserve, right?

I couldn't deny how much I was starting to like Persian Lawyer. For example, there was his ability to be both playful and firm with my girlfriends after a drunken bachelorette party, from which he was picking me up. They had texted him from my phone asking him to bring them cheeseburgers, and his response was close to perfection: *unfortunately, delivery boy never made it onto my resume :)*. It was only made better when, after he picked me up, he said, "Do you want a cheeseburger? I can take you for one if you do, I just didn't want to stop and get them for your girlfriends, I wanted to see you." He learned quickly that bringing ice cream to my apartment would always be a winner in my books, but so was cooking us incredibly healthy dinners. It was about balance and we were achieving it. Mostly.

Alas, our schedules caused us problems, as we'd both planned busy summers before meeting each other. Possibly because of the timing issue, we found ourselves getting into an unhealthy "*date*-date to *sex*-date ratio" as we called it. (At least I did.... I'm not sure he minded the imbalance between time spent having sex and time otherwise spent together.) We tried to rectify it and find time to see each other more often, but it was difficult. Though, every time I'd start to think that he was ready to call it quits, he'd surprise me. Like the weekend that I was in Kelowna with the Beach Girls (plus a sixth friend who'd joined and made me no longer the only white-blonde girl!) while he was in Vegas. I'd expected a weekend of us very much doing our own things and catching up afterwards, but it turned into a weekend of texting almost constantly and getting desperate to see each other back in Vancouver. I think I ended up round at his place ten minutes after he got back from the airport.

In fairness, sometimes we did more than just have sex, but it was always part of the buffet. Recently, I'd spent the day on a boat, with another Persian guy who'd started a cannabis business producing edibles. He'd given me a bunch of samples, despite my protestations that I didn't use cannabis in any form. But a few weeks later, Persian Lawyer (who also never partook in cannabis) and I decided to try an edible together. I've always been reluctant, knowing what a cluster-fuck alcohol can be—like why add another substance into the mix? But people assured me that it would be relaxing and I'd sleep great and have no hangover. Sounds amazing. So, on a Tuesday night (yeah, I don't know why we thought a Tuesday night was a good idea), Persian Lawyer and I ate a tiny piece of a ginger cookie laced with weed and then waited for whatever effect this edible would impose.

Two hours passed, with some great sex and a decent movie, and still neither of us felt anything. Kind of disappointed, we said goodnight and he headed for the elevator. But probably before he even reached the ground floor, I had moments where my brain would shut off for a millisecond, as if I'd blinked and everything had gone dark for a snap—but I hadn't blinked. It was like the living room TV losing picture, back in the olden days before digital. I also realised that I just felt generally kind of fuzzy.

I've since learned that the psychoactive cannabinoid in marijuana, THC, can expand your blood vessels, and the resulting blood pressure decrease can bring on symptoms of fainting and distorted vision. Perfect for me, clearly. Consuming cannabis in the form of edibles versus smoking it was supposed to prevent this from happening, most of the time, but apparently not for me.

I also learned that cannabis becomes about a million times stronger in the body, at least upon crossing the blood-brain barrier.

At the time, however, it was like momentary psychosis. I distracted myself with getting ready for bed, but I was fully losing it. I couldn't tell what was real and what was my imagination. I knew that I was in my apartment, but I wasn't entirely sure that I wasn't also walking through the lobby of my building naked. I was in my bed, but I wasn't entirely sure that I wasn't also heading for my balcony.... That was when I realised that I didn't trust myself to be alone.

I'd been relaying all of this to Persian Lawyer, over text, who said that he also felt kind of weird, but mostly just hungry. He'd had a snack on his short walk home, then the lunch he was meant to take to work the following day, all before tucking into a gallon of ice cream from his freezer, which he would never ordinarily do. Okay, so we were both feeling something now, though arguably he was having the better time. Why did I have to be the one losing my mind and not the one stuffing my face with ice cream? Upon realizing that I shouldn't be alone, I called him. Of course, I didn't want to sound hysterical, but I was *really* feeling it and he needed to come back and save me from...myself?

But it just rang to his voicemail. *WTF? DUDE, I NEED YOU!* I messaged him and said just that, but I got nothing back. Jesus, help me. Trying not to fully lose it, I attempted to quieten my mind and fall asleep, but every single noise was now super loud. If falling asleep meant slipping into a dream state then maybe I was already there. It was like a new dimension introducing itself in my mind; I'd moved from reality, to edible-induced thoughts, and now to a lucid dream state. Or was it a fugue state? *What if I actually had been in the hallway naked,* in some other version of that moment? *What if I actually had jumped off my balcony,* but also in some other version of that moment? *What if instead of hitting the concrete, I'd learned to fly, or else die?* It was too much.

Given that Persian Lawyer had gone MIA, I called Keith and Priscilla. They both lived relatively close and I knew that they wouldn't judge. Both of them were fairly early to bed, so I wasn't surprised when I got no answer. Next up, and I hated to do it (given that Sara had just moved back into his place), I had to call Damien. Thankfully, he answered. When I told him what was happening, his first response was, "Do you want me to come over?" No, I told him, just talk me through how to feel better, like should I drink water or what? *Wow, I am such a weed novice.*

Apparently though, there wasn't anything to do but let it work its way out my system, like some long-ass natural detox. I decided that maybe he did need to come over. He agreed, but as soon as he hung up, I wasn't even convinced I'd had the conversation in real life and not just my edible-induced thoughts. I even wondered whether he'd just offered to come over to get me off the phone...*Paranoia much?* So I called Sara and kept her on the phone with me until Damien arrived at my door, such was my inability to be alone with my thoughts now, especially as time slowed to a near standstill.

My brain kept snapping on and off; the everyday street noises and those of my building were now deafening, and my distrust that Damien was even on his way over kept growing. The ten minutes it took him to reach my house felt like the longest two hours of my life. All the same, armed with ice cream, he put on Netflix and talked me through all the tangible, real things around us, knowing that I essentially needed to be talked off a ledge. Eventually I fell asleep. When I woke up the next morning, Damien having safely returned home, I was still high as a fucking kite. But in my paranoia about anyone finding out that we'd taken edibles (as if anyone in Vancouver would bat an eyelid!), I headed into work despite almost being run over when I misread the traffic signal and dropped my AirPods in the middle of the road.

Finally, I heard from Persian Lawyer, who explained that he'd fallen into a coma after the last text he'd sent. When I'd called him, he could hear his phone ringing but he wasn't able to move from the chair; his body was completely detached from his mind. I was kind of mad that I'd had to fend for myself, but the reality was that we'd had a super-delayed reaction and mine was pretty extreme. Unsurprisingly, we both agreed that we'd never be touching edibles again (I don't care how many people tell me to try the gummies)! But having tried edibles with him was a testament to the fact that I trusted him and felt safe in his presence. But who the fuck does it on a random Tuesday night? We are idiots.

Despite needing to babysit while Persian Lawyer was in his edible-induced coma, Damien questioned my sanity about even putting up with Mutual Friend's bullshit when there was this lawyer on the horizon. Meanwhile, having told Sara about the situation with her friend, she'd said, "I'd love for you guys to get together. I know he can be a shit, but he can also be incredibly generous and sweet." It was hardly a resounding review but it didn't entirely put me off, which is unfortunate. After a few months on this particular merry-go-round, I was coming to realise that Mutual Friend's mood swings were becoming too much, and the issue of timing with Persian Lawyer and I was now well beyond *well-this-is-kinda'-annoying*.

As a result, I vowed to ignore Mutual Friend and try to address things with Persian Lawyer. He'd been feeling badly about his busy schedule keeping us from seeing each other, but he couldn't offer up much more. I explained that I didn't need more of his time per se; I just needed our time together to be about more than sex. As great as the sex was (and it was truly incredible) it was practically all we did. But if we could meet at lunchtime for sex, why couldn't we also meet at lunchtime for lunch, like most people probably did? He agreed, but a couple of weeks later, nothing had changed and it was time to address it in a bigger way.

I went round for dinner, looking forward to doing something other than having sex. I mean, we were also likely to have sex, but there'd be food too—a girl needs to eat! In fact, the sex came before the food, which was just as well; especially in that we chatted again over dinner about our scheduling problems. Eventually he starkly said, "It's maybe also partly that I don't want to make time for this right now." He explained that he had a lot going on, important life stuff, and he didn't want to sacrifice any of it. He also admitted to being jaded from his last relationship, even now. I appreciated his honesty and understood, but ultimately I didn't want to feel like a burden. I deserved someone who would prioritise me, all of which I told him. We finished up dinner, finished our incredibly mature conversation and said goodbye.

If I said that I didn't cry on the way home, I'd be lying. I loved how full his life was. I loved his closeness with friends and his dedication to family. His work was obviously important to him, and that was incredibly attractive. As an individual, Persian Lawyer was super motivated and driven—and don't even get me started on the sexual chemistry. But I knew that, at some point, someone would come into his life; and even if he couldn't find space for them initially, he'd make it work because he wanted to make it work. But that person wasn't me. We make things work with people because we want to make them a priority; because our lives would be worse off without them in it at all, even if they also create more pressure on our time. That's what I wanted to be to someone. Not a time suck, but someone with which to be and bear witness to life.

Twenty

There's Always Chicago

In trying to distance myself from Mutual Friend and now Persian Lawyer, I was back to swiping regularly and seeing who else popped up. (Ideally someone who wasn't dark and bearded—could I say that all Persian men were causing me problems? Is that too much of a generalisation? Or is that just what was happening?) I felt like problems had arisen with all of them in some way; either they were entirely blind to things or else they chose to ignore them, as if they were somehow "above" emotional issues. No man likes to admit it, of course, but I felt like saying, "Oh hi, toxic masculinity" to like the entire world.

However, with the men I'd been with whom were also Persian, I'd noticed this air of liking to promote having all their shit together. Often they *did* have all their shit together, in terms of work, family, and community—but having your shit together for a healthy, long-term relationship is an entirely different thing. In my experience, Persian men often say that Persian women are drama queens, and Persian women tell you to stay away from Persian men because they're trouble, which is hardly a resounding advertisement. Obviously, there was plenty to like and appreciate, hence why I ended up going out with so many Persian men in Vancouver! I get that we're born of our cultures and environments, and possibly Persian culture doesn't encourage the emotional awareness that I expected in a partner. It was okay for me to expect more, and it was okay for them to approach life in their own way.

I guess a frat boy from Chicago was pretty far off from a Persian dude living on the West Coast, so it was a welcome match on Bumble. He was in town for a week or so, on vacation, by himself. *Interesting.* When I mentioned meeting for drinks, he said that he didn't drink. *Also interesting.* When I suggested a time to meet up, he said that he was planning to attend a yoga class. *Even more interesting*. When we finally did meet up that Saturday night (after he had the good sense to ditch yoga for me), I walked up to meet him outside Science World. I was going to take him to Earnest, my favourite ice cream place in the city, and I remember how big his smile had been. Chicago Guy was a twenty-nine-year-old personal trainer—born, raised, and still living in the Windy City. With his shaved head and the bulging muscles beneath his t-shirt, he looked like he should have been in the US Army.

Our plans for ice cream and a seawall walk changed when he realised that there was a BC Lions game happening (Canada's equivalent of the NFL) and asked me if I wanted to go. So, we made our way back to BC Place Stadium, he bought us tickets, and we got to know each other while watching a "poor imitation of American football," as he put it. He was funny and very American: loud and ballsy and confident as shit. I didn't hate it (I just kept telling people that he was a tourist, particularly after he learned that I liked to fly a little more under the radar and playfully tried to embarrass me about it).

From the football stadium, we went to a bar—although he didn't drink. I asked him whether his body was a temple for his job or something else. He told me it was something else, a choice that he'd made a few years ago. But he was still happy to hang in a bar, so we crossed the road from the stadium and ordered pizzas. Also, I had a gin. When I'd gone to order a non-alcoholic drink, he'd told me not to on his account, that he preferred when people still drank around him.

There, sipping on my gin and ginger ale (and him on his water), we fell into much deeper conversations than we'd shared during football. We discussed family and our respective upbringings, learning that we both viewed personal growth as an incredibly important part of life. At that point, he admitted to being in AA for alcoholism, hence the no drinking; in trying to turn his life around, the one thing he'd really wanted was to experience more of the world, hence his trip to Vancouver. I didn't quite understand how Vancouver came to be his choice destination, but maybe it was the clean living of the Pacific Northwest and how it matched his new lifestyle. Given that I enjoyed spending time with him, I was glad his impulses had wandered across the country.

As we finished drinks, I finally admitted that my apartment was across the street. He made the obvious joke that it'd be rude not to walk me home.

When we'd been messaging earlier, arranging to meet up, we both agreed that this would just be a fun opportunity to hang out with someone new—for me to show off the best bits of Vancouver and give him a local's view. Looking back, I'm not sure if either one of us believed that was all it would be, but I was aware that our initial agreement would likely change if he came up. In his straight-talking American way, as we stood at the elevators in my apartment building, he said: "I'd like to come up. Of course, I'd also like to sleep with you. But if you only want the first part then I won't turn into a lunatic in your apartment. You could probably kick my ass anyway." I *definitely* couldn't kick his ass, but I liked his honesty. At that point, I wasn't sure what I wanted, but I did want to spend more time with him; so, conflicted, we went up to my apartment.

With all the men coming to visit, my concierge probably wondered what I was up to now and then. I wanted to believe that the staff likely weren't paying attention, but what else are they supposed to do while working there all day? I'd worked in hotel receptions before and knew my way around that particular block. There was a high possibility that they thought this was some kind of business activity, perhaps one that allowed me to afford my rent. I have no judgments towards sex work, but it did strike me that this assumption would never be made about a guy bringing home lots of women. If anything, the man would probably be thought of with additional respect. *Yet another wonderful double standard.*

More comically, if they had tracked my preference for dark-bearded men, were they now surprised by the shake up in the kind of guy accompanying me home? Chicago Guy and I spent the night talking. *Talking, talking and talking.* With no alcohol. I just had one drink at the bar, so this was potentially the most sober I'd ever been with someone at my apartment. Throughout all the talking, the thing that struck me most was his lack of judgment, along with his focus on how the past informed the present, thus our past experiences should be looked at as building blocks rather than attaching negative connotations to whatever happened *then*.

As we delved deeper, it was clear that he had a colourful past, although he never went into full detail. What was obvious is that I was still hugely enamoured by men whose lives revolved around fitness. The physical results of being a personal trainer were delightful under his light blue t-shirt. That, coupled with his way of putting me at ease, made me think that it wouldn't be the worst thing if we slept together that night. I presumed this was his plan, to ease me into bed, as it were. But I was okay with it, especially when he looked the way he looked and had treated me with nothing but respect.

My thought was that it wouldn't be the worst idea, was not only correct but wholly understated. The thing with active men is that their stamina and endurance in the bedroom are second to none. It was a fairly sleepless night, but his want for snuggles equaled mine. He didn't really have anywhere to be in the morning, so eventually we got out of bed and went to brunch.

While knocking back eggs benny at one of my favourite Yaletown brunch spots, Yaletown Distillery, he re-iterated something that he'd said the previous night, which I'd taken as a joke the first time. He was heading up to Whistler that afternoon, for a few days of mountain biking and white-water rafting, and he'd suggested that I join him. I reminded him that *some of us weren't on vacation,* but he said I could work from the Airbnb while he did the touristy stuff during the day. Then we could hangout at night. It was a lovely idea (if he was actually serious), but the reality was that I had to go into work on Monday and figure out whether I could work remotely for the rest of the week. Dropping him at the bus station later that afternoon, he kissed me goodbye followed by, "See you in Whistler." That American confidence.

By this time, I'd learnt to keep some of my dating escapades to myself—such were some of the opinions I'd heard upon sharing my "promiscuity" or other questionable choices. Ranging from the standard, "if you have sex too early, you'll never develop a meaningful relationship" to "are you not worried about your number climbing?" Also, there were all the fun judgments my friends made upon seeing one of my date's app profiles. Don't get me wrong, we're all judgmental; but is it helpful to say, "He looks like a douche" when you know I'm already going on a date with him?

Maybe I just didn't like people questioning my life choices—and who does, anyways? My friends' opinions were important to me, but if they had something to communicate to me in earnest, I was all ears. It's hard to know what to make of things when a stranger gets called a douche and I have to decide whether to take stock in the comment. Either way, when I arrived at a classic, Sunday afternoon pizza-and-beer catch up at Yaletown Brewery with friends, I told Damien the Whistler plan before anyone else had arrived. In his usual style, he said, "Yeah, that sounds like a great idea. If you want to get killed." His opinion wasn't softened when we discovered that Ferg, a friend of ours visiting from Dublin, would also be heading to Whistler on the same day.

Fast forward twenty hours, after much musing in my head about whether Chicago Guy really wanted me to join him, he told me to get out of my head and come to Whistler. That's how I ended up on a three pm bus into the mountains, with Ferg beside me. We enjoyed the Sea-to-Sky highway views and talked about dating—how Ferg had found it since moving back to Ireland and where I was with men. We got onto the topic of age, given my propensity for younger men, and I explained that it wasn't so much age but life experience that seemed important to me. I needed someone who'd been through stuff, who'd seen some shit and come out the other side, earning some emotional intelligence and maturity as a result.

In this way, I wasn't going after a particular age, but I found myself dating in the mid-to-late twenties range nonetheless. Often I was advised to date older men, in fact the comments came so frequently from friends that I ended up doing a controlled experiment to disapprove that I had any inten-tion to date younger me. My theory was that men my age, or older, might prefer to date women in their twenties. Thus I changed my settings to only see men between the ages of thirty-four and forty-two. Within one night, my matches dropped off enough that I might as well have been existing in a different dimension.

I'd never proclaim to receive one hundred matches a day, but if I went on a swiping spree, I was always guaranteed a good chunk of matches. This time, *nada*, nothing—even when I was "generously" swiping on men whom typi-cally I wouldn't swipe on! *Fucking rude.* I gave it a week; and in that week I had maybe twelve matches. I don't think anything came from any of them. I couldn't be sure of the reason, but clearly I wasn't ending up with younger men because I didn't swipe right on older men enough. Also, is it just a coin-cidence that men enjoy their sexual peak in their mid-twenties and women in their mid-thirties?

Regardless of the age difference between Chicago Guy and me, there were a few things that I hadn't anticipated. Spending two nights in an Airbnb with him was so easy, and after checking out my favourite pizza place in the village (Pizza Antico...GO!) on our first night, we returned home to watch my favourite movie. In the middle of the Anthony Hopkins and Brad Pitt *classic* (of which many people have never even heard), *Legends of The Fall,* I realised that we wouldn't be getting any sleep. And not because of sex. But because we found ourselves in what can only be described as the biggest *Come To Jesus* self-revelation session I've ever had with someone.

It started with him asking me whether I'd want to get remarried, followed by my thoughts on kids. While explaining to him my rational about having kids (or not) with my ex, he made a comment about how I'd made a hasty and cruel decision by saying I'd never have had kids with my husband. While his disagreement with my life choices was bad enough, what I liked about him most was his complete lack of judgment, which now had been thrown out the window. Taken aback, and hurt by his quick assumption of negative intentions on my part, I rolled over in bed and stifled my tears with the sheet. In my head, I knew that I'd be leaving now, in the middle of the night, if we were in Vancouver. *Fuck him, fuck Whistler.*

As I lay there silently, trying to stop my shoulders from heaving with each of my sobs, he turned towards me, put his hand on my arm, and apologised. He spoke quietly and deliberately, choosing his words as if they were some of the most important words in the world. He explained that he'd be the last person to judge me; he had too many things in his past to allow him to judge other people. Then he launched into two hours of bearing his soul, telling me stories from his past, the like of which I'd only witnessed in movies or on TV shows. He chronicled alcohol abuse and extreme drug use, brushes with the law, familial trauma, restraining orders, violent relationships, and an accident that ultimately resulted in him going to prison.

The charges that sent him to prison were put down as a misdemeanour, hence he could still travel the world and come to Canada—a future made possible only by his white privilege. The part he played in another man losing his life was difficult to hear him describe. The honesty he showed in sharing his story was bewildering, almost as if he needed to get it off his chest. But I'm sure he'd told the story before. Listening to him become more emotional as we lay in the dark (he detailed the aftermath, the court case, the victim's family-impact statements) I didn't know whether to be terrified of the man lying next to me in bed or to reach out and hold him.

The most recent part of the story was what I was witnessing right now: him sober, repentant, turning around what was otherwise a drama-filled life. His gratitude for this second (third? fourth?) chance seemed to know no bounds. Such was his understanding of how close to death and long term incarceration he'd come in this life. As for me, I had no clue what to say.

While I'm not often lost for words, in this instance I didn't have the vocabulary. I didn't think I had the life experience to provide me with anything meaningful to say. How do you respond when someone tells you things like that? Yet to have someone open up in that way, with details that I hadn't asked for and could have been kept hidden, he deserved my empathy at least. In some ways, I'd never felt closer to someone than lying in that darkened room with Chicago Guy, the movie long since paused, just a blink of light from the digital bedside clock.

He told me that he'd understand if I wanted to leave in the morning and return to Vancouver while he went rafting. I didn't respond to that comment, not knowing how I'd feel in the cold light of day and trying not to make promises I couldn't keep. By the time we started to drift off to sleep, wrought in emotional heaviness from a night of far deeper conversations than I'd ever anticipated, it was close to five am. I had to be up in less than two hours for a call; and he was getting picked up in two-and-a-half hours for his day on the water. I already knew it would be rough, and I didn't mean his rafting.

When we woke to my alarm, he asked me if there was anything else I wanted to know, and I said that I still needed time to process. The truth was actually that I didn't know how much more detail I wanted to receive. What benefit would that have? Was it necessary to know more in order to determine how I felt about him, or would that only fulfil outstanding curiosities? He had gone into incredible detail of rehab stays, nights in jail, court trials, and media coverage—and I didn't need to see all of his darkness. He kissed me before leaving, in a way that made it clear he thought that it'd be last time he saw me.

Despite last night's heaviness, he said that he was glad I'd come to Whistler and infinitely happy to meet me. He took off and I focused on work, which was difficult. Attempting to plan our marketing efforts at an upcoming tech conference, while my head was foggy and my mind wandering, was less than ideal. As I rationalised things over text with Priscilla, while not divulging all the details (because they were ultimately not mine to share), I realised that I didn't want nor need another detail. He'd made it clear how sensitive he was about people finding out unintentionally, owing to all the online articles about him, so I definitely didn't want to Google him—even with my browser search bar staring at me. I wanted to take him at face value. I believe people deserve second chances. If he was turning his life around, which is how it looked from where I was sitting, who was I to delve into his past? What good did that do?

He was relieved but surprised upon returning that night. He wanted to take me for dinner, but first he needed to find an AA meeting. There was one happening in Whistler Village, so if I didn't mind, he'd go there and we could have a late dinner afterwards. I'd never arranged a date around an AA meeting before, but I think the right answer in that situation is: *sure, do what you need to do.* But also I wasn't sure what to expect after the meeting. Was it like when I went to therapy and just needed to hide in a darkened apartment with a blanket and *Friends* afterwards? Did he really want to go out for a fancy dinner (his choice, from what I'd told him was available nearby)?

On the way to dinner, I weighed the appropriateness, or not, of me having a drink with dinner. He'd literally just walked out of a meeting intended to manage alcoholism. But given last night's nature, I could really do with a drink. I stopped short of ordering a whole bottle of wine for myself and instead just had a glass. Over dinner, I told him how I felt about hearing more details (which is to say I didn't want to know), thanked him for his honesty and said that I'd honour what he'd told me and go with that understanding, no judgments or assumptions. Given his stories, it would have been incredibly easy to jump to unfair conclusions, but I was heading back to Vancouver the next day and he would return to Chicago.

Leaving Whistler, I felt so many things. I was unsure about going back to Vancouver, as if nothing would be the same again. Sharing the last few days with Chicago Guy had left an indelible mark, or more like an impending doom, as if I knew this couldn't end well. Yet for moments, it had felt so perfect. It was one of the strangest juxtapositions I'd ever experienced, but I was also rational enough to see the red flags. There were concerns about him, about an "us", and I couldn't know anything for sure without heading into the belly of the beast. Unfortunately, sometimes the belly of the beast swallows you alive.

Could this particular fling go anywhere in the first place, given our geographical distance? Did it matter what I thought about his past, if I'd been granted an experience filled with new perspectives that week? He'd made inti-mations that I should visit Chicago, but the whole thing felt beautifully unfair, because it was so close to perfect. But if this didn't turn into something long term, I had a feeling that life just wanted to remind me that amazing experi-ences and relationships, regardless of how fleeting, were still possible.

Not to mention, new connections could pop up with fresh lessons at the most unexpected of times. People could be vulnerable and honest, and some of them valued growth and gratitude just as much as I did. While Persian Lawyer had seemed perfect with his controlled, quiet, and unassuming demeanour, Chicago Guy felt perfect with all his chaos and charisma. And if *I'm* being honest, it was maybe the first time I hadn't been excited about getting back to Vancouver.

Twenty-One

Broadening Horizons

Chicago Guy left that Thursday night. The next day at work, while trying to catch up on what the hell had happened last week, I got a message from a friend I'd met up with a few weeks beforehand. I'd continued to do the Damn Early Days program with the Chasing Sunrise group, making the time to write for my blog at a damn early time every morning. I'd become more comfortable with the idea of going on their trips, so when I saw a post on the Facebook group about an overnight hike to Panorama Ridge, I figured it was a good place to start.

Panorama Ridge is a mountain ridge, up near Whistler, overlooking the crystal blue waters of Garibaldi Lake. The hike makes for a 30-kilometre, 11-hour round trip with 1520 metres of elevation gain. Not to be fucked with by amateurs, this intimidated the shit out of me, despite my active lifestyle and my now entirely under control fainting problem. I didn't want to be that person who slows down the group or has to be airlifted off the mountain after cracking open my skull. It was a bold hike to start with but I'd always wanted to do it. I mean, I could have started out with a day hike, arguably. I'd never hiked overnight. I didn't even know it was a thing. It sounded like the sort of expedition to lose someone off the cliff-side or face a nocturnal bear attack. But the thought of witnessing sunrise from Panorama Ridge was too good to pass up. I decided to go for it and throw caution to the wind. Time to get back to saying yes to things that scared me—and not just men.

Shortly thereafter, I was signing up to get picked up at nine pm by someone I'd never met (such is the way this group works, throwing everyone in a WhatsApp group to figure out ride sharing), along with another girl. At the last minute, one of the group leaders, whom I'd met numerous times at those early morning Real Talks, hopped in our car as well—at least there'd be someone I knew on the hour-and-a-half drive to the trailhead. I hadn't expected that we'd be singing at the top of our lungs from the sunroof before we even got halfway there, however. Such is the beauty of making new friends.

The start of the hike was more onerous than I'd imagined. There were six kilometres of switchbacks, which I've since discovered are my absolute nemesis—just back and forth as you head up the side of a mountain. Although in this instance, the complete blackness after leaving the trailhead at midnight made the switchbacks difficult to discern. Thankfully, thirty people with head torches create enough light for safety, but not enough to be fully aware of your surroundings. It was disorientating, but I found solace in the darkness, lost in the conversations I overheard while moving my way through the group. Meeting people and connecting with nothing other than one shared experience, all while breathing out your ass and heaving yourself up some crazy elevation gain, really levels the playing field.

Somehow, by the time we came through the last of the grass-covered meadows (but let's be honest, I could have been *ANYwhere*), I realised that our group had split into three sub-groups. Apparently some naturally occurring process of selection had placed me in the front group. By this time, it was too late to drop back, with such distance between us and the middle group, and I just wanted to get the damn thing over. I wanted to stand at the top. For fear my body would realise what was happening and refuse to go any further, I didn't want to stop. Plus, some of the guys in my group had done it before and knew the route perfectly, even in darkness, which I was impressed with, especially when the last part became a scramble up loose rock as we summited the ridge.

So yeah, I'd decided to stick with them. As our front group of six guys, plus me and one other girl (who'd done this hike three times already that summer!) reached the top, there was something incredibly euphoric in realising that I'd not only managed the hike but fucking crushed it. I hadn't struggled once; I hadn't paused; I'd kept putting one foot in front of the other and now I was chilling on top of Panorama Ridge waiting for sunrise. *How was this my life?*

The only problem was that sunrise wasn't forthcoming. BC had been plagued by forest fires that summer, so we knew going into the hike that the air quality was incredibly poor; but we decided to do it anyway and hope for the best. We did not get the best, not by a long shot. As light dawned, we realised that we couldn't see shit. *That crystal blue lake?* I had no idea where it was even supposed to be. *Views over to Whistler mountain?* I wasn't even sure which way was north. It was like we were on the moon. It was eerie and disconcerting, resulting in far fewer Instagram-worthy pics than we'd maybe all hoped. But still, *I'd hiked Panorama Ridge through the night!* I wasn't even that mad about the lack of views. My sense of accomplishment was worlds greater than any disappointment.

With daylight upon us (if you could call this hazy orange glow *daylight*), we decided not to spend too much time on the ridge. We started to make our way back down, in differing groups to how we'd reached the top. Shortly before reaching those bastard switchbacks (equally awful going down as going up, and arguably worse now that we could see their ridiculous, neverending zig-zag), I caught stride with a girl I'd hardly noticed until this point. She'd kept mostly to herself, as far as I'd seen, but we bonded over this being the first Chasing Sunrise expedition for both of us.

Darlene had moved here from Toronto and worked at a law firm. She was a quietly determined and independent female and seemed fit and capable. I wondered if any part of her had worried about undertaking the hike, like I had. By this time, I'd done the worst part so maybe she'd never know that I doubted myself. Again the mountainside trail kind of levelled the playing field, the physical exertion stripped us back to vulnerability central, and we found ourselves sharing experiences about moving to Vancouver, dating, and evolving new friendships as we moved through our lives.

I had recently met with Laura for a *Come-to-Jesus* brunch to unpack our changing relationship and attempt to understand from where the distance we were experiencing had come. There was an acknowledgement about our lives simply taking different paths: Laura was now pregnant and I was seemingly more likely to be found hiking a mountain in the dark than drinking wine at happy hour. We weren't the same people we'd been upon arriving in Vancouver. The growth that we were both entitled to had ultimately left us further apart as friends. Unknowingly, we'd also been triggering each other in ways that we hadn't realised until discussing it over eggs benedict at Honey Salt. Again, difficult conversations for the win.

Darlene and I talked about how friendships need as much work and attention as romantic relationships, that despite them seeming as if they should be easy, often boundaries must be set and annoyances discussed. On the other hand, some friendships, as the saying goes, are really just for a *season or a reason*. I had struggled to think that Laura and I wouldn't or couldn't get back to how things had been, but despite whatever distance, I would always be right at the end of the phone if she ever needed anything. I had a feeling that would be reciprocated from her. There was comfort in knowing what a huge part of my life she and Sam had been when I first arrived in Vancouver, and I often wondered if I'd have settled as well without them.

It was clear that Darlene and I had a lot in common, and not just because we'd been insane enough to sign up for a massive hike in the dark with strangers. But all of the people I encountered in Chasing Sunrise were clearly looking for something that was missing from their lives—a sense of adventure, new experiences, new friends, freedom, safe spaces.... With Damn Early Days, Real Talks and now this first CS trip, I was finding that I'd never been surrounded by people who were so actively and openly looking for *personal growth*. This buzzword, which I used to feel pretty indifferent towards, was now incredibly relevant to my life.

A few weeks later, just after Chicago Guy had returned to the east coast, Darlene messaged to ask me what I was doing that long weekend, and we made plans to get coffee and see a movie. That is, until we were persuaded/ coerced/sold on the idea of going on the CS road trip that weekend, specifically by another guy we'd met on the Panorama Ridge hike. He was trying to get another car together and suggested that we go with him. Then we'd just need one other person to make a car of four.

The road trip was leaving on Friday afternoon and going to Banff and Jasper. I'd been desperate to explore the Canadian Rockies since I got to Canada, not least because of my namesake lake which had always been on my bucket list. I'd gone to Jasper for a work conference but hadn't seen a whole · lot of the surrounding area. This trip could change all that. Except for the fact that when we were discussing it, we would need to be leaving Vancouver in like four hours. When have I ever decided to go on a weekend trip with mere hours notice? When have I ever not been packed for a trip a week in advance? When have I ever... oh right, that's the point, *new experiences*. Fuck it, I'm in. Darlene's in. We're doing it. Some random guy called James is in too. We arranged pickups and the next thing I knew I was leaving work early to go home and see if I had everything I needed for a camping road trip in the

Rockies. Surprisingly, I did have everything I needed—this from the girl who didn't even have shoes to go on a hike when she first got here!

Three hours later, I got picked up at five past six and we drove to get Darlene and pick up mystery guest number four.... As we drove the block from Darlene's place to James' place, we discussed what we'd do if he was a total bore or a nutter. We would be in the car with him for three straight days! We had no good answers for either scenario but thankfully James turned out to be this super-cheery English guy who seemed ridiculously easy going. We were one of six or seven other cars, and with a roughly planned route provided for us, we would meet up at certain spots but otherwise the time was ours to do as we pleased. All the same, it's a fuck tonne of driving for one weekend.

From our first drive to Emerald Lake for sunrise—to Johnston Canyon and then Banff Hot Springs, to our first night camping, as Darlene and I cramped in the shared tent, to visiting Lake Louise (massive tick on the bucket list) and Moraine Lake, to driving up the Icefields Parkway to Jasper, to more hot springs and a final night camping in a campground that came with a massive "warning: bear in the area" sign—we never stopped talking. We took all of our excess energy and channeled it into conversation (apart from when we were taking strategic naps to rotate the driving responsibilities). We started with basic intros of ourselves as we were leaving Vancouver—as well as why James had brought one fully-cooked chicken and one fully-cooked ham as car snacks—but as we covered the two-thousand kilometres of distance in three days, we also covered conversation topics from food (and kombucha) preferences, Canadian and British cultural differences, favourite insults, controversial opinions, and a lot of dating and sex stories.

To say that we were well-bonded by the end of the trip is an understatement. James admitted that he wasn't sure what he'd gotten himself into when the conversation so quickly plummeted to depraved jokes and we admitted that there weren't any plans to get drunk or high on the trip—which seemed quite foreign to him, an Englishman who'd arrived in Canada not long ago. We really were all just about enjoying the experience. The friendships made (James was literally my new favourite person) and developed (Darlene and I were infinitely closer after sleeping in the car on the second night—outwardly because of the rain, inwardly because of the bear warnings) were only matched by the unbelievable natural beauty surrounding us at all times. I'd never seen anything like it. Like, it was literally *AWE-inspiring*. As tired and dirty as we looked coming home on the Monday night, I wouldn't have traded it for anything.

There was something about spending time in nature, outside your comfort zone, learning about people and learning about yourself. It was one of the most enjoyable and rewarding experiences of my life, and I'd done it with three hours notice. While explaining to my car mates how big of a deal that first hike to Pano Ridge and now the Rockies trip had been for me, I realised that this is what self-reflection felt like. This was what recognising growth meant. Sometimes the change wasn't so obvious, and sometimes it showed itself as a big, fuck-off hike or road trip.

Chicago Guy had been receiving a running commentary (when we had signal) of the adventures, not least because he was desperate to see it for himself, so sending envy inducing pics was only right. Communications were maintained once I came back, but it wasn't long before we realised that our daily schedule really didn't align and the reality was that I wasn't going to Chicago anytime soon. On top of that, with him wanting to go back to school, he was hardly likely to make frequent trips to Vancouver. We'd both realised the same thing, but he took the approach men seemed to love the most and just started to get harder and harder to reach. I, on the other hand, took my "if you think we're *not* going to have a final conversation, you're out your fucking mind" approach. We finally chatted it through and resigned ourselves to the fact that it had been a fun weekend dalliance, and perhaps nothing more. We were both grateful to have met each other—and there *endeth* the story.

A week later, I received a random text from Persian Lawyer, as fate would have it. My willpower, weakened by the copious amounts of alcohol I'd consumed at a music festival, led to my ending up at his place. But not without me (attempting to) creating some boundaries. If I was coming over on the way home, it wasn't going to be a fuck and run. He'd actually have to commit to spending time with me—a date, staying over, I don't know. Without a whole lot of prompting, he told me that he had a fresh towel waiting for me. (Raincouver earned its nickname that day at the music festival; I was a soggy mess, which I'd told him.) He wanted me to stay over and in the morning we'd go for brunch. This was more than he'd ever committed to while we were seeing each other, since I'd never even stayed at his place. I was shocked but delighted.

It was a perfect night, apart from the pigeons nesting on his balcony, with their nest directly in my eye line as we had sex. Not only did I not appreciate five sets of beady eyes on me in those intimate moments, but I also hated birds. I'm terrified of them. I will scream like a small child if one comes near me. But feathered "friends" aside, it was lovely to be back with him. After a night when he'd actually snuggled into me, something he always said that he could never do, he cooked me breakfast before taking me out for coffee and apparently the best almond croissant in the city, at Beaucoup Bakery.

He wasn't wrong, the crispy pastry and creamy almond-filling were divine. What wasn't divine was me wondering what the fuck was happening. Especially as we then went to buy flowers as a hostess gift for a party he was attending that night. *Why were we all of a sudden in couple-central?* It was the place I'd wanted us to get to but the destination never seemed like an option. Rather than silently wonder and be grateful for the hint of commitment from him (if you could even call twelve hours of effort commitment), I decided to address it in the car as he drove me home. *Why now? What's changed? What do you want?*

He said that he was coming into a slightly quieter time with work and social stuff, and he thought maybe he could give more time to us, but ultimately he didn't think anything had changed that much. *So...what the fuck are we doing? Why the fuck did you message me?* Oh right, you were horny and I seemed like a good option. Okay, great.

He said that he wanted to see how things went, but we fell into the same routine, meeting for sex and not much else. One night, when he'd claimed to be out for dinner but was heading home because his uncle was staying with him, it was more than a little surprising to bump into him in a bar. Again, I could have just ignored it; I could have waved politely from afar. But no... ginned up (is that a verb? It should be "verb; to be emboldened by gin"), I went over and enjoyed the look of shock on his face when I said: *Hi, it's good to see that you're enjoying your quiet night at home* (in my most sarcastically sweet tone). Before he could utter a response, I returned to my friends enraged, and the rage wasn't helped when they told me that Mutual Friend could be on his way. Two Persians from my past in one bar? Yeah, it was time to go home.

Persian Lawyer texted to ask me where I went—he wanted to explain. I told him that there was nothing to talk about; I was sick of him and didn't want to see him again. It felt melodramatic, like I was that "crazy girl," but I was past caring at that point. Burn the whole fucking thing down, what did I care?

Having lunch the next day with Priscilla (at the bar where Persian Lawyer and I'd had our first date, randomly), my phone dinged with a text from Persian Lawyer, mid-story about the night before. "Can we meet for coffee? I didn't like the way things ended last night." Finally, someone else who likes to have final conversations, and I'm obviously a sucker for punishment, so off I went. I knew how it would go: we'd agree (again) that we had to stop this; it wasn't going to work because one of us (likely me) would get hurt. I admitted to being an eternal romantic optimist, so I wanted to believe any smidgen of good intention from him. He did the whole, I-just-don't-want-to-hurt-you-but-I-really-don't-think-I'm-ready-to-date-right-now" thing and the whole conversation went down exactly as I'd expected.

Eventually, you do the whole on/off, on/off thing so many times that it really does get ridiculous. As I sat there outside Starbucks on the corner of Robson Street with him, drinking coffee on a fall Sunday afternoon, I was sad that it was over, again, but I felt like I'd already mourned it a number of times. The worst had passed. It was now just a realisation that I had to find some strength from somewhere and walk away from it, from him, for good.

As we parted, he said, "I'll probably see you around and bump into you at some point," just like what had happened the first time we tried to cut it off. Instantly I said, "I really hope not" because truly I didn't want to have to call on my self control to stay away from him again. I knew I wouldn't have that capacity forever.

Twenty-Two

New Views

The end of September was a difficult time. I'd finally closed the door on Persian Lawyer, and it marked five years since I'd moved to Vancouver. I was incredibly proud of the life I'd built for myself, but there was also a sense that it wasn't entirely what I'd imagined nor hoped for by this point in time.

If someone had told me when I arrived that I'd still be single in five years, no closer to having a meaningful romantic relationship (whatever that looks like), I would have been pretty goddamn upset. As it turned out, however, that was exactly what I was facing. My naivety about dating, soon dashed as I started my dating journey, led me to believe that I'd be in a relationship in no time, if I so desired.

Many people have said to me: "You could be in a relationship if you settled for less than you want," which isn't a suggestion; it's just a statement that I'm looking for the right thing for *me*, and in looking for that maybe I *should* expect it to take longer. But my expectation was that I'd have found a partner who provided what I hoped for in a partnership, while also being able to provide for their desires in return, and that hadn't happened.

To make things even trickier, the core group of friends I'd made upon moving to Vancouver had almost all gone through significant life changes: marriages, babies, engagements, even a breakup and a reunion for the same couple. I couldn't have been happier for all of them, but it had been significantly difficult for me not to compare where I was at myself. Admittedly, there was envy there—the devil of all emotions—but it was mostly just sadness and disappointment (and maybe a hint of fear). Granted, I'd only been dating again for two and a half years, but if it hadn't happened in that time, I wondered if it ever would. That thought in particular was creeping in more and more frequently.

As I was conducting my five-year Canadian life review, resetting my expectations and reconfirming what I already knew deep down: that I had achieved a lot in five years and shouldn't be comparing myself to anyone else. I came to realise that my unspoken expectation that I'd be in a relationship at this point had led to my unconsciously putting other parts of my life on hold. When I moved to Vancouver, I chose to live downtown, because it was something I'd always wanted to do—to live downtown in a North American city. So, great, check that off the bucket list! Moving into my second apartment and building Ikea furniture for my five-hundred square feet of personal space, I'd written myself a narrative that I didn't even know at the time. "This place is perfect for me until I get into a relationship. Once that happens, we (whoever "we" is) will build a home together and I'll have space for a dining table. We'll host the best dinner parties on the block."

Fast forward all these years later and the relationship was no closer, neither was a space that felt like home, the dining table or those dinner parties— which I so desperately wanted to have in my life again. They were something I'd been missing since my marriage ended. While the relationship wasn't something I could fabricate myself (and I'd definitely tried), the home, the dining table, and the dinner parties were entirely in my control. Living downtown had made complete sense for a number of years. My proximity to some of the best happy hours in the city was fully utilised, often three or four nights a week, and my friends made jokes about me not going over bridges (i.e. never leaving Downtown). At onset, they probably weren't too wrong.

But in recent years, as my interest in the outdoors and watching as many sunrises and sunsets as possible (something which brings me untold peace) grows, the match made in heaven between me and downtown living has started to wane. Yet if you asked any of my friends, or even me, until recently, you'd have been told I was the quintessential "Downtown Girl." Such was the narrative to which I adhered and everyone who knew me had fully bought into it. Once written, they never questioned me again. Once I'd even uttered the words, "I don't think I can ever see myself moving out of Downtown."

What I hadn't questioned was *why*. Why couldn't I see myself moving? Was my life Downtown everything I wanted? Was I truly living the life I wanted? No, I was living the life I felt that I should be living at the time, as a single female, as if somehow I should only be living in a shoebox-sized apartment and enjoying nights out in Yaletown bars drinking wine. That was my narrative. And no one had forced it on me; it just happened and for a while it fit. But now, it felt like I was trying to squeeze a non-shoebox shaped life into that apartment.

One random Saturday morning, while wandering around Kitsilano with Darlene and James, both of whom I'd been seeing a lot of since our Rockies road trip, I suggested that maybe I should look at apartments in the neighbourhood. We were sipping coffee and enjoying the beach views two minutes from where they both lived. But even as I said it that day, I didn't truly believe I'd end up moving. I definitely didn't expect to view twenty-one apartments in the next seven days and then sign a lease on a new one the following Saturday.

It was a transformative week. Not only were apartments less expensive (or old and crumbly) in Kits than I had imagined, but Kits wasn't as far from Downtown as I'd thought. Clearly, I had been holding out on myself. I'd been holding out on giving myself the life I wanted, instead waiting for someone to join me before the next stage of my life could begin, the stage that included a home and a dining table. *"Could begin" according to who?* I was more than horrified upon realizing that I'd subconsciously told myself that having more space, a dining table and a home, were things I couldn't have by myself. Partly that came from a financial perspective, but it was a misinformed perspective.

A quick look at Craigslist and a cancellation of a gym membership later, and I could make the numbers work. Maybe, just maybe, my often severe disappointment from failed dates and potential relationships wasn't just about being no closer to a relationship; the loss was how the relationship dream seemed to vanish along with the home dream. The two seemed intrinsically linked in the depths of my brain. How had I let that happen? And without even noticing? The realisation kind of threw me into a shock for a while.

Signing the lease on my new place partly came down to logistics. It was such a good find, and I needed to sign before it got snapped up. But I also didn't want too much time to talk myself out of it. So strong was the narrative about me being a "downtown girl" that every friend I told about my idea to move to Kits reacted with shock.

In reply to every reaction like that, I told them that I couldn't remember the last time I'd been to a happy hour in Yaletown, reminding them of just how often I was leaving my apartment to chase a sunrise or a sunset (both of which were much more accessible from Kits). It didn't take long for them to come to the same conclusion as me. Downtown didn't fit my life anymore. Somewhere like Kits made much more sense. And it literally took all of two seconds for my friends to agree, yet until that point we'd all just been following the same old story: *I'm Downtown Girl, I don't cross bridges, I live at happy hours...*

To be clear, there's nothing wrong with doing any of those things. They were all true and genuine for me, for a time, and I loved them while it made sense. But it didn't make sense anymore. The speed with which the subsequent move happened was probably the only thing that surprised people more than the move itself, myself included. Still, I kept waiting for the other shoe to drop, to realise I'd made a terrible mistake.... But the shoe never dropped. Fully settled into my new place, with an extra two-hundred square feet and a beautiful marble dining table that Damien and Darlene helped moved in before anything else, I accepted that maybe there wasn't another shoe to drop. Both shoes were firmly removed and my feet were fully ensconced in the sand of Kits beach.

It was a stark lesson in reassessing who I was, where I wanted to be, and whether I was being true to myself. Whether it's about a living situation, a job, a relationship, or whatever, too often we get into a comfort zone, a rut or habit, call it what you will. Breaking out of that habit can feel uncomfortable and, at times, unnecessary. But being brutally honest with yourself, coming to the realization, and doing something about it is truly liberating.

What may seem like a small change to some (I mean, I only moved a ten-minute drive away!) was genuinely life-changing for me. It felt like closing the loop on my move to Canada. I'd given myself the life I wanted, the life I'd been unconsciously wanting for a long time—and how fucking great is that? I got to do that for myself, by myself. Granted with a lot of help from friends and their cars and moving muscles. But the point is, I didn't need a relationship for any of it, which I'd somehow brought forth as a condition. *What the hell was that? 1950's me?*

And of course, just as I was gifting myself the benefit of independence, Persian Lawyer popped back up like clockwork. Replying to an Instagram story of mine (yes, we still followed each other and it was detrimental to the soul), he started flirting almost immediately. The next day, I cut to the chase and essentially decided to tie him down or chase him off. I suggested that we meet up for a drink, to which he replied, "I've actually just started seeing someone so I don't think it's fair to anyone if we do that." My eyes stung with tears as I sat at my desk. *How? Why?* I really thought I'd moved on, but I guess it was never fully off the table in my head. But now it had to be. I don't fuck with other women's men—it's a code, and we'd all do better if we adhered to it.

So, I told Persian Lawyer that the news was exactly what I needed to hear; it confirmed what I'd always said: that it wasn't a timing issue but a person issue. He didn't want to make time for me (and that was totally okay) but for the right person, he would always make time. Persian Lawyer said that he didn't know why I so strongly believed that, because apparently it wasn't the case, but he was happy that we'd spent time together and hoped there were no hard feelings about whatever did or did not happen.

This right here is one the biggest problems with so many men—wanting to be the good guy, so much so that they won't call a spade a spade. But I get it, oftentimes they don't want to give a girl the truth in case she "goes crazy," yet that's really just code for them not wanting to deal with the repercussions of their actions. In their defense, we sometimes don't do ourselves any favours by letting our emotions get the better of us, and some of us give *all* of us a bad name. But I'd always been clear about my need for clear and concise communication. It's not a crime, not having strong feelings for someone, so just be fucking honest!

With that behind me, I decided to concentrate on creating a sanctuary of peace in my new apartment. I vowed not to have any men over to my new place, unless I thought they were serious. Also, I vowed not to let Mutual Friend know where I lived, even though I was only three blocks from his place. We'd seen each other after I'd signed my lease and before I'd moved (yes, it was still a casual thing that happened when one (or both of us) were needy), but his horror that I was moving to his neighbourhood was enough for me to keep away from him, despite our close proximity.

I took two full weeks off over Christmas to enjoy my new surroundings, making the most of my ski passes for Grouse Mountain and Whistler and hosting my very first Christmas Day, including brunch with Damien and Sara and a drunkenly-cooked Christmas dinner with Keith. I worked out or skied every day, and by the New Year, I hadn't felt more at peace, possibly ever. I was also in the best shape of my life. Up until the last month of that year, I'd been feeling like I hadn't had many successes lately; but upon further reflection, the move to Kits coupled with the Chasing Sunrise trips, learning to set boundaries with men, and creating my own sense of peace had all been huge wins. Going into the new year felt liberating in a karmic way, like I was finally coming into my own after some tough times. Let's just say that I had high hopes for 2019.

Part 4

Twenty-Three

Not What I'd Planned

The peace I'd manifested at the end of 2018 was beautifully unfamiliar. I'd lived for myself and by myself ever since moving into my new apartment, which I'd made to feel cosy and super homely. While describing my new place to friends, I discovered that "homely" in North America means close to ugly, boring, or plain; while in the UK it means somewhere that feels home-like. Here they call it homey.... *Okay, Merriam Webster's*—another one for the "same language, different meanings" list.

With my mum's sixtieth birthday trip to Dubai coming up in February, all I wanted to do was concentrate on keeping my peace until that glorious week in the sunshine with my family. Even when Mutual Friend messaged me, a few days after New Year's, I told him where my head was at and we agreed on the importance of me keeping my peace. We both knew us seeing each other didn't play into that so well, so he left me alone. I'm not entirely sure what I was still doing on dating apps, and even less sure why I ended up agreeing to go on a spontaneous ice-cream date on the fifth of January, in the wintry Saturday cold.

Perhaps I was reacting to the guy I'd been ghosted by in early December; could a frosty cone put some ice on my heart for a while? In his defense, I'd showed up to our second date *drunk* from my office's Christmas party the night before, dressed in my ugly sweater gear and prepped for this year's Twelve Pubs of Christmas. So like, I probably would have ghosted me too.

Any swiping I'd done was without any real intention of going out. But when I started chatting with a match on the first Saturday of the year, he suggested that we meet for ice cream that afternoon. My kryptonite got the better of me, and I figured that if he wanted to drive from White Rock (a city about forty-five minutes south of Vancouver), and all I had to do was walk ten minutes to get ice cream, I wasn't going to argue. Since I'd moved to Kits, my go-to spot for ice cream had switched from Earnest to the local Kits spot called Rain or Shine. This was to be my first date at Rain or Shine, whereas I'd had too many to mention at Earnest. It felt good to start fresh here too.

In person, White Rock Boy's profile could have gone either way: either he'd just posted a couple of flattering pics or he was entirely underselling himself. Meeting him on the street, I remember being struck by his handsomeness, thus learning that it was the latter. He was classically good looking, in a wholesome sort of way, which his Bumble profile did not do justice. When we hugged hello, it was a warm and lingering hug, almost like you'd expect from a friend—again, wholesome. There was a sense of familiarity from the instant I met him, making it easier when I started walking him through the flavours & highlights of one of my favourite neighbourhood haunts.

The ease and fun continued as we sat in the ice cream shop for over an hour (long after our waffle cones were finished) and then seamlessly moved from there to dinner—his suggestion. It was getting later and he knew that neither of us had plans. The chat moved from lighthearted to life-affirming over dinner. We talked about our past relationships and why they'd broken down, dating in general and what we wanted now. At this point, I knew I'd met someone different. Never before had a man admitted to me, especially not on a first date, that he was not only looking for a long-term relationship but a future wife. Currently, it was one of his two life goals, which he wrote out on paper everyday.

To say that I was stunned but equally delighted by this detail is an understatement, albeit that marriage is a complex topic for me. I kept my jaw off the floor and the conversation moving, but there was something about the moment that made me wonder if this would be different. Dammit, there I go getting ahead of myself. All I'd done was come out for some ice cream!

Dinner then turned into drinks. He suggested the bar across the street, but I had to decline because I'd learnt the hard way (what with December's ghosting date) not to shit at your local. The bar is called Local for a reason; I was in there multiple times a week, thus you don't take random dates there. Instead we went to another nearby place and I made myself a vow to essentially go against all my usual instincts and have two drinks maximum. Regardless of how much I liked him, I wouldn't invite him back to my place (which would be harder than it might sound because my place was just a block away from the bar). But I truly wanted to keep my new apartment as a sanctuary and maintain at least an element of peace. My last apartment had ended up like a revolving door of men; and while I didn't regret any of it, there was something nice about knowing that my new place was almost virginal. Even if I was not.

So, despite drinks going by in a flash (because we never stopped talking) the night ended with another warm hug. We said goodbye outside the bar, five-and-a-half hours after we met. I was a little disappointed that he didn't move in for a kiss, worrying for the first time that we weren't on the same page. As he turned to leave, however, he said that he'd be back in the city the following week, so he'd probably see me then. He also said that it might end up being sooner…. I liked the idea of sooner.

Despite my initial efforts to do the opposite of everything I usually do on first dates, I did send a text not too long after we parted, as usual. In my text, I said thank you for the ice cream and the dinner (which he'd paid for) and the great night. He replied saying that it had been fun for him also, and he'd chat to me later. I figured that'd be the last of our communication for the night. But another text quickly followed, suggesting that I follow him on Instagram to check out videos of his puppy, about whom we'd talked extensively.

It sounded like such a line, but he seemed too wholesome for that. *Was that just my naivety talking?* Either way, we ended up messaging each other for the rest of the night until I went to bed. I had to actually cut myself off from talking to him, as I lay in the dark vowing to sleep, because I had too many questions. I wanted to know everything about him. Our hours of non-stop talking that night hadn't been enough. I was *fascinated* by him.

When he made a flirty comment about me getting into bed, my mind relaxed about us being on the same page about liking each other. It was a bit of a relief, for a couple of reasons: a) the lack of an end-of-date kiss hopefully didn't mean anything, and b) I liked someone who was flirty & sexual in messages. Though I still wasn't sure about the ideal time to initiate such messages, having them start *after* the first date was much later than some of my prior experiences.

White Rock Boy (nicknamed after his hometown of White Rock, which is *literally* just a stone's throw from the U.S. Border) was thirty years old, a custom-home designer/builder, and very much a country boy with a love for city living. He drove a Jeep, listened to country music and was getting a gun license, but he was also an entrepreneur who'd lived in San Diego and wanted to move back to Vancouver in the coming year. He came across initially as quiet and mild-mannered but with opinions and stories, and the ability to drive the conversation forwards with confidence, no matter the subject.

I'd often joked with Priscilla that I needed a country boy—someone with small town values and a wholesome upbringing—but I'm still a city girl at heart. I was never sure how that future would work out of for me. Meeting White Rock Boy, I wondered if this could be my perfect crossroads, my happy medium, my country boy. In the days following our first date, we arranged to see each other the following weekend, sooner than he'd suggested when we said goodbye at the bar. For the remainder of the week, I woke up every morning wishing that it were Saturday, like a kid in the run up to Christmas. It just couldn't come soon enough. I hadn't felt that giddy about someone in a really long time—I figure it must have been the country boy thing.

We messaged a lot that week: some flirty messages on the first night and then others that helped us get to know each other. That feeling of wanting to know everything about someone—every memory, every story, every win, every scar, all the light, all the dark—it's like receiving a paint-by-numbers kit with just the outline. The more you assign new colours, the more it comes to life. By the time Saturday arrived, I could barely wait to see him at six pm. When he said he could get to Vancouver earlier if he came straight to mine and showered there, I wasn't mad. I just asked if he always invited himself to shower at women's places on second dates. His reply? "Only the sexy Scottish ones." *Oi. Stop.*

He ended up arriving around half past four in the afternoon, while I was out shopping with Darlene and trying to keep my excitement in check. Even as we looked at furniture in the shops on South Granville, my mind was racing about how the night might go. He came to pick me up from the furniture store, but I figured that he'd just text me once outside. I was more than surprised when he nonchalantly strolled into the store with a hug for me and a hi for Darlene. I was struck again by how handsome he was. *Jeez,* I needed to get a grip on myself.

We got into his Jeep and drove off. When he reached over and squeezed my thigh, I thought that my heart, or my vagina, might burst. His touch was electrifying. I'd been waiting to have physical contact with him since our polite hug goodbye seven days ago, but this felt like an actual physical spark. In my head, all I could do was wonder when he'd kiss me. How the hell would I keep my shit together for that? I hoped it wouldn't happen in the car. In-car first kisses are always sub-optimal.

Once he'd showered from his day of snowmobiling (definite country boy), we had a drink at mine before going out. There was some light grazing of hands as I passed him another beer, and he jokingly grabbed my ankle at one point, which rested beside him on the sofa. His little moves only heightened my sense of excitement, making me wonder when the hell he was going to kiss me. I got my answer as we prepared to leave for dinner. He offered his hand to help me off the sofa (not that I needed it, but I wasn't going to pass up an opportunity for physical contact), pulling me into him as he pulled me upright, putting his hand in my hair (something he'd mentioned doing over text) and gave me the sweetest first kiss. It was light and so perfectly placed on my lips, and he simultaneously pulled me closer to him with his free hand.

I've had weak-knee moments, but this was practically rag doll, instant-Jello Lou. There's something about a good first kiss—when the anticipation has been building like fireworks and colours, marching bands and cheering crowds. In that moment, I was almost glad that we hadn't kissed on our first date. Unfortunately, the sweetness didn't last long. Clearly, we'd both been waiting for that one thing to happen, the slight opening of the door. But now the floodgates were open and before I knew it, he had me pinned up against the doorframe with his leg between mine, and the kisses weren't so sweet anymore.

During our five minute, very hot and very heavy make-out session, I wasn't sure that we'd make it out to dinner. At times, we both seemed to long for the bedroom, but instead we stayed in my hallway kissing, knowing we should stop but evidently unable. The lightness of our first kiss had become urgent and obsessive, as if we couldn't get our hands on each other enough.

Eventually, we made it out for dinner to Las Margaritas, a local Mexican place in Kits (by then, I'd recovered from the trauma of my day-of-two-dates—you know, shitting myself on a Mexican dinner date just a few years earlier?), which, again, seemed like a weird option if we were planning to have sex later. *Were we?* I didn't know; he'd been planning to drive home after dinner but anything could happen after our pre-dinner escapades. As we ate, I learned that he thought I was hilarious. Like, he actually said that. He had mostly dated "country girls," it seemed, so meeting a *tell-it-like-it-is* Scottish girl was perhaps a novelty to him.

After dinner, we walked back to my place via the beach. It was a cold January night, but he bundled me in his lap and plopped us down on a bench. We sat there intertwined, with him kissing me like he had in my apartment. The crispness of the air seemed to soften, the darkness enveloped us both like mist rolling in off the mountains, and we only tore ourselves away to get more "comfortable" back in my apartment.

Back on the sofa, we decided that he'd stay and "save himself the drive home," especially since he needed to be in Vancouver for lunch the following day. Part of me was screaming at myself to revert to one of my *reverse-Lou* tactics, while the other wanted nothing more than to get him into bed. (The latter part won.) I'd been concerned that this reserved country boy might not be up for much in the bedroom, but I needn't have worried. We had sexual preferences and libidos that matched perfectly, and his incredible rugged body was ideal for snuggling. His biceps made for perfect pillows.

The next morning, I discovered another match in our personalities—a love of early mornings. Awake and in need of coffee just after seven am, most people would have just rolled over; but we satisfied our morning sexual cravings, followed by a caffeine fix. What a perfect Sunday morning: sleepy morning sex followed by coffee, a walk downtown for breakfast, and more coffee as we headed home, followed by us getting back into bed for some more "exercise."

I was already exhausted, with a snowshoe hike planned for that afternoon, though the tiredness was entirely worth it. While I summoned the energy to hike through the snowy mountains on a gloriously sunny Sunday, he headed off to lunch with his buddy. I tried to play coy when I got interrogated mid-snowshoe adventure; but with friends there including Damien, Darlene, and James, plus the fact that I was bursting to talk about how great he was, it was hard to keep it chill, despite the near zero temperatures on Cypress Mountain.

If I couldn't play it cool with them, I would at least try to play it cool with him that afternoon. I'd focus on time with my friends and text him that night, if anything. But that plan was thwarted when he texted to ask me about my hike when we were halfway through, thus our ongoing text conversation took off down the runway. When it comes to digital communication, sometimes I struggle to set and respect my own boundaries. I've always been a *reply-in-2.5-seconds-or-2.5-days type of person,* so usually I do the former because the latter seems rude. But maybe it's not so much rude as necessary sometimes.

After a whirlwind weekend, my lack of sleep and general exertion left me feeling under the weather, so I worked from home on the Monday. That day, he posted a pic on his Instagram story, which he'd taken on our walk the previous morning. Given his profession (architecture is his jam), the new twisty skyscraper of Vancouver House under development beside the Granville Bridge had caught his eye. I replied to the story with: "Were you on a hot date when you took that?" Because, yes, even bleary-eyed on a Sunday morning, I tried to consider myself hot, such was the nature of my "fake it til you make it" confidence.

When his reply popped up as a text, not an Instagram DM reply, I had to re-read it a couple of times because the words didn't make sense. I'd expected it to read something like, *Oh yah, she was a real beaut';* a descriptor I'd already learned that he used for buildings, jeeps and women. Instead, it read: *She was just an old friend. I hadn't seen in her in a while, but yes it was a date. But I wasn't doing anything wrong because things are still so early with us.*

Oh-h-h-h this was awkward now. He'd just unwittingly admitted to having a date yesterday afternoon, while I was up the mountain—that was my first thought. Like *oh wow, this joke has backfired real bad.* I also felt for him, because he'd so regret sending that text. Then I recalled that not only had he specifically, on numerous occasions, referred to having lunch with a *buddy,* but he must have texted me while he was with her. *Oh* this did not feel so good. I replied, "Weren't you with me when you took that picture?" I could almost hear the penny drop all the way in White Rock, like that time I sent Malaysian Persuasion a screenshot of our convo, which I'd intended for a friend. In those moments, there was nothing to do but hold up your hands.

Wow, I'm an idiot, he wrote next. I agreed with him on that. I also agreed that things were still early with us, so no, he absolutely didn't need to tell me about the date—just as I hadn't told him about my date on Thursday (made in a futile effort not to rush into things mentally with White Rock Boy, though I kept that to myself). Because that's what you do: you go on the dates but keep it to yourself, unless of course it's an exclusive situation! What annoyed me more was that he'd consciously tried to mislead me in saying that lunch was with a "buddy." Even if she were an old friend, he never would have referred to her as a buddy if he didn't want me to think it was a guy, not a girl.

He called me to talk it through, which I liked. A lot of guys would have hidden behind their phone screen. He conceded that I was right, and he was sorry. He'd thought about telling me the night before but decided against it, because he didn't think he owed me anything. I agreed, but I always think that sounds kind of rude. *I don't owe you anything…. Yah, well, fuck you.* He apologised again, and I re-iterated to him something I'd already expressed during our dates so far—that I needed honesty, communication and consistency.

We were still in that gray area, between casual and having some skin in the game (mostly feelings and ego). It can be hard to know exactly how much you owe someone at first, not to mention what to expect from them. Despite gray being my favourite colour (calm down designers, I know it's technically a shade), I absolutely hate "gray areas." But in this shaded area, I always tried to ground things in the thought: *How would you feel if the shoe were on the other foot?* Would I act without reproach in this situation, or how would I want to be treated? I don't know if there's ever a wholly right answer, and sometimes I probably expect too much. Other times, I've possibly not considered someone else's feelings enough—but I do my best with being human.

Later that afternoon, as all these thoughts swirled in my head, he texted to say that he was coming into Vancouver, so would I be in for him to drop over? I wasn't sure what had cropped up all of a sudden in the city—maybe another hot date? But I said sure, he could drop by. So, when he arrived on my doorstep with a pint of ice cream from Rain or Shine, I was pleasantly surprised. He felt shitty about what happened and wanted to apologise in person. *He drove forty-five minutes for that?* Okay, I could take that kind of apology. Especially when it came armed with blueberry balsamic ice cream.

That said, I was less impressed when we ended up having sex and the condom split. *I'm sorry, Monday, are you fucking with me?* Because when a boy visits to apologise for something he did, who wouldn't want to seal the deal with a trip to Shoppers Drug Mart for Plan B, on a rainy Monday evening, when you're already feeling less than one-hundred percent? But he dropped me home and apologised like wild, knowing how much Plan B can fuck you up. I told him it was fine. I took the pill and went to bed. I was doing my best to forget this day entirely. Things with White Rock Boy were in very early stages, and his apology seemed genuine. Perhaps I really could chalk up his snafu to stupidity, and I believed in modern medicine. I was sure there'd be nothing to worry about in nine months (and there wasn't).

Putting that behind us, things progressed and we started spending weekends together. With the distance and his dog, there was some planning required, but we made it work. It started with me heading to White Rock on a Friday, faded into him coming into Vancouver on a Thursday, and then eventually I was going there on Wednesdays evening to work for the rest of the week. Then he'd drive me home on Sunday and stay a couple hours—which became him staying until Monday—and on Tuesday he'd leave. So yeah, we were spending weekends with each other, but really our weekends included the majority of the week. Thank god I was able to work remotely.

We went out for dinners, showed each other our respective neighbourhoods, ate a lot of ice cream, went on long dog walks, cooked a lot of steak, drank wine, had a lot of sex, sang along to country songs in the car, spent Sunday mornings wrapped up in each other, and we talked about life and family and future plans. The only weekend we didn't spend together was when I went away for Damien's birthday at the end of January.

One of my favourite groups of friends—Damien, Sara, Alana and this new addition to the group, a lanky English geezer called Jamie—had booked a weekend of skiing over the border in Washington State, at Mount Baker, to celebrate Damien getting a year older. Meanwhile, White Rock Boy had a course to attend in Vancouver starting on Friday. I casually suggested that he should just stay at mine, to save him driving back and forth. Although selfishly, I'd offered because that way I'd see him before I left *and* when I got home. I didn't think twice about it; such was the time we'd spent together by that point. However, an always amusing South African colleague of mine, who was always interested in hearing the latest and (not so) greatest dating stories, was convinced he'd steal my identity.

Thankfully, my identity wasn't stolen, but before I even left on Friday, I realised that we had a problem. Going onto Bumble at work to show a friend his profile, I saw that he was three kilometres away, which was also the distance to my apartment. Had he been swiping on Bumble while staying in my apartment?!

In fairness, he could have done what I had, which was to open the app and look at something, without swiping, but I just knew in my gut that wasn't it. So I texted him. Maybe I should have left it, but the weird feeling in my stomach wouldn't let me. Was he going to go out on another "buddy" date while staying under my roof? The thought of it made me feel sick. The reply that came back was very matter of fact: *yes I still have the apps…we never had a conversation about it.* Right, yeah, I get that mate, but you're at my fucking house!

I told him that if he was happy for us to see each other so often and to stay at mine for a weekend while I was away, but not happy enough to commit to stop swiping on other people, then maybe we should slow things down a bit. He could take time to see what else was out there (if that's what he needed?) and then we could pick things up again if/when he felt sure. I truly meant this too. While ordinarily I would have been terrified of giving someone the option to leave me, in fear they actually just might, I'd always had this sense of peace with White Rock Boy. There was no feeling of needing to second guess or force it. It felt like a great place to be and a brand new sensation for me.

I texted him in my most calm and rational tone. Is that even a thing? Apparently not, because he received it as an ultimatum, which apparently he didn't appreciate. It escalated as we went back and forth during our work mornings. It felt like a fight, and it wouldn't be helped by me losing signal for the weekend, somewhere in the shadow of Mount Baker. I offered to call him before I left for the weekend, but he declined and said that he didn't want to talk to me, such was his dislike of the way I'd gone about the situation. *Um… ok.* I chose not to respond with the "what the actual fucks" in my head and told him we'd chat about it when I was back.

That weekend, I just had Wi-Fi in the cabin. I'd message White Rock Boy while listening to Damien's running commentary about how much I was on my phone; so I guess it's fair to say that things had returned to normal between me and White Rock Boy. But when I got back to my apartment on Sunday, the first thing that hit me when I opened the front door was the smell of weed. *Ah fuck. Fucking weed. Again. Why did this keep causing me problems?!* I could choose to ignore it, but no, it was my apartment.

Had he really smoked weed in my apartment? He was still at his course when I arrived home. I knew he smoked and it had never bothered me, but in my apartment? Like did he just have no respect for my home at all? Had he been enjoying a weekend of swiping and smoking while I'd been *shoop-shoop-ing* my way down the slopes? Or had he simply rolled a joint on the table and taken it outside? Could it smell that much still from simply rolling a joint? Honestly, who was I to know.

Walking back over the Burrard Bridge after I met him from his course, I asked him whether he'd smoked in my apartment, simply to communicate that I'd appreciate if he didn't do it again. While I didn't mind him smoking, I still found the smell kind of triggering, due to my ex. As a non-smoker myself, I shouldn't have to put up with it in my own home. He told me that he hadn't smoked—he'd just had a joint in his pocket, which must have made the apartment smell.

Of course, I was instantly transported back to conversations with my ex-husband. When he'd tell me one thing but my gut knew it wasn't right; I'd feel like a child trying to argue with a parent, feeling that for whatever inexplicable reason, they had the upper hand. I was also aware of how little I wanted to rock the White Rock Boy boat. I saw so much potential; we were aligned on so many things. But I could feel when someone was lying and the end result was that I carried the wool they thought I could pull over my eyes.

A week later, we dug into the weed thing more, after he lied to me about smoking before picking me up. Sitting on the floor next to his couch, I asked myself questions about what it was that I disliked so much, where it came from, what the emotion was, and why it triggered me sometimes and not others. Perhaps it wasn't marijuana at all but rather dishonesty in general. Regardless of whether someone is okay with cannabis use, it's not cool to smoke in their personal space without permission; and if I could understand that someone had a right to ghost me if I showed up for a date drunk, then surely he could understand that I might not appreciate him showing up high.

All the same, I realised during this self-analysis that my memory of my ex and weed was that he always lied to me about it, and thus I connected him lying about it to him lying about fucking and sexting half the women in Edinburgh. So yeah, it makes sense that I could associate covert cannabis use with lying and cheating. White Rock Boy was amused by my ability to uncover this revelation and my own delight in doing so. Then all we had to do was figure out how to get around that. The answer wasn't for him not to smoke; I never wanted that. I realised that all I needed was for him to be up front about it. Not in a "miss, I smoked today" way but in a "my day was good, I went to the gym, smoked, took the dog for a walk" kind of way. We high fived on the solution and he said it sounded easy enough. Then we decided to rearrange some of his furniture. In the midst of doing so, he went out to smoke. Nothing covert about it, it was as overt as you like and I thought I was fine, but according to him, when he came back in I was different towards him. My argument was more to do with the fact that I was left to rearrange *his* furniture than about him smoking, but he wasn't convinced. So we went to bed hoping this was something that would get easier.

But the next day, I went to visit Granny Carmelita (my adopted Canadian Granny that Jess was kindly still sharing with me, who also lived in White Rock) and when he came to pick me up, something was just different. He was agitated and keeping a noticeable distance from me. Of course, he charmed the pants off Granny in the five minutes that we chatted on her doorstep, but there was a palpable difference in him from when he'd dropped me off. I asked him what he'd gotten up to while I'd been with Granny, and he told me that he'd washed the Jeep. That was it. Half an hour later, when he finally kissed me, I tasted it. The smoke.

Ugh. So I asked him, and he said that he'd smoked while I'd been at Granny's. Why couldn't he have just offered that up when I'd asked him what he'd been doing, as we'd discussed? I didn't want him to feel like he had to report to me, but it was the best way to start to get around my issue with it. Anyways, I didn't think it was that big of an ask and he'd agreed! So why try to keep it from me after we'd had that conversation? Once again, I was transported back to those feelings of being at a complete loss for what to do. It's like that feeling of knowing you should probably run, but you don't want to; so instead you just stand, feeling torn, feeling stuck, feeling as if you're drowning and there's no fucking service to call and ask the universe for help.

I didn't know how to react, so I went silent. Usually I'm a talker, a resolver, but this time… I just…*froze.* My body vibrated with conflict and frustration that the issues from my marriage were still plaguing me. I didn't want to be that girl who brings her baggage into new relationships, but as much work as I'd done on myself, with Julia's help, it was difficult to know where my head was at until I rode the waves of a relationship. Other than with Filipeen and Italian Lebanese, I hadn't had the opportunity to do that much. There were still so many unknowns. At the first hurdle, White Rock Boy had reverted to the type of guy I was desperately trying to avoid—choosing the "easy" thing above trying to move our relationship forwards, and then getting annoyed when I reacted poorly.

It was a tough day, ripe with silence. I asked him to drive me back to Vancouver and was almost entirely packed before he asked to talk about it. I explained my frustrations, reiterating what I needed and that if he couldn't provide those things, maybe we needed to call time on things now. He assured me that this wasn't what he wanted; we could work it out sooner or later. I'd agreed to stay after all, but who knows if I'd be able to get out of my head.

As it turns out, my head was holding me captive. We spent a painful afternoon shopping and going to meet his friends. It was a weird time to introduce me to his friends, but I did my best Oscar-worthy act of pasting on a smile. There was still something in his want to introduce me that I liked, as an indication of his dedication to progressing things. Maybe it was the sign I needed that day.

I left on Valentine's Day to fly to Dubai, a flight I'd booked back when I thought I wouldn't have any Valentine's plans (*whoops, spoke to soon*), and by then he'd met some of my friends as well. We had plans for him to come along to the Rugby Sevens in March (I'd bought his ticket for his birthday, which he'd celebrate while I was away), and we'd had a conversation about not being on the apps anymore. He told me that he didn't need to see what else was out there; he was enjoying getting to know me and that's what he wanted to focus on.

I was hopeful that the break imposed by my trip would give us time to reset. When I got back at the beginning of March, we could start fresh, having hopefully missed each other as much as we expected. Dropping me off at the airport, I already knew how excited I'd be to come home and have him pick me up. The thing I'd always dreamed of since I moved to Vancouver: coming home to someone. Little big dreams.

Dubai was amazing, of course. *It's Dubai.* I spent a full week with my family in total luxury, bathing in the sunshine of Atlantis The Palm. Making memories with my niece is forever special and only makes me wish I could do it more. Despite my jet lag, celebrating my mum's sixty years on the planet as a family, putting so much of the past behind us, was a glorious moment of coming full circle. From Dubai, I went back to the UK for a few days, another surprise for my mum, and threw a party for her at the house. While we wanted to be selfish and celebrate her birthday just ourselves, with all the friends and family who think so highly of her, we couldn't not celebrate with them as well.

As always, it was a busy and emotion-filled trip home. I'd be in Edinburgh for just four days, including the day I'd flown out, and it took its toll. Not least because, before we even left Dubai to return to the misery of the UK in February, I could sense that something was off with White Rock Boy. The FaceTime chats we'd promised each other happened only once, and despite his assurances about not wanting to chat (because he wanted me to spend time with my family), I found it hard to believe when he said it at six am, my time, as all my family members were sleeping. Maybe he wasn't thinking about the time difference, but I'm pretty sure I mentioned being up with the sun.

The emotions and copious amounts of alcohol got the better of me, the night of my mum's birthday party. Drinking with my godmother (who has been my mum's best friend since they were five) and her twin daughters until stupid o'clock in the morning, I would have loved to have just taken myself to sleep afterwards. But waking up the following morning, I had a picture of White Rock Boy in my head, on a FaceTime screen, in a red sweater or jacket...Had I dreamt that? *Please God tell me I'd dreamt that.* One swift check of my phone later, and nope, I'd apparently FaceTime'd him three times... *Oh Jesus.*

I knew it couldn't be good. I'd been in a headspace that wouldn't have allowed for a cheery and easy breezy catch-up. So, I pre-empted the impending fiasco by sending a text, saying that I knew we'd talked but I didn't remember what about. I was sorry if I'd said anything uncalled for and presumed we'd have stuff to talk about later, but I was looking forward to doing it in person at home.

None of it was good, came his reply. Well, no shit Sherlock, that's why I apologised. *I know, it's rarely good when you call someone blackout drunk,* was my actual response. It wasn't a good day. I was hungover, and the guilt of being hungover is always elevated when I'm in my mother's presence. My mum is incredibly tolerable, but I'd always been aware of how disappointed she got when people over-indulged in alcohol. Despite having a bar in her house and being a huge gin fanatic, she was a proponent of drinking in moderation—something I'd struggled with since I was seventeen. Back then, I remember going to some school classes drunk, as a way to cope with my parents' divorce. This was made easier by being at boarding school, because there simply weren't enough teachers to track your every movement.

To the hangover I could add a healthy dose of guilt, the reality that I had no idea where things stood with White Rock Boy, and the realisation that blacking out was becoming an all too regular occurrence when I drank. Blacking out refers to the body's inability to form and store new memories, often when the blood-alcohol level raises too rapidly. It's also known as alcohol-induced amnesia or a sign of binge-drinking. *Hmm.* I mean, I knew I was a classic binge drinker, but the increased frequency of drink-induced blackouts, even after a relatively small amount of alcohol (sometimes after just three glasses of wine), was definitely playing on my mind. When I could remember, that is…*sorry, bad joke.*

I told my mum about the FaceTime and her response was as expected: "Well, I hope you haven't ruined things with him because of it." *Oooft.* In some ways, this was just my mum's tough love. But in others, she was expressing disappointment that, at age thirty-four, I was unable to control my drinking. She'd bore witness to the habit for over seventeen years now, so I could understand her frustration. To say that my flight back to Vancouver the next day was a struggle is an understatement. Emotionally, I was all over the place—and White Rock Boy had gone MIA.

Texting with Darlene, I expressed my confusion and concern, saying that, while I hadn't heard from him, I presumed he'd still be picking me up at the airport. Except there was no text before I got on my flight in Edinburgh and no text before I boarded the plane in London to Vancouver. I figured that I should prepare for the worst. But surely if his intention was not to pick me up, he'd let me know. The wheels had barely touched the tarmac at YVR when the text pinged through on my phone. There it was: *I won't be coming to pick you up. I'm working and I'm leaving right when I'm done to go and see my brother.* I should have known that he wouldn't be there. He'd given no indication since dropping me off that he'd be waiting when I came home; and yet my naivety, my hopeless romantic optimism thought that maybe, just maybe, he would come.

Whether or not things would work out or whether I even wanted them to work out, I still hoped for my airport pickup. Instead, as we moved along the runway towards the terminal, I felt stranded, tears filling my eyes. By the time I was walking through arrivals, tears were rolling down my cheeks and I couldn't stop them. I must have looked like I *really, really* didn't want to be in Vancouver. I had a hot pain in my chest and a fog in my head, this time one that wasn't just jet lag.

Having friends who can pre-empt an SOS are the people you really need in your life. While White Rock Boy wasn't at the airport, Darlene was. Grateful doesn't even explain how I felt. The regular updates on the situation, which she'd been receiving from me, meant that she was a bit more of a realist about the situation than I'd been. Getting into her car, my heart broke. It wasn't the airport pickup I wanted, but it was the one I needed.

Twenty-Four

It All Falls Down

I wouldn't see White Rock Boy again. He would ignore my texts, become unavailable, and not respond to my calls. In the jet lagged, devastation-filled nights that followed my return to Vancouver, I downloaded Bumble and Tinder again, not with a view to date but to prove something to myself. I made the settings as specific as possible (with age and distance) and found him on them again in less than five swipes. *Was he ever really off them?* Either way, it was clear nothing was left between us.

But still, I just needed to hear it. In my moments of desperate hope, I'd think that maybe he just needed some time and space; but in my moments of reality-soaked devastation, I knew it was over. A week and a half later, we spoke on the phone. With the Rugby Sevens weekend coming up soon I was unsure whether he was still planning to come or not, despite the writing being right there on the wall, or rather in his silence. But I couldn't give it up. Whatever tiny, miniscule amount of hope I had that things could spring back to life, I clung onto for dear life.

Friends would tell me that I deserved better than somebody who left me stranded at the airport (he wasn't to know Darlene had been my saviour in a Ford Escape). They would ask why I'd want to be with someone who'd essentially ignored me since I had come home, despite my attempts to make sense of things. They'd told me to forgive myself for the drunken FaceTime. But of course they would—they're my friends. In my head, I knew that drunk call would haunt me for a long, long time. The worst part was not knowing what exactly I'd said; I could only guess, and self-guessing a memory that isn't there only makes the mind go wild.

When we finally spoke on the phone, he mentioned that he'd started feeling differently about me before I left on my trip, but he didn't know how to bring it up. I reasoned that letting things go down the shitter while I was trying to enjoy a family vacation definitely wasn't cool. He said he thought that "we both fundamentally want[ed] the other person to change." I had never once said nor thought that about him, but obviously he had about me. When pressed, he assured me that there wasn't someone else. But I didn't honestly know what to believe.

It hurt, it all hurt. Every single part of me. To be so explicitly rejected by someone, to have someone choose you one day and not the next. My body was fatigued, my mind fogged, and my emotions so heightened that I could barely function. To complicate matters, when I'd returned to work post-vacation, my new boss at the company I'd taken the challenging job with told me that she didn't think my heart was in it. It was not the first time she'd asked me whether I really thought the company and I were a good fit. It blindsided me, because I'd never questioned my dedication to my work, and I didn't think anyone else did. She obviously felt differently. I then found out that she'd been asking people about my timekeeping. Being based in L.A., she couldn't have known that I was often the first person in the office every morning, turning on the lights, all for her to throw me under the bus in meetings.

After my first conversation with her, I'd vowed to knuckle down upon returning from my trip, to ensure she knew my value and contribution. But I hadn't expected to be in the middle of a heartbreak at the same time. My appetite had entirely vacated my life; my ability to get any more than three hours of sleep was gone, unless distressed-dream-filled sleep counted, and my head was consumed with thoughts about why this had happened. *Why wasn't I good enough? Why did I get drunk? Why had he changed his mind about me? Should I fundamentally be a different person? Was I still so damaged that no one would ever choose me?*

Two weeks later, I had a work trip to Austin. The value of my joining the trip was being questioned by the exec team (or so my boss told me) so I had "better make sure it was valuable." She asked me whether I realised the trip was so soon after my vacation. *Yes, I did, which was why I'd brought it to your attention when WE both agreed it was worthwhile for me to go,* even though it was so soon after my return from Dubai. She was nitpicking everything, questioning all of my work and putting pressure on me before I even boarded the plane to

Austin. Life stress had started to physically manifest itself with me becoming sick as a dog just in time for the trip.

Thankfully, I was travelling with Kim, a colleague who became my friend when we travelled together for work to Montreal, last May, when I'd been with Italian Lebanese and instead I'd celebrated my birthday in Quebec with Kim and her now fiancé, who'd joined us in Montreal. Even before we left for Austin, Kim knew the stress I was facing at work, her sympathy aroused again upon hearing about the situation with White Rock Boy.

By the third day on Texan soil, I was so sick and stressed. I could feel a black wave of nothingness coming at me, like an abyss rolling into my beautiful Fairmont Hotel room. Unfortunately, I didn't know how to escape it. It had been hovering as a cloud for the past couple of weeks, but as my Slack messages piled up on my phone, emails bundled into my laptop, and the pressure of needing to get value from my time at SXSW (the conference we were attending), I completely lost my ability to think clearly. I was in a constant state of panic as the cloud descended into a black mist all around me.

I tried to get a Skype appointment with Julia, in hopes that some therapy from afar might talk me off the ledge. But Julia was busy. To make things worse, my sinuses were inflamed so I couldn't breathe through my nose. Kim suggested that maybe I should go use the sauna and try to sweat out all the toxins swirling in my body. I knew the real toxins were the ones in my brain, and that's how I found myself sitting alone in the beautiful spa with fifties' décor at the Fairmont Austin (if you're ever in town you should go), in the middle of an emotional breakdown (but avoid that part). Once the tears started, I was at a loss to stop them. They were like Niagara Falls. The difficult thoughts I'd been having got darker and darker by the minute, to the point where I couldn't see myself making it out of Austin in anything other than a body bag.

It was a scrolling rotation of shitty thoughts. "I'm devastated by White Rock Boy; my job isn't safe; maybe I don't love my job; maybe this isn't the space I'm meant to be in anymore; maybe these are not my people. My finances are a mess because I'm fiscally irresponsible and missing a life purpose. I don't have the capacity to learn anymore. When did I stop being curious? The event of a romantic relationship and a family are completely illusive. Stress is making me sick; my own life overwhelms me; I'm completely disillusioned by the Internet, Instagram, and online dating. I just feel broken. Why am I so broken?

How do I make it all stop? I need it all to stop."

I was sitting in a luxury spa, in a five-star hotel, in a city I'd wanted to visit forever–but every single one of my thoughts had gone dark. It's true what they say: money can't buy happiness. With my phone trembling in my hands, I reached out to Darlene and Priscilla in Vancouver, but I couldn't explain the depths of my feelings over text. There was little they could do from afar, apart from assure me that things weren't as bad as they seemed. But their claims fell on ears deafened by a sense of loss and desperation.

I stayed in the spa for hours—thankfully all the while alone because most people were likely in Austin getting *value* out of SXSW—until the panic arose once again. I'd just remembered that I had a meeting to take with a contact at the conference. The thought of missing it and possibly having to tell my boss terrified me, much more than the dread and lethargy filling my body at the thought of facing the world. The rest of Austin was a blur. If it hadn't been for Kim, I probably wouldn't have made it home in one piece. Her ability to speak rationally enabled me to simply put one foot in front of the other, which in itself was a struggle. We'd chosen to stay an extra two days after our work commitments ended, thinking we'd fill them with fun and food and partying, but I'd never *not* wanted to be in a party city more in my life. If I could have afforded a change of flights, without alarming work, I'd have gone home earlier. Instead I barely left the room, all the while trying to fabricate a great time on Instagram—such was my need to seem functional on this work trip.

We barely made it back from Texas, with delayed flights galore, and the weekend after Austin was Rugby Sevens. Against my better judgment, I went. But I was still raw and barely had my sanity intact. I felt sure that I'd lose it at some point. But maybe a weekend with friends would make things better. I figured that I should probably keep my drinking to a minimum, yet James suggested the opposite, so my losing it happened even earlier than anticipated as I lost it at him in the car, catching both him and Darlene off guard. So yeah, I was still on an emotional teeter totter.

As intended, I kept my drinking under control during the day. But as we left the stadium later on, clad in our eighties' workout gear (our costume of choice that year), I decided to let my guard down and throw back a few drinks at Brewhall, a craft brewery in Olympic Village. Around the same time, I made the questionable choice to message Malaysian Persuasion, inquiring as to whether he'd been at the rugby festivities like last year. Talk about grasping at straws, but there's nothing like an alcoholic crutch to get men back on the brain. Despite my brevity in reaching out, I was surprised when he replied. Sometimes, in these situations (where I clearly can't save myself from myself), I hope the guy will do the saving for me and simply *not* reply. Alas, that rarely happens.

He hadn't been at the rugby but he was at a club downtown. As my drunkenness increased, my infinite wisdom became finite: I decided to turn up at the club he had mentioned. I know, so much was wrong with that decision, and of course that's when the blackout starts in my memory bank. Oftentimes I have snippets of memories from nights like that, and others are pure blackout. Honestly, I think the blackout is kinder—snippets are torture. I could remember him meeting me in the parking lot outside the club on Davie Street, in addition to us entering and him paying the cover charge because I had no cash. I remember almost falling over on the dance floor, and the next thing I knew, I was struggling to unlock the side door to my building, with him behind me asking whether I was sure it was the right key, or the right building (he'd never been to my new place). Then I remember looking at him from the perspective of me lying on my bed, either partially or fully naked, I wasn't sure, and him saying "I should go."

There are lows and then there are *LOWS*. This was definitely a *LOW*. I knew even while it was happening that I was emotionally devastated; this was just my way of "dealing" with the feelings, but that didn't make it okay. To be that much of a mess and embarrass yourself in front of people so thoroughly.... Well, I presumed it qualified as embarrassing because it clearly wasn't a glowing representation of my otherwise lovely self. I'd carried the whole thing out in eighties' workout gear, but I was nowhere near anyone else in costume. All the *too-cool-for-school* twenty-something-year-olds were looking at this thirty-four-year-old with disdain. At least, that's the way it happened in my head.

I didn't tell anyone what happened the following day, but I did show up for rugby again. People just thought I went home after the bar, so I chose not to correct them. Instead I just lived with the shame and added it to the growing pile of absolute shit that was stinking up all my thoughts. Work was still an ongoing stress, and my boss had been suggesting I look for other jobs. After one call with a potential business partner, she sent me the contact's LinkedIn profile on Slack, along with the note: "Maybe a job like this would be good for you?" Like, *WHAT'S THE BIG IDEA; I HAVE A JOB!*

I'd never dealt with conflict and stress like this at work. Granted, it wasn't helped by the emotional distress from my personal life, but I felt victimised by my boss for some reason. I was dreading going to work every day, like panic-attack shit. I'm not sure whether she truly just didn't think I was good at my job, thus hoping I'd quit and save her the hassle of dealing with me. But the professional thing to do is treat your employees professionally; if that is somehow not possible perhaps have them report to someone else, if in fact they're doing their job well. Maybe my boss was just as toxic as my ex-husband; she was under a lot of pressure at work, but we all were. It was a very "dynamic" place to work, but was she just taking it out on me? I shared it with HR, who told me to maybe try communicating with her differently. Um, I think we're past it being a communication problem.

By the end of March, I couldn't understand what had happened to my life. I had gone away to Dubai and my life had fallen apart under the Arabian sun. I'd had no time to enjoy the post-vacation glow; my New Year's peace was gone and the previous years of work I had done on myself were feeling futile. I was emotionally incapable of dealing with where I found myself. So, as a distraction, Darlene and I decided to visit Whistler on the last Saturday in March. I always loved the head-clearing effects of throwing myself down a mountainside, being just on the right side of losing control. That said, it was scarily comforting to know that I could have chosen to "accidentally" lose control, and I don't say that lightly. By the time we were making the two-hour drive up the highway, I found out that Mutual Friend was also going to Whistler that day (through mutual friends, of course).

He had in fact come back into my life, just as White Rock Boy was exiting, as if he had a sixth sense. Sometimes I wondered where he got his insider info, but I knew Sara would've never shared anything about me with him. I'd seen him a couple of times recently in the midst of the growing pile of shit accumulating in my life, mostly for sex and watching movies. Always we hung out at his place, the epitome of casual—but one time I'd helped him pack for vacation, as well as lending him a suitcase and driving him to the airport the next morning. He was going to Hawaii for a family wedding. We had a very couple-y kiss at departures, and I returned his car to his building's parking garage.

While nothing serious would ever happen with him, there was a familiarity between us that felt nice. Despite my usual dislike of going to guys' apartments, his place brought me a strange sense of comfort, and I always had the best sleeps in his bed. He never asked anything of me, and we never talked about life outside those four walls. He had no idea about my work stress or my heartache, though he commented a couple of times that I seemed "sad" or "quiet." All the same, he never wanted to actually know about my feelings; it was just an observation, not a concern. In every other area of my life I felt like I always had to be "on", but with him there was this sense that I could just "be". As unconventional as it was, I found unexplained comfort in being with him, as if we were somehow kindred spirits. We had a come-to-Jesus chat about our expectations from each other and mutually admitted that we each were using the other person. *Well, at least we were honest.*

As we got off the gondola on Blackcomb Mountain, some of our other mutual friends were the first people I ran into. As we headed off in the direction of our different runs, we loosely arranged to meet up at the end of the day, in the obligatory après-ski bar in Whistler Village. After a gloriously sunny day of skiing, getting to the Longhorn Saloon felt well-earned, and the crazily warm March day had the patio packed. People, ski jackets, hats, scarves, helmets, and gloves discarded all over the place. Darlene and I made friends with varying groups of tourists; and across the bar, I could see familiar faces gathering, including Mutual Friend.

What should have ended for Darlene and me with a drive back down the Sea-to-Sky Highway turned into us crashing at the Airbnb the boys had booked for the night. After some futile attempts at declining, we accepted their offer. Darlene had never experienced the right of passage that was partying at Longhorn or other Whistler Village bars, but Mutual Friend made it clear that he absolutely did not want me staying. All the same, he'd grabbed me for a kiss me as I passed him on my way to the toilet one time, ensuring, of course, that nobody in his group saw. Those kinds of head games were the absolute last thing I needed. So, in a show of defiance (and maybe just a hint of pettiness) I turned right around and accepted the offer to stay. I knew it wasn't the smartest idea, but fuck it—at this point, how much worse could things really get?

Well, apparently much worse. We all headed to the nearby sushi restaurant to eat before returning to the Airbnb. I don't eat sushi, but an empty stomach wouldn't be a great combination with copious amounts of beer, sake, and shots. (We were going out again later.) Plus, dinner was awkward as fuck. I sat between Mutual Friend and one of his best friends, who was maybe hitting on me, being unaware of the history between me and one of his closest buddies. I could sense Mutual Friend getting frustrated. In my pettiness and general dislike for the male species, at that point in time, I didn't do anything to quash the tension.

Not to mention, Mutual Friend was making offensive side comments to Darlene all night. They'd always had a strained "relationship," ever since being introduced on Halloween and alcohol had made for a terse first meeting. As we left the restaurant for the Airbnb, I remember trying to talk to Mutual Friend about it and set some ground rules for the night: like a) *be nice,* and b) *either we're together or I'm free to do what I want, and so are you.* He couldn't have it all ways with me: kissing me but telling me to leave *and* being mad when I started chatting with his friend.

I'd love to further recount the conversation here, but the blackout happened right in the middle of it. The only snippet I remember is being back in the bedroom of our Airbnb—the door closed on Mutual Friend and me. I remember shouting and things being thrown, but that's *all* I remember. Until, that is, my drunken blackout cleared (who knows how much later) with Mutual Friend in the single bed and me in the hallway, discovering that the Airbnb was empty, whereby it had previously been teeming with our friends. My phone was dead and I was partly undressed. I didn't understand how the fight had happened, or where everyone else had gone, but I found a charger and tried to organise the racing thoughts in my head.

Whistler wasn't that big, so there were only a few places everyone could be. I would probably find them, *right?* In my drunken haze, I went downstairs and opened the front door, still missing half my clothes, and found myself gazing upon a maze of other condo buildings, pathways, and treetops. That's when the freezing alpine temperature hit me. I had no idea where in the village I was right then. In Whistler, once you're in one of the building complexes, they can be almost impossible to exit—like a labyrinth of Western Civilization—especially if you'd entered while black-out drunk.

Thankfully, I made at least one good decision, choosing not to leave the Airbnb in search of our friends. At least I was sobering up, albeit I was still freezing. I couldn't work out the heating—hell I could barely find my ski pants—and the only warm body in the whole place was Mutual Friend.

Despite not knowing quite what had happened last night, I was pretty sure we weren't on speaking terms. Still, I was so cold, and genuinely worried that the alcohol and plummeting temperatures would put my body into a hypothermic state. So, mostly in survival mode, I climbed into bed with Mutual Friend. It was a precise representation of how desperate I felt in life. There we were, lying together in the single bed, where we couldn't help but have physical contact, with palpable hatred between us.

The rest of the night played out with a couple of friends coming back, me having a partially coherent conversation with them, and Mutual Friend waking up to tell me that I'd ruined his weekend—in fact, pretty much his life. He hated me. Meanwhile, I was told that no one knew where Darlene was. I tried to find her, remembering where I'd plugged my phone in to charge, as more people came home. Someone was snoring like a steam train. Eventually I heard from Darlene, who was coming home with one of the guys she'd found somewhere in the village.

Once she was back, we made a plan to leave as soon as she could drive, meaning the following morning. Back in the cosy single bed, Mutual Friend then threw out some of his friends, who were snoring while we talked. He moved to the other bed to get away from me (which he explicitly expressed), and then he climbed back in beside me three minutes later because he was being "bitten" by something. Eventually, we were having depraved, hate-filled sex that of course one of his friends walked in on. I'd never been walked in on having sex, but here I was at thirty-four popping that cherry. *How? How is this my life?!*

When day dawned, Darlene and I made our silent escape. I couldn't wait to get away from the mountains. The black cloud I'd been wrestling had followed me into the alpine and burst into flames. Evidence of my concerning mental state lay all around me, like ashes the morning after a fire, a dumpster fire, and something like that is hard to ignore for long. Before the Peak of Whistler was even out of sight in the rear-view mirror, I declared to Darlene that I was done with drinking. Rock bottom had been achieved. I'd scoped out the real estate and found nothing there for me—no water, no growth, no light.

This was not the Lou I knew from my own past. I could forgive myself for my actions because of my extreme stress, but I couldn't keep choosing to put alcohol in my system when, even sober, I was struggling to cope with my life and emotions. It was all too much. Something had to change—and it had to be me.

Twenty-Five

Where Do We Go From Here?

In the weeks A.W. (After Whistler), my boss got let go, despite her vendetta against me. It turned out that nobody on our team cared for her management style, and while I would never want anyone to lose their job, it was a huge relief. More turmoil would still come at work, as they searched for a replacement, but hopefully the new hire wouldn't use the undertone of someone who didn't think I should be in my job.

I fully set out my no-drinking intentions with friends, rather than waiting until a night out and "disappointing" them with news of not drinking. I chose to proactively explain what had happened in Whistler—without the gory details, just that I'd reached rock bottom, right near the base of a mountaintop. Most people aren't super supportive of a random dry January, or even giving up booze for a great summer body, but funnily, when doing it for mental health reasons, no one tries to coerce you into having "just one."

The social stigma attached to drinking, and even more to not drinking, is beyond incredible. It's a fascinating social construct that we're unable to break down. It was easier to stop drinking in Vancouver than it would have been in Scotland, such is the strength of the drinking culture at home. I was grateful for my friends' support, but I vowed that it wouldn't stop me from going out. Instead I'd just drink soda and lime, relishing the thought of driving myself home and spending considerably less money than usual, all while knowing that I wouldn't be waking up hungover, with the after effects of my poor choices to deal with the next day.

I surrounded myself with good people, clean living, and positive mindsets. I was on the road to recovery, trying to be kind to myself while working through all the ruffled feathers from the first three months of 2019. However, another few weeks passed by and I was still struggling with how things ended with White Rock Boy. I was sleeping less than five hours a night, despite getting healthy in other areas of my life, which was not medically recommended at all. Arguably, any benefit from not drinking was likely cancelled out by the lack of sleep, because our brains get much more done at night than most of us learn in high school. My thoughts about the situation were dark, twisty, and unrelenting; everywhere reminded me of him, such was the way he'd become ensconced in my life, my home, my neighbourhood, even within such a short space of time.

I was told over and over by friends that I needed to stop letting him take up space in my brain—that despite what I thought, I didn't need him to provide closure. It was up to me to provide that closure to myself. I'd done everything that people suggest in those situations—written a letter that I'd never sent, wrote down my feelings in a journal, deleted and blocked him on everything, worked out until my body was exhausted, got my hair done, had therapy, talked about it, cried about it…. But it was still literally making me sick. People were worried about me, and I was worried about me too.

In consequence, I did the only other thing I could imagine: unblocked and messaged him on Instagram. Sincerely, I explained that I was struggling with how things had ended and would appreciate time to talk things through, while respecting his decision to end things and not looking to change that. If I'd reached out even a week earlier, it would have been with the wrong intentions; I would've still hoped that maybe, just maybe, he might change his mind. Perhaps the universe would offer him an epiphany that worked in my favour, but seeing him one last time was still enough. Hopefully, I'd know then that we weren't right for each other. For some reason, I'd built things up in my head, thinking that he must hate me, and apparently I can't deal with people hating me.

If only I could have reached that place by myself, without having to involve him, as all those self-righteous-as-fuck Instagram posts tell us we should. But dammit I was failing and needed closure. I attempted to orchestrate our meeting in a neutral location, but somehow he ended up in Kits. After rejecting his suggestion to join him on a shoe-buying errand (did he think this was some kind of jolly?), we met at a bar. It'd be the last time we'd make memories in yet another of my neighbourhood spots; already, we had a few memories from this bar. I was optimistic about reclaiming so many old locations, spots that'd be haunted until we addressed things once and for all.

My heart was racing as I prepared to meet him. Of course, I got attacked by a crow as I walked up the street. But my severe fear of birds only steeled my nerves further, as I tried to gauge his reaction to seeing my face, and mine to his. Would it all come tumbling out in tears? Would I want to strangle him? Would I feel nothing? *God, please, let me feel nothing.*

Seeing him was strange, like a familiar face that I used to know. He was still handsome, yes, but the warmth from the first day we met was missing. There was a coldness, and I wasn't sure whether it emanated from him or me. But my Lord, he was still handsome, his frame still imposing as he sat in the booth. I might have been distracted by his backwards baseball cap (thank you Lord for the backward baseball cap!), which didn't make him look great. Hence I focused on his forehead and tried to explain how challenging the last couple of months had been—without seeming melodramatic and needy. I simply wanted to give context as to why I'd been struggling to move on.

I asked him some questions that were bothering me, dealt him some home truths about his incredibly poor handling of the situation, and explained that I was no longer drinking. The FaceTime between us was certainly related to my decision. Finally, I said that I appreciated him meeting me. When he ordered a second drink, I wasn't sure why. Did he think this was a pleasant social situation? I'd said my piece; now I was ready to leave.

We made small talk while he drank his second drink, but I had no intentions of waiting from him to finish. I felt better, like a weight had been lifted. He hadn't really provided any earth shattering additional insight into what the fuck had happened, but he did say he wasn't in a good place. To some degree, I just needed to know that I'd left no stone unturned. I still didn't know exactly what I'd said on my drunken FaceTime call, and perhaps I never would. Maybe White Rock Boy was a notch more sensitive than I expected and my big mouth had pricked his heart. Honestly, it was hard to tell.

Abandoning the dregs of his beer, we walked out of the bar, and he playfully bashed my shoulder as we stepped onto the sun-drenched street. He looked at me sideways and said: "Despite everything, I'd still really like to *play* with you..." *Hold the motherfucking phone. Shut the fucking front door.* Like, I just explained that after we'd broken up, I essentially had all the makings of a mental breakdown, and now he was asking if we could have sex? *Seriously, shoot me to the fucking moon and back.* Does he have no duty of care to my mental health at all, so little that he'd suggest we climb into bed together?

If I'd clung to any shred of attraction or respect for him these past couple months, it had just been fully wiped out. Who doesn't love sex? Trust me, I remember how good the sex was between us, but to put that above my topsy-turvy mental state was unthinkable. I couldn't help but hear my ego shouting *fucking dickhead!* like a banshee, but boy did it give me the closure I needed. Yes, I did exactly the thing that people advise against doing, and it got me exactly what I needed! Take that, preachy Instagram "relationship coaches." Though if I'd done it a week beforehand, I might actually have taken him up on the suggestion of sex.... So maybe the preachy relationship coaches had a point.

Regardless, it was the end of a super-shitty chapter of 2019. My birthday was coming up at the end of May, and I knew the day would be tough. I was feeling better, but ultimately things were still raw. Marking another turn around the sun gave me mixed feelings. Things seemed so completely not where I'd hoped / thought / they'd be. *Wow, I really do love checking my life off against perceived "normal" timelines....* But my friends rallied around me as reminders of how much love I have in my life.

That Friday night before we celebrated my birthday the following day, and after a huge cluster-fuck at work that afternoon, I found myself alone on Kits Beach, tears staining my cheeks as I watched the sunset on my thirty-fourth birthday. I wondered what the hell had happened. How had I got here? I had so many questions and so few answers, and all of them were incredibly isolating. The following morning, on FaceTime with my mum, I was unable to verbally accept her birthday wishes, due to my sobbing. If you're looking for a sure-fire way to concern your mum, well, this is a pretty good one. I didn't know if I could manage brunch with eighteen friends, and Priscilla had to talk me out of my apartment.

One pep talk and two blocks later, we were at Local for brunch, that place I'd specifically not wanted to go with White Rock Boy on our first date. See, sensible. My friends were treating me with kid gloves and normally I would have re-established my independence, but on this occasion I was grateful. I wasn't myself. I felt like a fragile, beaten-up shell of a person, far from the self-affirmed thirty-five-year-old the world expected. As the rain poured down—because of course it would—brunch came to an end and everyone looked at me for next steps.

Except I didn't have anymore plans for my birthday; mostly I wanted to head home to bed. Instead, I jokingly said: "Well, the Raptors [basketball] game is on in four hours…" I thought everyone would laugh and we'd go our separate ways; but instead, there was almost unanimous agreement that it sounded like a great idea. So we hunkered down for the long haul. It was like my friends had cleared their days for me; their only intention was to be wherever I went. *Jesus, I loved them dearly.* Shortly thereafter, the bar filled up for a hotly anticipated end-of-season game for Canada's only NBA team.

Naturally, my birthday wouldn't be complete without testing my emotional fortitude a bit more. First, Sara told me that Mutual Friend was coming to the bar. I should have known (it's his Local too). We'd done a great job of avoiding each other these past two months since Whistler, but we were bound to be in the same vicinity eventually. Of course it would happen on my birthday. I attempted to handle it with dignity, and said a casual "hello", while restraining some friends who barely knew him but were throwing shit across the table in his direction nonetheless. (Of course he'd get sat beside us.) Sara did her best to referee the situation, but it felt like an unnecessary blip on my day.

As I turned my gaze away from this particular ghost-of-my-past and looked left into the parking lot, I appreciated the view of the hot bearded guy coming inside. Wait, what, no… that hot bearded guy was Persian Lawyer. *BECAUSE OF COURSE IT WAS.* Thankfully the bar was full and turned him away, but not before my heart rate rose so significantly that I decided I needed a shot, despite my non-drinking status. My friends had been supportive of my not drinking, but they were extra supportive when I *did* want a drink, so a round of shots was ordered for the table. It was my one and only on the day.

Some of us took a reprieve from the bar, watching the blaze of sunset from the beach before heading back in for more drinks. I'd only fallen more in love with watching sunsets and sunrises, the more I fell out of love with the qualities in the men I was meeting. No matter how challenging things were, I always found something poetic and relief-inducing in what they signify: a fresh start every day, and a quiet come down every night. The sunset takes the challenges of that day when it goes, and the incoming sunrise always brings a clean slate.

Eventually, twelve hours after arriving at Local for brunch, I left to go home. Damien and Sara were the last people standing, and I was escorted two blocks home by James. Keith offered to stay over in case I didn't want to be alone, and my heart filled up with the love and support my friends had for me. Not having family nearby can be very isolating; in times of real need, you're without the omnipresent crutch of people who have no choice but to help you. But in the friends I found myself surrounded by that day, I knew these were people I could rely on for good, people who would hold my heart as it hurt.

The rest of summer was a lesson in living quietly and prioritising my own self-care. I'd worried that living sober would be too hard (such was its importance in my life B.W. [Before Whistler]), but I felt much better not drinking. I wasn't heightening the emotional rollercoaster I'd rode for so long; I wasn't making stupid drunken decisions about men, ones I'd feel ashamed about once sober, in the cold light of every "morning after." Being fully in control of myself and my emotions was a novel feeling for me, and I was warming up to it.

I dated a little that summer: a half-black rugby player from France who turned out to be younger than his Bumble profile suggested, a Persian guy (of course), and a personal trainer whose lanky hair and mansplaining were all the turn-offs I needed, not just from him but dating in general. I didn't feel ready to put myself out there again, nor could I be bothered by it. But in the midst of swiping, I also came across another familiar Persian, OP. I hadn't seen him on dating apps for a really long time; in fact, I think I'd blocked him after the disaster of our last encounter.

But for whatever reason, I swiped right, more out of curiosity than anything else. Later that day, we'd matched and were chatting, both equally surprised that the other person had swiped right. In our initial conversations, he mentioned how much his life had changed since we last knew each other— where he lived, his job, his outlook on life—it had all been altered by some pretty heavy stuff. He was sorry for the way things had ended with us; he knew he was in a bad place back then and just wanted a chance to explain.

To say that OP coming back into my life was a whirlwind is an understatement. When we met, he even *looked* different. He had a wild, unkempt look about him. He tried to give me context about what was going on in his life, during the time I'd been part of it. I could understand all of what he said, and I told him so; but that information would have been useful back then. Instead he'd chosen to leave me in the dark, despite assuring me that he'd never just disappear. He was incredibly apologetic, at the end of the day. So, after a first date (was it still considered a first date if we'd already had one, albeit years ago?) that lasted far longer than either of us expected, followed by dinner and a sunset on the beach, we had some tea back at mine. (I wasn't the only one who had given up drinking.) He told me that he wanted us to try again. If I gave him time to show me that he'd changed, he promised that he wouldn't disappear again. This was unfathomable to me. At the end of every failed relationship that I'd hoped would go somewhere, I always had daydreams about the guy coming back and expressing his deepest regret and undying love for me. Of course, it had never happened until now (and still, I was only seeing the first part).

I asked him not to make promises that he couldn't keep, but I was willing to give him a second chance. It didn't even take a moment's thought for me. To some extent, we'd always had such unfinished business that it was almost like, "of course this was going to happen." With how much he'd changed, mentions of the books he'd been reading, and thoughts from Brene Brown, I could tell that self-growth was a priority for him. It was something I was looking for as well. Plus, I'd forgotten how incredibly secure I felt in his 6'5" frame. He made me feel tiny. I never felt tiny, even after my body had transformed into the lightest and smallest version of itself.

But fast forward one week (*ONE WEEK!*) and we'd encountered why things weren't going to work. I was naturally apprehensive about whether I'd get absolutely clobbered again by the situation, and given how the year had started, I wanted to avoid that at all costs. Seemingly, his "give me time to show you I've changed" was in fact nothing more than "I just want you to accept that I've changed and I don't get why you're so hung up on the last time…." *Oi*. I'd hoped not to drag the past into the future, but there were a lot of emotions that week, especially after we slept together again. Fuck, I'd missed him. But fuck, we needed to take this slow.

Seemingly, it was too much for him. As quickly as he came back into my life, he left again, telling me that he couldn't hang around. It was a mistake. I was clearly harbouring too many feelings and he wasn't prepared to go through any of them with me. *Well great.* Let me just erase this memory from ever fucking happening. But in amongst the surprise (should I really have been surprised, didn't he have some priors?), I also realised that it was exactly what needed to happen. He'd always felt like an unknown to me, always such a mystery; and while it clearly wasn't meant to work out, at least I had an understanding of what the fuck had happened two years earlier. We'd gone full circle, and I felt like the universe was trying to give me some closure, at last allowing me to find some peace.

Or maybe not. At the end of the week, things with OP had reached their final resting place (*in the shitter*). I was taking my mind off things with an All Girls Weekend in Kelowna, just me and my Beach Girls. I'd relaxed my non-drinking to allow for some wine tasting, but I still kept to no wine drinking. So instead of attending our usual hungover, boozy brunch of Kelowna weekends past, I went to a Sunday morning hot yoga class with Dez and Mel. As we came out of the studio in Downtown Kelowna, sweat soaked from working out at thirty-two degrees Celsius, there was a group of Persian friends right in front of us, both men and women, hugging goodbye (or maybe hello?). Before Dez could finish her joke ("Lou, they look like your people!"), one of them turned around and caught my eye. Persian Lawyer. Jesus fucking Christ.

If we'd been a second earlier, or later, we'd have likely missed each other. I hoped that he hadn't seen me, at least not recognised me looking like such a hot mess, but he did a double take and moved three feet towards me. For fear of just how horrific I looked, I put my sunglasses on and tried to make pleasant small talk, all while my heart pounded in my chest (which was no longer the result of the workout). I don't know what we talked about, but I know that I introduced him to Dez and Mel, hoping they'd smile politely and not ask any questions. He told me how impressed he was that we were working out. Other than that, I don't remember what we each said. Honestly, I think I blacked out.

As he went off to catch up with his friends, who'd said their goodbyes and were splintering off in different directions, Dez asked: "So which Persian is that?" *Crap, he was barely out of earshot.* I'd introduced him using his real name, which they'd never heard before; so for the duration of the conversation, they'd been wondering which of the dark-bearded flings from my past accounted for this particular fellow.

It was a head-fuck that I didn't need, only heightened when the following evening, having left Kelowna that morning, I received a message from an unknown number saying: *Hey, not sure if you kept my number, but funny running into you in Kelowna. How've you been?* I'd secretly hoped this wouldn't happen. I'd hoped that somewhere in that group of friends, there was a girlfriend who'd keep him from messaging me. But I knew, deep down, that I'd likely be getting a text if he was single. It was too much. Two old Persian flames in a week. Universe, if you're trying to send me a message, please, change your strategy.

Similarly to OP, Persian Lawyer came back into my life for a short enough period of time not to totally fuck with me, but long enough for me to get some closure (which I didn't know that I needed from him). That first night of messaging, he fell back into the flirty and suggestive messages we'd been so fond of a year ago. It was surprising how easily it had been to rediscover familiarity with both OP and Persian Lawyer. Maybe with the levels of intimacy we'd shared, the feelings would always be there, like an historic ring in our tree stump of life.

When we met a week and a half later on a sunny Sunday morning, I wasn't sure what I was meeting him for, really, but the ease with which we chatted in the car on our way to Steveston was further testament to how some things never change. As we walked around the fishing village, we caught up on jobs, trips, and family. I admitted that for the last few months, I'd been going to a yoga studio downtown that I knew he sometimes frequented, all the while hoping I'd never run into him. But then I'd run into him outside a yoga studio four hours away in Kelowna...*What are the chances.*

As we walked through the throngs of tourists, sipping our smoothies, he told me that his sexually suggestive messages the previous week arose from a complicated situation he'd found himself in with the girl he'd been dating; and that if we'd acted on them, it would have been a mistake. Clearly, he was struggling with his current relationship. He explained how he and this girl had been having problems and were trying to figure out how best to move through them or else move on from them. So, I found myself essentially counselling Persian Lawyer on the girl he'd started dating right after we stopped (shortly after he'd told me that he just wasn't ready to date).

He did apologise for some of what had happened between us, accepting that he'd kept coming back to the relationship knowing that it wasn't going anywhere. I wanted more than he was ready to give. But he said the sex had been such a huge draw for him (*of course*); he'd always found me to be smart and funny, thus spending time together was easy. I explained that intending to be the nice guy didn't automatically make you the nice guy, and he finally accepted my point of view. As I'd pointed out at the time, it's not that he wasn't ready; I simply wasn't the right person, as proven by him choosing to seriously date someone right after me.

When he dropped me home, the sick feeling I had in my stomach told me that I'd overextended myself in that situation. I knew that in trying to be "cool," and nice, and mature I'd asked more of myself than I was emotionally able to give without being detrimental to myself. No matter how far past things with Persian Lawyer I'd gotten, giving him advice on how to make things work with another girl was beyond my limit.

In the same week, because life seemingly likes to fuck with me, I had to contend with Mutual Friend reappearing. We'd had no contact since the total dumpster fire in Whistler, other than the brief hello on my birthday, but when he needs something, he needs something. And this time, it was a suitcase. Yep, luggage. The case I'd lent him for his trip to Hawaii had been so amazing that he needed to break our pact of silence to borrow it again. When I reminded him that apparently he hated me, his quick as a flash response came back, "Yeah, but I love that suitcase." Fuck, he did make me laugh sometimes.

Obviously, the suitcase was an excuse for Mutual Friend to reach out, as would be the case (pun intended) when he again messaged me a month later, asking how I'd made his bed so well that one time (I'd put clean sheets on the mattress before promptly getting under the covers). Yes, I'd now essentially become his mom: getting him ready for vacations, making his bed. Except that every time we met up, we'd always end up having sex too. We seemingly couldn't keep away from each other and were resigned to the fact. I struggled with it at first, especially after betting Damien and Keith money that I'd never sleep with Mutual Friend again. It was a toxic situation and seemingly going absolutely nowhere, although I'd never actually broached that subject with him, but eventually I got to a place of acceptance with it. I couldn't deny that whenever we saw each other he was exactly what I felt like I needed in that moment. As long as I knew exactly what it was and exactly what I was getting, while also ensuring that I was in no way harbouring hopes or feelings beyond convenience, then I was chill. And that's what it was: convenient, with a side of lending luggage and helping with laundry.

While arguably I could have ignored the comebacks from OP, Persian Lawyer, and Mutual Friend, I realised that there's something about me that will always want to know where someone is now. Even with my dad—while I didn't want to re-establish that relationship and hadn't since those few emails back in January 2016—there was something about closing the loop, eliminating unknowns. The same thing applied to my marriage; I'd ensured that was done to the doneth degree. I certainly didn't always like this proclivity, but it was just another thing to learn about myself. Accepting that instead of trying to change it was liberating.

Twenty-Sex

Then There Was New York

After putting all those "ghosts of years past" to rest, my summer of clean living was a dream. Living so close to the beach, I spent most evenings and weekends with a blanket on Kits Lawn. My mornings were either spent running or leaning into the challenge of a Barre class, or perhaps miracling at how much I'd grown to love hot yoga. Meanwhile, I chose to ignore my stress from work. My bully of a boss was gone, but working in a fast-paced, cutting-edge industry with big goals always brings turmoil. Thankfully, my new boss believed in work-life balance and, more importantly, she believed in me. But I still wasn't convinced that my job was safe, given the rate at which people were being let go, for seemingly innocuous reasons.

I'd also made some great friends at work—and that summer, it was finally time for Kim and John's wedding. From discussing their engagement back in Montreal, over a year ago, to Kim talking me out of my head in Austin, I couldn't have been more excited about celebrating with them. However, this would be my first sober wedding and I wasn't sure how that would feel. I was going with Dustin, another colleague and friend, so at least I wouldn't be flying solo. But I was adamant that I wouldn't drink, even when Kim suggested that instead of driving Dustin's car, he and I just take the hired shuttle. Their wedding was taking place in the breathtaking shadow of the mountains north of Whistler, and I didn't relish the idea of being at the behest of a group bus situation. Part of the joy of not drinking was having complete control. Driving Dustin's car, thus allowing him to get his party on, meant that we'd actually have some control over our comings and goings.

As well as the beautiful setting, the gorgeous couple and tasty-as-hell doughnut wall, there was an added layer of excitement in the air. (Or was it apprehension?) Months and months prior to the wedding, Kim mentioned that one of the groomsmen would be a perfect hook-up for me. He was a best friend of John's from Vancouver, but he lived in New York. Kim said I'd find him attractive, and I laughed, asking how she knew that I wouldn't be in a relationship by then. *LOL.* Joke's on me.

Going to the wedding, single and sober, I wasn't sure what would come of it. During the rainy but atmospheric-as-shit ceremony, it was hard to tell which of the bow-tie clad groomsmen was N.Y. Boy. This was cleared up when the wedding party was introduced at dinner, in pairs of bridesmaids and groomsmen. One particularly fun-loving pair shot-gunned a can of beer each, while the MC described the male half of the couple as a cross between Arnold Schwarzenegger and Ken Doll. He was all muscles and blonde hair. Yup, that was probably the guy Kim picked out for me. There were no Persians in the wedding party, after all.

As the night went on and the cumulative intake of alcohol increased, N.Y. Boy wandered my way with the opening line of: "I think I'm supposed to talk to you." It hadn't been lost on me that multiple people knew about Kim's plan to set us up, so I shouldn't have been surprised that he knew too. Kim and John, but particularly Kim, pride themselves on having set up multiple couples— and not just for casual dating, but couples that went on to have serious relationships and loving marriages.

He was outrageously good looking, in *this are-you-actually-real* kind of way. Kim had told me that he "looks like a potential douchebag, but he's actually not." We did some very casual chatting in amongst being dragged onto the dance floor by friends, called for photos and coerced into more shots at the bar. (Him, not me.) When it came to booze, I'd managed to get the Aussie barman into collusion with me; whenever I ordered a gin and soda, he'd just give me soda, no gin. Previously I'd met a lot of Kim and John's friends; in fact, two of them had joined my birthday brunch. All the same, I didn't go into the details of why I wasn't drinking; on this occasion, it was simply easier to be one of the gang.

The reality was, despite my initial concerns, I loved not being drunk. I'd probably have embarrassed myself in front of N.Y. Boy if I *had* been drinking. Instead I was feeling great about myself, yet I know how many people use alcohol for social situations. Moreover, I did not let Kim down in the partying stakes, which I think was her concern when I'd offered to drive. In reality, I ended up being one of the last ones on the dance floor, playing chauffeur to the wedding party and returning my friends to the bridal party Airbnb.

Alas, this actually proved tricky at one am in the middle of nowhere. As everyone split themselves between the remaining cars, the bride and groom came with Dustin and me; and (surprise surprise) N.Y. Boy climbed into our car as well. In the foggy black of nighttime, winding along the base of some gorgeous mountains, it took all my concentration not to be distracted by the amusing drunken chatter—not to mention the fact that, in my rear-view mirror, I could see the right pec of a certain groomsman, busting out of his now beer-stained white shirt.

Back at the Airbnb for the bridal party, which was an outrageously large stone-clad mansion, we had an after party in the kitchen, with a fully-stocked fridge, snacks galore, and a perfect dance floor for Shelby to exhibit her skills as DJ Shelbz. In my sobriety, I was surprised by how much fun I was having, despite being sober in comparison to everyone else. The cheese selection helped, definitely.

N.Y. Boy would take the opportunity to speak to me again as well. Our conversation hadn't gotten very far at the wedding itself, after he suggested that we return to the party before being thwarted by friends. His inebriation was endearing—although Dustin did get a great photo of us chatting, in which I appeared either bored out of my brains or else thinking of ways to kill him. I put his inability to make a move down to his complete lack of game, on top of his blood-alcohol level. Or maybe he simply didn't want to make a move while he was drunk.

During a group lap dance for a passed-out bridesmaid and her boyfriend (who were sprawled out on the couch), N.Y. Boy and I went out in rain, chatting together beside the hot tub. It was more out of necessity than a romantic notion, as he seemed altogether tongue tied in proximity to other human beings. How could a man this good-looking be so shy? I'd find out later that he'd even said to Kim: "Help me, I don't know what to say." So you see, it doesn't matter how attractive we are—we all struggle with the same kind of shit.

We tried to take cover under a tree, but instead we got soaked by the rain-drops falling from the branches. He exclaimed for possibly the tenth time that he was perplexed at why Kim and John wanted to set us up, because they'd never tried to set him up with someone before, so there must be something special about me. In my sober sarcasm, which I knew would be lost in the corridors of his drunken brain, I told him that yeah, I was pretty special. I was actually fucking amazing and he'd be lucky to date me.

As much as I was joking, it was probably the closest I'd ever felt to owning that kind of statement. With this model-esque man standing opposite me, in no way did I feel out of my depth or insecure. I had my sober mind, my body in the best shape of its life, and I was reaping the benefits of these life choices. And shit, did that ever feel *good!* We had a drunken but sweet kiss, which reminded me of the moment you get to be alone with your high school crush at the dance. It's usually not the greatest kiss, but you're glad to get it out of the way. Shortly thereafter, we went back inside and I couldn't help but wonder how long we'd been out there together. We'd lost Kim and John to their beds, someone was sick by the front door, almost everyone else was passed out, and Dustin was more than ready to return to our own Airbnb.

Again, I provided the chauffeur services with Dustin in the passenger seat. We took N.Y. Boy, DJ Shelbz, and her groomsman boyfriend back to their Airbnb. As we loaded into the car, N.Y. Boy leant forwards from the backseat and whispered in my ear that we had a problem. My initial, sober, *person-in-a-car-full-of-drunk-people* thought was: *Oh god, please don't be sick in Dustin's car,* but thankfully he followed it up with, "I don't have your number." *Oh* finally he has some moves? Or was it game? Or was it just desperation?

Either way, as we said goodbye at the final stop of Dustin & Lou's Post-Wedding Taxi Service, I took his phone from his hands and called my own number. I wasn't sure if he'd ever find it, because I hadn't saved it. I'd just called it, and there was no signal out in the boonies, so who knows if it ever rung through. All this to say that I was more than a little surprised when a text came through from a New York number just nine minutes before four am. It read: *Hope you got home safe. I'm off to bed… happy I met you :) Night.*

N.Y. Boy was leaving on the Tuesday morning back to (you guessed it) New York. I decided to take the bull by the horns and ask him whether he wanted to meet up before he left. He'd planned to spend Sunday recovering and Monday golfing with family, but we thought maybe Monday evening would work. When his return from golf coincided with my bedtime, I explained that I was heading to bed early for a run the next morning, but if he wanted to join me for the run, he was welcome. I fully expected him to politely decline. Instead, I picked him up the following morning at sunrise for a seawall run. Honestly, anyone who's willing to do that, especially before a five-hour flight, gets huge brownie points in my book. He also looked exceptionally good in workout clothes. There was obviously an attraction between us, and as the early morning Vancouver sunlight danced off the water in False Creek, the commonalities between us were clear. It helped that he was sober this time.

As we ran toward Granville Island, we talked about how it felt to move and live away from family (him from Vancouver to New York and me from Scotland to Vancouver) and how important working out is to us both. As we walked back with coffees from Starbucks, we discussed how much we both wanted dogs, my decision to give up drinking and his want to do the same, and our general mindsets and outlooks on life. The only problem with the date (was it a date?) was its brevity, because soon he had to head home and get ready for his flight.

At the wedding, his drunkenness had resulted in a somewhat repetitive, albeit adorable, loop in conversation. He loved dogs and was desperate to get one. He was more than a little enamored by my jumpsuit, and he was intrigued as to why Kim and John were so adamant that he meet me. Nonetheless, by the end of our sunrise coffees, I think their adamancy on the last point made sense to him ;). The only issue seemed to be our living on opposite sides of the continent. But his family was still in Vancouver so he came back sometimes, and he also suggested that if I found myself "wanting to do an exploratory trip to NY" to let him know. *Ugh! Kim! Why were you setting me up with someone who lived so far away?*

If nothing else, N.Y. Boy was a reminder that there were seemingly good men out there, men who were smart, driven, polite, funny, and really fucking hot. Granted, they didn't seem to be living in Vancouver, but at least I knew they were out there. *Somewhere.* With all the turmoil and troublesome ghosts I'd been dealing with that year, it was just what I needed.

My summer of fun continued with a trip to Lisbon, where an old friend from my international school in Egypt was getting married. With two outrageously wonderful grooms, I figured it'd be nothing less than fabulously over-the-top fun, and I was right.

The trip was particularly special because I hadn't seen some of my Egyptian friends since my wedding, nine years earlier; and others I hadn't seen since living in Egypt, twenty-one years earlier. There's something about inter-national schools, where the intimacy of shared experiences often results in never-ending bonds. Other guests at the wedding were fascinated to hear that we hadn't seen each other in so long, not since we were children, yet our friendships held their energy for the duration.

I'd added to the friend fest by having Darlene join me on the trip. She was always keen for some European travel, and while I was more than happy to enjoy the wedding by myself, it was always nice to have a pal join me for the rest of the trip. Plus, choosing an Airbnb with someone else is far more fun; and I compounded the love fest even further by inviting Lisa, my best friend since I was four years old, to join us from Edinburgh.

Lisa arrived while I was at the wedding on Saturday night. By the time I returned from my night of dancing, after too many pastel de nata to count and enough flowers to make Elton John envious, she and Darlene were best buds. It made me more than happy. The whole trip did. To have so many people from different parts of my life in one place, especially somewhere as beautiful as Lisbon, was truly special. It was also the first time I'd visited Portugal since getting divorced. My ex's family home was in the south of Portugal, and for a while his sister had lived in Lisbon. Laying those ghosts to rest and reclaiming Portugal with my own memories was yet another liberation.

My heart was so full from the trip. I had heaps of fun with people I dearly loved. I felt happy and free like a child. Darlene commented that she liked "Lisbon Lou," who definitely had more chill than I'd been able to channel for the past year. It was another lesson in not needing to drink to have a good time. Did I have a glass of champagne at the wedding? *Yes.* Did I have a port? *Of course.* Did I have half a glass of my favourite Portuguese wine from years gone by? *For old time's sake.* But my default mode now was that I didn't drink, and it was an anomaly when I did—a setup I was enjoying. You know what they say: *Everything in moderation, including moderation.*[5]

On the day I flew to Lisbon, I'd finally had my promotion at work confirmed. Since my new boss had started managing the team in April, she'd been trying to promote me, in both title and salary. The salary negotiations took longer than the title assignment, and I'd only gotten confirmation that they'd signed off on it as I sat in YVR airport. It felt like a huge achievement, but I couldn't help but feel a little bitter, considering how hard we'd fought for the increase.

---

[5] Attributed to various people, at different times, including Oscar Wilde, Horace Porter, Petronius, and probably a bunch of others from other races, cultures, and time periods! This one is a universal tenet.

Surely if people knew your value, there shouldn't be a need for so much discussion? Either way, the change in title and considerable salary increase would make a big difference for me.

N.Y. Boy and I kept in touch. I continued to learn about him while we texted and sent each other dog memes on Instagram. At one point, I hoped to swing a trip to New York, but he had to be in L.A. for a conference during that time. Instead he asked me if I wanted to meet him there. I thought about it and came pretty close to booking the flights; but after returning from Portugal, I asked him if he was still imagining that as the plan. His response of "I don't mind either way" was not exactly my druthers.

A very good friend of mine—who goes by the nickname Arms and is the living definition of a successful Tinder fail (we met on Tinder, had one night of fun and then became exceptionally good friends, even after he moved home to New Zealand)—has always hammered home the "fuck yes" argument. In his view, if something isn't a "fuck yes" then it's a "fuck no"; and from that perspective, travelling to L.A. for N.Y. Boy was a "fuck no" for me. He wasn't in a "fuck yes" space about seeing me, evidently, and that factored into my decision.

Of course, I understand that getting to know someone in a city where neither of you live might be stressful, especially if one of you is on a work trip. I wasn't sure what exactly I was looking for at that point, but it wasn't some lukewarm sentiment about wanting to see me. At one time I'd have accepted it, grasping at any breadcrumbs that guys threw down, but I didn't have the time for it now. I was worth more than an "I don't mind." So I politely declined, saying something about needing to buckle down at work, which wasn't entirely untrue.

Work had been crazy and although my boss had offered me the time off, I knew it wasn't great timing with a bunch of deadlines coming up. That, coupled with the *meh* response from N.Y. Boy, made me decide against the trip. But a few weeks later, my boss asked me if I still wanted a weekend away, telling me about a conference she thought I should attend in New York at the beginning of October. *Oh...well...if you insist.*

But given my experience on the last time I travelled for work, I was a little apprehensive. I double checked with my boss that my trip would be valuable, while taking a couple of days to think through the implications. I also messaged N.Y. Boy, saying: *Apparently the universe does want us to hang out. I might be coming to NY early Oct.* His response was far more effusive than I'd expected—like, if he'd replied like that about L.A., I'd have been boarding a plane the following week.

When I confirmed my trip dates with N.Y. Boy, four nights across one weekend (two for pleasure and two for work), I hardly expected to be invited to stay with him for all four nights. In fact, I'd already booked a hotel. Of course, I was hoping to see him while I was there, but staying at his place seemed like a reach. Staying with him the whole time hadn't even crossed my mind, but I get that New York is expensive, and people who live there end up hosting friends from out of town all the time. And we were "friends," right? Regardless, there was something in his easy breezy nature that made me think I should do it. And *fuck-yahs* breed *fuck-yahs*.

When Kim and John returned from their honeymoon, it was fun to tell them that I was staying with N.Y. Boy for four nights! But as the trip got closer, I questioned myself a couple of times about whether I'd lost my mind. I'd now cancelled my hotel, and although I could always rebook at one of the thousands of hotels in Manhattan, I also had an old school friend living in New York, if I was really in a pickle. I still wondered if staying four nights with someone I'd only met twice was really a great idea; but deep down, I wasn't concerned. *Maybe that's what concerned me?*

When a friend asked me, "what happens after New York?" I knew this was the bigger concern. What if I let my heart (and my vagina) rule everything and then came back to Vancouver, because I would **have** to come back to Vancouver, and be heartbroken. Was I setting myself up for failure? Was I doing what I'd been trying to avoid all year, inviting heartbreak into my life? Could I see it in the distance already, rolling into the station like a train?

Right before my trip to New York, Mum was coming out for her annual visit. As always, we had a blissful ten days together. Showing her my new apartment in Kitsilano after she'd gotten so familiar with the downtown area reaffirmed to me what I already knew: my life in Kits suited me perfectly. My mum commented on how much more relaxed and happy I seemed, clearly relieved that my drinking was now under control, even though it caused her a conundrum at Duty Free. She always brought me gin, so this time she brought me whisky.... *Yeah,* only a Scot brings someone whisky after hearing they're no longer drinking.

On our road trip to BC's Sunshine Coast, I celebrated six years in Canada. It felt like a huge milestone. Here I was at six years in Canada, with my mum by my side, having built an incredible life here. Thankfully, my mum's rational and pragmatic mind was also in favour of the New York plan. Over the years, she'd gotten used to me doing things that didn't always "make sense" on paper. I was happier when I led with my heart rather than my head. It was my heart that brought me to Canada more than half a decade ago; my head had just worked out the details. Even broken, my heart had known what to do.

Mum left on the Sunday and my flight to New York was on the Thursday night. It's always difficult saying goodbye to her, especially without figuring out our next trip first, but I was grateful for my upcoming sojourn on the East Coast. The thought of seeing N.Y. boy in the big city kept my mind occupied and my chin like a statue in the air. I'd somehow decided to run a half marathon in Brooklyn during the trip—you know, just super casual. Actually, I'd been training for one already, to be held that October in Kelowna, but I was sick of training and the thought of running a big race in New York was too exciting to pass up.

I did a random check online, and one half marathon popped up in Brooklyn on the Saturday. I couldn't say no, so I told N.Y. Boy: "FYI, this is what I'm doing Saturday morning, so maybe we could do brunch afterwards." But what he heard was: *I'm running a half marathon and it'll make me question your masculinity, if you don't join me.* So he decided a week beforehand to run his first ever half marathon with me...*Oh god,* what if it killed him? What if I killed John's friend?! But again, someone who's willing to bash out a half marathon impulsively? Super attractive in my eyes.

We also got tickets for the New York Giants football game. It would be my first NFL game and the MetLife stadium seemed like the perfect place to pop that cherry. It was shaping up to be more than a good weekend, like actually a dream weekend. If someone said, *tell me about your ideal weekend,* there would have been a workout (half marathon, *check*), watching sports (football game, *check*), great company (our text convos made me confident, *check*) and maybe some sex (actually, I wasn't sure if that was in the cards). The reality was, he'd been super nice to invite me into his home, but his intentions and wants were a mystery. I sensed that they were good, but beyond that who knew.

Taking the red eye to New York, I was a mix of nerves and childlike excitement. New York is one of my favourite cities in the whole world, having first visited when my mum took me for my sixteenth birthday. Arriving at his Sixth Avenue apartment in Chelsea at nine am and picking up a key from his concierge, I was basically living someone else's life. That was before I walked into his apartment and saw how clean and stylish it was. Raising my eyes from the cushion-clad sofa, the picture window in the corner gave me the most breathtaking view of the Empire State Building. *What the fuck. Who lives in a place like this?!* Granted, he was a financial analyst and presumably did pretty well for himself, but this was blowing my mind.

After picking up coffee and a croissant from Eataly—located just kitty-corner from the Flatiron building—I spent the day working on the sofa in the shadow of the Empire State, anticipating just how weird seeing him walk into his own apartment with me on the sofa would be. I had showered and changed before he came back from work, looking forward to our plan for the night: walking to a sports shop for some pre-half marathon buys, followed by dinner.

Just after six pm, he came home, still laden with his bags from the day and smiling ear to ear. His smile looked like an ad for Invisalign. I'd forgotten how it got to me. Lord, I could have jumped his bones in that moment, but I was aware that I didn't want to take anything for granted. Maybe he was just being *really* polite in inviting me to stay. Maybe he had absolutely no intention of anything happening. Maybe he was simply being nice to someone from home, a friend of Kim and John's. Or maybe I had no need to "maybe" myself.

As we wandered through the streets of New York, traversing the beautifully lit artery of Washington Square Park, the city was bustling with people finishing work and starting their weekends. There was an ease to our conversation, but I couldn't help but assume that we were both on our best behaviour. We shopped for energy gel and apparently an entire new set of running gear (for him), but I stopped him at new shoes, insisting that running a half marathon in new runners was a sure-fire invitation for misery.

As it turns out, he'd be moving out of his beautifully modern apartment with its jaw-dropping view into a walk up in Greenwich Village (Jesus, could he get anymore New York?) on the following weekend; so on our way to · dinner, he asked if I wanted to see his new place. Did I want to have a nose around another (no doubt) stunning place that he'd soon be calling home? *Um, yah.* True to form, it was also pretty nice, albeit less of a wow factor than walking into his current apartment earlier that day.

From there, we started with our carb load. He'd found a perfect, darkly-lit Italian place, the type where you can't see the whole space because of the shadowy vibes. We sat at the bar, eating multiple pastas and all the bread, until the conversation moved to somewhere I guessed it would soon arrive eventually: "I don't know much about you...." I'd given him very vague stories up until then. I'd never mentioned my divorce. I'm not even sure I'd mentioned Egypt. I was always an open book, but with him, there was something that stopped me from going all in so quickly. Perhaps he didn't make me feel as if I had anything to prove or explain.

Even when I did tell him I was divorced, I held back a lot of the details. I didn't feel the need to share them in the way I often did, and part of me didn't want him clouding his judgment of me based on those old stories. Despite me knowing that they inherently make up different parts of who I am, perhaps by not sharing some of myself, I could avoid getting unnecessarily hurt in this situation.

Before we'd gone out for the night, I'd asked him where I should put my stuff, given that I was sleeping on the sofa. I didn't want to leave it lying around, nor did I want to take up space in his bedroom. That's when we had the interesting discussion re: "listen, you're not going to sleep well on the sofa, so take my bed." I insisted that I hadn't come to throw him out his bed, so the conversation changed directions to "okay, we're both adults; so if you don't mind, why don't we just share my bed?" He was right, we were both adults. But if I climbed into bed with him then surely I'd want to jump his bones. Certainly I didn't want him to think I had any expectations just because he'd invited me to stay. *Tricky....*

Also, I never considered that we'd have to get ready for bed together, after coming home from dinner and buying pre-run breakfast stuff at the grocery store. So, I did the same thing that sixteen-year-old me would have done: I took my PJs into the bathroom to change. Had I bought new PJs and spent ages deciding whether they exhibited the right ratio of cute versus sexy? Yes. But in that moment, they made me feel frumpy as hell. Although maybe that was a good thing, because my head was already whirring with thoughts before he even stripped down to his boxers.

Dear God, send help. No man who isn't a fitness professional should have a body like that. You know when people talk about bodies chiseled from marble? Well, this was one of them—and this particular body was getting into bed beside me. We were both fully sober and aiming for a good sleep before we casually ran twenty-one kilometres the next morning.

I remember thinking: *Close your eyes, Lou; just close your eyes and pretend you're at home, by yourself; pretend that this heaving warm mass of golden muscle lying next to you is just a hug from the universe.*

Alas, it was no good. Sleep was difficult to come by—and I was running a half marathon in the morning! We slept with about a foot of space between us, and I didn't dare let there be skin-on-skin contact. It was simply too tempting. Morning would surely be an interesting time. I always get crazy nervous before half marathons, despite that this was my seventh one. I don't know if I'll ever get used to them or come to consider myself a runner. This was his first half marathon, so despite his male ego, he admitted to having nerves. He'd simply never run that far of a distance. But he was, very visibly, one of the fittest people I'd ever met; so I wasn't too concerned about him dying anymore.

In the Uber to Brooklyn, my mum FaceTime'd me. She was at my brother's that weekend, so she and my niece wanted to wish me good luck. I suspect that Mum was also secretly hoping to get a glimpse of N.Y. Boy. (If that was her M.O., well, she must have been delighted when he leant his head into the frame, introducing himself to both of them.) We'd already established that we weren't going to run the race together. I don't like running with people, apart from the training runs I'd done with Keith, and neither of us wanted the distraction. But I can still say that competing in a half marathon with someone whom you don't want to absolutely suck in front of is a sure-fire way of running a personal best....

Five years after my first race—seven half marathons later—and I'd finally finished in less than two hours! Given that I'd cut off the last two weeks of my training, and how shockingly difficult I'd found the *initial* month of my training, running a new PB came like an electric shock. Like *shit*, I've got the power! But a perfect Brooklyn morning, with views of Manhattan and the Empire State Building, plus some smoking-hot motivation, were apparently all I needed. Was my jubilation in any way dented by the fact that N.Y. Boy ran it four minutes faster than me, on his first attempt at a half marathon? Absolutely not. I was just glad he didn't die, and I was pretty happy that the memories of his first half marathon would always include me.

Driving back to Manhattan, our focus was on showers and brunch. When he suggested that we go for massages, I could have kissed him. I mean, I'd felt that way since I'd seen him yesterday, but the feeling reached a whole new level when he booked us a couple's massage in Midtown. Um, a couple's massage. *What?* "Is that like in the same room?" I asked. I knew the answer, because I'd worked in a hotel spa many moons ago, but I wanted to make sure that HE knew the answer. Just in case it was a mistake. Nope, apparently he knew, it was fine. Good Lord, are you trying to test me?

After the most blissful of showers (taken separately, to be clear) and Korean BBQ that entirely satisfied our famished post-run bodies, we walked up to the spa on West 35th Street. As we completed the waivers, I realised that I wasn't sure whether N.Y. Boy knew how old I was. Given his career in finance, I figured he'd work it out from my 1984 birth year on the form. Had I been intentionally secretive with him, or had I just not got round to mentioning some stuff, like how many years I'd been on the planet? Was it important? I guess it depended on how he felt about a seven-year age gap. Yeah, he hadn't even hit his thirties yet...

I knew that we'd have to get pretty much naked in front of each other. But when we got into the room, I couldn't tell whether the rose petals scattered everywhere made it better or worse. There was no "good way" to do it, other than just strip down to my thong and get under the covers in one quick movement. N.Y. Boy was polite enough to turn the other way while I attempted the move; and once our sixty minutes of muscle tending were up, he very sweetly offered to hand me my bra before I emerged from my envelope of covers.

Talking about whether we'd go for a walk or back to his apartment, I made just one request. I needed sugar, something sweet, a doughnut or a cupcake or *whatever.* My need for sweetness matched his need for chips (crisps for my UK readers) and I realised that I'd truly met a kindred spirit. We'd run a half marathon that morning, and now we were encouraging each other to buy every single thing that we even remotely liked the look of in the grocery store—chocolate muffins, pineapple, a red velvet cupcake, mangoes, cheesecake, and two types of chips. There wasn't a single thing that we said no to for ourselves nor each other. Someone who inspires me to run over twenty kilometres in less than two hours, then actively encourages me to gorge myself, is the sort of person I want in my life for good.

Never mind the fact that he was incredibly generous, polite, funny, and hugely driven when it came to his career. He was motivated beyond most people with respect to fitness and really not terrible to look at. But someone that supports me in keeping fit *and* stuffing my face? Yes, where do I sign?! As an individual, I never want to stop growing or experiencing life, but I want to have fun doing it. I want someone who joins me on those experiences and walks (or runs) by my side through all the inevitable ups and downs. I want someone to do the work alongside me. I've done so much work on myself, but I don't feel like I've truly had the chance to do the necessary work in a relationship with a willing partner. That excites me. I want to want to be a better person for me **and** my partner, and things with N.Y. Boy seemed promising in that way so far.

After a few hours on the sofa, stuffing our faces and watching Netflix, we went out with some of his friends for dinner and a comedy show. I was surprised by how well I was feeling after all those miles on the legs that morning, but when we left the comedy show at midnight, I was more than a little tired. It wasn't surprising that when we got into bed that night, again with me attempting to ignore this next hit of bare skin, it was clear that neither of us were looking for any form of exertion. My reticence was down to tiredness but I didn't know if that was the sole reason for his. He did open up his right arm, however, and while initially I thought he could just be stretching, soon I realised it was an invitation for me to move into the space. *Oh lord,* now we were snuggling? And I was supposed to remain seemingly unbothered by this? *Was I unbothered by it?* I couldn't be sure. But we were both...just...so...tired....

We woke up a little further apart, but having bridged the physical gap last night, the following morning I felt more comfortable grazing his thigh with my hand, along with whatever other skin-on-skin engagement I could maneuver. Secretly, I was absolutely hoping for some morning sex. (I mean, up until that point, I'd secretly been hoping for any kind of sex. But lying in bed on a Sunday morning, with the sun peaking through the blinds as we chatted ourselves awake, with nowhere to go but brunch before the football game that afternoon, was the perfect morning sex setting.) Still, there was not a single movement on his part to indicate that he was feeling the same way.

Yeah, I was confused as fuck. Granted he'd invited me to stay; and granted he'd offered to share his bed; and granted he'd booked us a couple's massage;

and granted we'd fallen asleep with me in the nook of his arm; but I still didn't feel clear about his feelings. I'd reached a point in my life where, if I met someone and I liked them, all bets were off and I'd end up in bed with them. But here I was in bed with a guy and unable to put myself out there enough to show that I wanted to do more than snuggle. Could I tell him that actually I wanted my legs snuggled around him?

Choosing to remain silent, I got up to shower and prep for brunch in Chelsea, despite my lack of sexual satisfaction that morning. It was entirely idyllic, from the deconstructed French Toast we shared, to the cosy but chic farm-to-table decor. We talked a lot about our families over brunch and I was building the picture of a man who, at only twenty-eight years of age, had a strong sense of what was important in life. He would do what he needed to provide the life that he wanted for himself and his future family.

We both acknowledged how well we felt after running a half marathon, though I may have been fairing a little better than him, such is the benefit of training. In his matter of fact, loves a challenge and can seemingly do anything way, he said, "I think we could do a full marathon." Was he kidding? Sure, we'd done pretty well at 21.1 kilometres, but 42.2 kilometres was a whole different ball game. It had never even been on my bucket list, despite people asking me the question after every half marathon I'd completed. Keith was always telling me to go for it, but there was something different about the way N.Y. Boy approached the conversation. I'd had the mindset of "but why would I want to do that?" for a long time, while his was more like, "but why couldn't you, if you thought your body could?" There was something crazy persuasive in his reasoning. I told him to pipe down and talk to me again after his two days of muscle stiffness had fully kicked in.

By this time, I was becoming increasingly aware that it was Sunday afternoon and I had just two more nights with N.Y. Boy. Also, tomorrow we were both at work; so realistically, if anything was going to happen, it would have to be that night. Because who wants to be hooking up on a Monday? *Jokes,* I always do, but really I was just hoping we'd sleep together more than once. So that afternoon at the football game, I leaned just a little closer and manufactured a couple more opportunities to touch or compliment him. *God, who was I?* When had I last tried this hard? Why couldn't I just lay it on him?!

We decided that night to order food and watch a movie—but some of his friends gatecrashed our plans and we all ended up in the gym many floors below his apartment. My confusion turned to frustration and I ran eight kilometres on the treadmill outrageously fast for someone who'd just completed a half marathon. I was also simultaneously texting Darlene, who was talking me off a ledge; and Kim and Dustin were astounded and in disbelief that we hadn't hooked up yet. *Yah,* you and me both.

By the time we were alone again, it was after ten pm on a Sunday night, with work the next day. I was pretty sure the opportunity for anything more to happen between us had passed. I would be lying if I said that I wasn't disappointed, but I had to be grateful for the weekend regardless. It was a huge amount of fun—living in New York like a local, even just for a few days, was a dream. If nothing else happened then so be it; at least that way our feelings wouldn't get confused by sex, and everyone could go home happy and unscathed.

So when he offered his arm again when we both got into bed, I envisaged the same falling asleep mid-conversation as the night before. But what had been a solid static hand on my shoulder at Saturday's bedtime, became light and enquiring fingers stroking my arm. *Um. Wait. What was happening?* At first I thought about ignoring it, such had been the rollercoaster in my head for past forty-eight hours, and because I still thought maybe he just wanted to...stretch his fingers?! Soon my sensibility and my libido got the better of me, and I knew there was absolutely no way I was going home without getting a whole lot more intimate with N.Y. Boy than a bedtime snuggle.

I turned my head towards him and tilted my chin up. There was still a moment when I wasn't sure he'd actually kiss me, until he did. It was sweet and hushed and slow. Allowing my hands to wander the contours of his muscles, I didn't hate a single second. It felt like we were discovering each other for the first time. This was true, physically, and I was learning things I never could have known about him in conversation. For being so late on a Sunday night after a fairly active weekend, I would have forgiven him if it hadn't lasted all that long; but he was dedicated and clearly wasn't going to let things fizzle fast after such a long build up.

The sex was in line with everything else that weekend: pretty fucking great. What I loved just as much was how we talked for at least an hour afterwards, strewn across his bed, his pillows and duvet entirely displaced. We discovered that we'd both been unsure of the signals from each other. He said I was a closed book, which I admitted was unusual for me. We laughed as we each recounted parts of the weekend when we'd each, respectively, thought we'd been super clear, but the other person had completely misread or missed the signals. Wow, we were dumb. Though we agreed that getting to know each other up until that point had been enjoyable without the complications of sex. It felt a little purer, a little more genuine. Besides, if we'd had sex earlier, I would have seen a whole lot less of New York City.

The next morning, he went to work and I went to my conference. A day full of email marketing best practices kept my brain occupied while my body longed to snuggle with N.Y. Boy. It'd be my last night in the city, and having been treated to almost everything that weekend (did I mention he was generous?), I was treating him to dinner. Except that it was dark and raining by the time he returned from work, and I felt bad about making him go out on a Monday night. If he was anything like me, weeknights were not to be fucked with, especially after entertaining an out-of-towner all weekend. Instead we decided to stay in, get pizza, and watch a movie. We ate pepperoni pizza and watched *A Time To Kill* (how had I seen a movie that someone else hadn't?!), laying on the sofa with our limbs entwined and our hands wandering. It was a perfect last night. I may have even thought about never leaving.

Going to bed, stuffed full of pizza and having dozed off on the couch, sex didn't seem likely—but I may or may not have made it clear that we'd be having morning sex in a few hours. I was worried that if we didn't do it again, my mind might think that I'd created the memories from Sunday night. I needed to cement them in my brain, and there were things I wanted him to do to me again. If I could wake up that way everyday, I just might.

Saying goodbye as he went off to work the next day, it was unlikely he'd get home before my flight that evening. I was mentally preparing myself for that, but a tiny part of me still hoped for another five, or even just ten more minutes with him. Before I left, I went back to the sports shop from Friday night (which now felt like a week ago), and bought the shoes he'd been looking at. I left them in their sleek black box, along with some more energy gels and a card, perfectly placed on his crisp white bed.

The card thanked him for his hospitality and tried to explain how much fun I'd had and how I'd enjoyed getting to know him more. I also set out my feelings: that I wanted to spend more time with him, *somehow,* somewhere. We'd spent so much of the weekend not sure of how the other person felt, and I just didn't want to leave New York without being clear about my feelings.

Even if I wasn't sure about his, I didn't want to leave anything unsaid. I practically had to tear myself away from his apartment, locking the door with Vancouver calling me home. It was a huge emotional rollercoaster. I'd had one of the most incredible weekends with someone who'd brought me back alive, motivating me to do and be more, whose kindness was like nothing I'd ever known from a guy.

I had no idea what was to come for us when I left New York, but I knew the weekend had changed me. I'd been settling for a bunch of shit with guys, and N.Y. Boy made me realise that I should be expecting and getting so much more. While his looks and ridiculously sculpted arms had been an initial draw, there were now a hundred other things I'd list before those that attracted me to him.

Just before I boarded my red-eye flight, he texted to say that he'd just found my gift. To say it landed well is an understatement. I was reminded of how good it felt to give someone not only a physical gift but your honesty. Arguably, it's easier on paper than in person, especially when you draft and edit it a million times before eventually inscribing the card. Being that vulnerable with him had felt scary as shit but also empowering. Standing in my feelings, asking a N.Y. Boy for more of his time.

Getting a row to myself on the flight home felt like a just reward, allowing me to sleep for the entirety of the six-hour flight home. Going into the office only a few hours after I landed, I vowed to put New York to the side and let it to unfurl in whatever way necessary, focusing on work and not forcing anything that was out of my control. Things felt positive, things felt optimistic; and I was excited to see what the future held.

Twenty-four hours later, I lost my job.[6]

---

[6] But whatever, I also wrote a book.

Epilogue

Lessons

Life is a rollercoaster and there's no denying the fact. Songs have been written about it (yes, I just made a Ronan Keating reference and my sixteen-year-old self is so fucking happy right now). In coming off the extreme high of New York, I stumbled into the shattering moment of my new boss explaining that the business needs had changed and there was no longer a requirement for my role. While I hadn't felt secure in my job for a long time, since all the drama with my old boss in March, it was still a shock. No matter how much you might need to leave a job, it's never a fun way to go.

After the initial panic of losing my source of income, I decided to take a moment to breathe and make a meaningful next step. I'd never been great about saving, which didn't help, but rather than just rushing into any other job, chasing a paycheck like a crumb of cheese, I decided to pause. I wasn't desperate to throw myself back into a situation that could lead to my role being eliminated again, after all.

But I struggled. I struggled with my ego, with fear, and with my doubts. How at thirty-five years old was I in this situation? How was this my life? How could I have no job, no financial security, and no relationship (despite a wonderful weekend in New York with a wonderful human). If there'd been a challenge to my sense of self, after all these years of apparent self-growth, this was it.

I could choose to lament the situation (like, hadn't I already been through enough?) or I could see it as a blessing in disguise, knowing that the universe was doing for me what I was slow to do for myself, removing me from a work situation that was not aligned with who I was nor what I wanted in life. Gratitude, the greatest lesson I'd stumbled upon in the aftermath of my divorce, had lived with me every day. It was now my greatest strength.

Now I had the opportunity to make a decision for myself, and I was beyond thankful for all my friends reaching out, offering help looking for jobs, taking me out for coffee and asking if I needed help with rent. I was grateful for the city and the apartment I now called home; they were sanctuaries of comfort and beauty and calm. I was grateful for so many things in my life, and the loss of a job paled in significance. Since separating from my husband, I'd learned that gratitude was more than a great mind hack—it was a necessity.

Once again, life was showing me that there's no set timeline or "right way" to do things; there's just the way you end up going. You could describe my entire life as "it didn't quite go to plan"—at least not the plan I'd envisaged. Some things we can control and some things we cannot, but ultimately, we each tell our own story. We each get to write it however we please. Other people's stories are not the be-all-and-end-all; and society's narrative is not all that important. What's important is what *we want* the story to be.

The story I'd thought I wanted included a flourishing corporate career, a stable but epic romantic relationship, and financial security to enable a comfortable (and borderline luxurious) life. That was not the story I was living, and I had to come to terms with that in the starkest of ways. However hard it was to accept my progress, did I really want my story to include rushing into another soul-sucking job? No, I wanted to write this book. Did I struggle with giving up a career and becoming an unemployed, unpublished writer? You bet your ass I did. But that storyline, the one where I took a risk, shut out the doubts, and did something that I knew deep down was resonant, felt much more like the story I wanted to write.

In making that choice, I had to feel grounded in my sense of self. Throughout the stories in this book, I was discovering and learning about myself, building out the different aspects of who I'm becoming in this life. The situations I found myself in provided an opportunity to truly see the extent of my growth. We find our truest strength in our darkest moments. It was empowering as shit, seeing that life had served me a crappy hand in the relationship department and I was dealing with it. I was not only living but thriving. So was that a crappy hand or an opportunity? The more we get challenged, the more we learn and grow from those challenges, the more we realise our capabilities:

Challenges are just growth opportunities, and I truly wouldn't change any of mine.

Finding myself further away from the three pillars of life as I'd previously considered them—career, love, financial freedom—I somehow found myself happier than I had been in a long time. I felt freer and more connected to myself. I felt more alive. Work had always been a second priority for me to living life itself, but in writing this book and finding a passion, I was more motivated to get to Starbucks at seven am to write than I'd ever been for a job. Time to reflect was perfect for my needs.

In aligning with my strengths, I've become more assured in asking people to meet me there, both in friendships and relationships. But people can only meet you as deeply as they've met themselves. Understanding that it's not necessarily about them not wanting to meet you where you're at, but rather about them still trying to get there themselves, makes it much easier to take a softer view of a situation. When you come at situations from a place of kindness and want to understand, you allow yourself the space to learn from a situation without the emotional content being an energy suck. Being hopeful about relationships is a wonderful and admirable thing, but when we make that hope dependent on someone else choosing us, or meeting us precisely where we are, as I've done a number of times, we lose the ability to show up for ourselves.

Most of the men I've dated have been good men; they just weren't aligned with me, my life or my needs. And that's okay. When I stopped trying to rationalise why that was or how I could change it and just accept it, it became much less devastating when things didn't work out. The ones I talk about in this book all taught me something about myself, and regardless of how they ended up, I appreciate all of those experiences. Despite some in-the-moment declarations to the contrary, I've never let my experiences make me bitter or hateful. I've come to realise that the ability to be open and optimistic despite my history is one of my gifts.

Clearly, romantic relationships have, at times, been a huge energy suck in my life. Thinking back to when I started dating, I'm shocked at how timid and underprepared I was. Back then, I was so lonely, with such feelings of unworthiness and a longing to be healed that I would let almost anyone into my life, just hoping they were the fix I needed. As I gained confidence, red flags became deal breakers, rather than just things to note and brush under the carpet. But I had to start somewhere, and the lessons I've learnt and am still learning couldn't have been found in just any other way. Through dating, we find out a lot about ourselves, even if sometimes the overriding feeling is: *When is this ever going to happen for me so that this nightmare can end?*

Are we so conditioned by fairy tales and rom coms that we seek the unobtainable? Or are we right to expect that the right thing feels nothing but right when it happens? Nothing but heart-bursting, soul-filling greatness? That's what I want. In addition to my own peace and self-achieved happiness, I want someone who makes my heart burst, who fills my soul and gives me nothing but what I need. I want someone who builds me up but holds me down; with whom I can build a life, an empire, a family. Someone who never makes me question myself or them; who could never see a way to hurt nor disappoint nor lie to me, and all of these same things I'd promise to them.

Are those just over-inflated wants, unattainable levels of respect, and impossibly high standards? I want to think the answer is no, and I'm told (and I read) all the time that this is the least we should expect. While I'm fiercely independent and entirely self-sufficient, admitting that I want to be someone's queen is something I do happily. I readily own the fact that I want to be treated the way I want to treat someone else. Putting someone else's needs and wants and happiness equal to my own is entirely where I want to be. I want someone who makes me feel like doing that is a privilege and not a chore. And I truly believe that can be found. I can absolutely be alone, but the truth is, I don't want to *have* to be.

Of course, there's hard work involved, compromises, give and take. I'm not naïve; I've been there and done that, possibly more than I should have. But none of it scares me. I want it back; I want to embrace it. At times, I wanted something to work so badly that I let the red flags slide, instead of asking myself if the connection served me and my true feelings. When I'm not asking myself those questions, usually it's because I already know the answers. As incredible as someone might be as a person, sometimes it's not meant to actually *be*—no matter how epic of a story you've already dreamt up in your head. Chasing unavailable people, or people who don't align with who you are, is akin to self-abandonment. Every time I did it, I got further away from my true sense of self and my real opportunities to find love, those that I know exist out there for me.

Instead of searching for someone and living eternally in limbo, I choose me. *Finally.* I am the love I was searching for. And I'll continue to choose me every day, because our relationships with people are reflections of our relationships with ourselves. My relationship with me is the most important one I'll ever have. There will only ever be one *me.* Even if there's someone else who joins for the ride, for some of it or all of it, it's still just me. It took me a while to get truly comfortable with that.

I chose me when I moved to Vancouver, when I started therapy, when I let go of relationships that I'd been fighting to keep, and when I gave up alcohol. I've had some questionable relationships, but my relationship with alcohol was certainly the least healthy. When my parents were divorcing and I first dipped into the sauce, I became that girl who would end the night crying. I hated her so much, but I knew she was hurting beyond what anyone could have known, including me. Whether it was my parents' divorce, my faltering marriage, the aftermath of it all, or the loneliness I felt trying to rebuild my life, there was a lot to work through in Vancouver.

My mental health is a fine balance of being aware and trying to manage unnecessary impacts on my life. It came into my awareness right around the start of my relationship with alcohol, and the two aren't unrelated. Being sixteen and on antidepressants was debilitating, and emotional traumas cause your mind to race. Your thoughts become jumbled and your brain is forever triggered. As I got used to dealing with that state of mind long term, it showed up in my sheer volume of feelings. I don't think it's a coincidence that I feel things incredibly strongly; my heart is forever on my sleeve, and my book is always open (unless you're N.Y. Boy, it seems).

My highs are galactic and my lows are Atlantis. What I used to think of as an inconvenience, something I needed to "get under control," I now view as windows into my soul. To be so aware of my feelings is only a problem when I don't know what to do with them. Being able to dig into them now and learn is something I don't take for granted. You truly can't experience highs if you avoid the lows. They go hand in hand. Avoidance can't be selective; we don't know whether a situation will end up as a high or a low in the end. Who wants to avoid everything anyways? And ultimately we can only love as deeply as we feel, and I'll no longer shame myself for doing both of those things extensively. I'd lived in a shame state for so long that escaping it felt like a mental breath of fresh air.

Making the shift from always feeling wounded and trying to fix myself, to instead just trying to understand myself, being kind with what I was feeling and why, allowed me to instead see my flaws as lessons and my vices as directions. Accepting these things, which I had so desperately tried to shed from my being for so long, allowed me to get closer to who I am, closer to how my soul truly is. And it wasn't necessarily the trauma that made me stronger and more empathetic, it was the way I handled the cards I had to play. It was my dedication to figuring out who I was, as all these different scenarios played out in my head. Mentally, it was a fight-or-flight option and I chose to fight.

Moreover, discovering my physical strength and stamina was a gift I gave to myself. While I don't think self-confidence should come simply from one's physical appearance, I'm much happier feeling healthy and looking fit. I don't need toned thighs or an outline of an ab for me to love my body or for a guy to think I'm attractive, but I want physical fitness for myself—to know that the hard work, dedication, and sweat are all mine. Feeling better in my body, coupled with finding my voice and learning to communicate what I needed, I also discovered a surprising comfort level with my sexuality. As women, we've historically been so conditioned to be available for sex but not to enjoy it or act like we enjoy it. To be sexy but not sexual. We're expected to want sex in association with breeding but not for the sake of just wanting it. Well, you know what, I want it; and I don't necessarily want it for the sake of offspring.

I don't care what my "number" is in relation to sexual partners—it's irrelevant. My want and enjoyment of sex is something I own entirely. I've been incredibly lucky with certain partners, even the ones who taught me what I *didn't* like. The oxytocin released after sex is maybe my favourite drug, and sometimes getting my fix of it made for poor decision-making; but utilising it in moderation is one of life's great joys. I so wish for women to own their sexuality more often, feeling free to explore it and having safe spaces to share and swap stories. I've loved feeling more secure in asking questions of my girlfriends, talking about preferences and sharing things like porn websites or new sex toys. Women supporting women, especially in their sexual awareness, is what I'm here for right now!

In the times when my priorities have shifted between wanting a relationship and purely a sexual liaison, I still always know that there is sex without love and there is love without sex, and more importantly, there is me without both. I also know that *just* good sex will never be enough, I will ultimately always want more. I want my soul to be met by somebody else's soul. I want to experience growth, to be taught and guided, connected with and understood by another person. These days, the same goes for all my relationships.

Socially, Vancouver is known to be unfriendly—difficult to crack cliques and sometimes unwelcoming. But I have not found that. I have made incredible friends here and not once did I feel unwelcome. Would I ever have thought that I'd go to a random Facebook group meet-up or climb into a car with strangers for a road trip? Hard pass on both, but they provided me with some of the best friends I've met in Canada. No one around me has been selfish with their circle, and for that I am endlessly grateful. Being so far away from family means that my friends here are inherently a second family. We celebrate birthdays and Easters and Christmases together. Finding a new sense of family has taken some getting used to, but I'm blessed for the experience all the same.

Being away from family hasn't necessarily become easier, but I am more used to it now, knowing I'm here in Vancouver for good. My family never questions, at least not too hard, my non-traditional choices, like if dialing down a job search in favour of writing a book is really the right thing to do. It's hard not to feel overwhelming gratitude for the freedom and support they provide. I know a lot of mothers who couldn't stand back and watch their daughters make decisions like mine. But arguably, my mum was more concerned about me getting my first tattoos at age thirty-five than any of my other life choices.

My mum instead acknowledges that my ability (in fact any woman's ability) to pick myself up day after day, despite being depleted in a multitude of ways, and remain open and warm and loving, is a sign of incredible strength. I don't think I was ever, or could ever have been, ready for the shit I've gone through, but clearly I was built for it. Everyone is just doing the best they can with what they have, in whatever situation they find themselves. Some people do better than others, and some need more help. Some people can't find ways through at all, and a lot of those people face systemic disadvantages and need our help. I want to be someone who, at the end of their life, can say they did all the things and felt all the feels, while facing what life threw at her and being unapologetically herself. I want that to be the overriding feeling, rather than lamenting the difficult parts along the way.

I've done and seen things, and experienced things that I'd be jealous about if it were somebody else. Moving to another country? Making a whole new network of friendships? Road trips in the Rockies? Dating some ridiculously fine men? Skiing in Whistler? Being loved so fiercely by my family and friends, and from so far away? Discovering and loving my own sexuality? Getting to see my strength and resilience in real life? I am so fucking lucky. But I hope this book paints both sides of the coin—because yes my life is as fun as it looks on Instagram, but there are also a lot of challenges. I don't post pictures of myself having meltdowns on social media, but that doesn't stop them from happening sometimes.

I'm still looking for someone whose drive inspires mine and wants to build an empire with the unique sum of our love and passion. Road trips, sunsets, creating traditions, weeknight dinners, missing each other, encouraging each other to work out, eat ice cream, be heard, seen and accepted and make somebody else feel that they are heard, seen and accepted. Like a *friggin'* star in the big black and blue sky, I want someone who can take in all of my darkness and all of my light, and I know this awaits me somewhere down the line. Perhaps it will be for a reason or for a season, or perhaps it will be forever, or perhaps it will teach me to give forever to myself. In a way I think I am already learning.

Even with all the personal challenges I've been through in the last decade, I'm grateful for the love and the life that I have been given; and I am blessed for the opportunity and privilege to strive to create the life I truly want, and have time to put a cherry on top, and there is no more beautiful place than here to end this chapter of my story. Creating Life 2.0 has been the greatest gift and challenge that I never expected, and I wouldn't change it for another million more matches or swipes on Bumble—like, not in a million more years. I'm grateful for the girl I was because she taught me to be who I am now.

Gratitude above all else. *Beannachd leat!*[7]

[7] Scottish Gaelic! Meaning "see you" or "blessings be with you." <3

Your living is determined not so much by what life brings to you as by the attitude you bring to life; not so much by what happens to you as by the way your mind looks at what happens.

- Khalil Gibran

About Louise Johnson

Louise Johnson was born in Edinburgh, Scotland. Since 2013, she has called Vancouver, Canada home, where she lives on the unceded and ancestral territories of the xʷməθkʷəy̓əm (Musqueam), Sḵwx̱wú7mesh (Squamish), Selilwitulh (Tsleil-Waututh) Nations. In tandem with furthering her career in Sales & Marketing, Louise wrote her first memoir in 2019, following a traumatic divorce and a transformative six-year period. Her writing style is unabashed and her stories are anything but sugarcoated. As a writer, Louise believes in conveying her experiences using a mixture of stark reality and dark humour; and as a woman, she's not afraid to tell the truth, especially if that truth is hard.